Supporting a Shared Vision of a Better World

"The Earth Charter... is a comprehensive statement of the norms and values required for effective global governance. It may be considered a guideline for humanity in the twenty-first century. Only with a shared vision, and shared effort toward the realization of that vision, will we be able to greet a more hopeful future. For this reason, it is imperative that the Earth Charter be given the support and recognition of the international community."

*SGI President Daisaku Ikeda in his 2002 peace proposal, The Humanism of the Middle Way: Dawn of a Global Civilization*

Since 1997, Soka Gakkai International (SGI), a worldwide network of engaged Buddhists, has been involved in promoting the Earth Charter in countries from the USA to Malaysia as a people's movement and as a process of dialogue for change and transformation. The SGI will continue to promote the Earth Charter throughout the UN Decade of Education for Sustainable Development (2005-2014) and beyond, through awareness-raising activities including exhibitions, and by encouraging individuals everywhere to make the Charter a personal pledge and commitment.

# THE EARTH CHARTER IN ACTION

## TOWARD A SUSTAINABLE WORLD

This book is dedicated to the yearnings of youth for a just, peaceful, and sustainable world – and especially to the young people of the Earth Charter Youth Initiative who represent the high hopes and practical idealism of their generation by putting the Earth Charter into action.

# THE EARTH CHARTER IN ACTION

## TOWARD A SUSTAINABLE WORLD

Peter Blaze Corcoran, *Editor-in-Chief*

Mirian Vilela

Alide Roerink

KIT Publishers, Amsterdam

# Colophon

KIT Publishers BV
Mauritskade 63
P.O. Box 95001
1090 HA Amsterdam
The Netherlands
E-mail: publishers@kit.nl
Website: www.kit.nl/publishers

ISBN 90-6832-177-3

© 2005 KIT Publishers BV, Amsterdam, The Netherlands

Publisher: KIT Publishers, Amsterdam. In cooperation with the Earth Charter Initiative, San Jose, Costa Rica

Editor-in-Chief: Peter Blaze Corcoran (Director of the Center for Environmental and Sustainability Education, Florida Gulf Coast University, www.fgcu.edu/cese)

Editorial Team: Peter Blaze Corcoran (Senior Advisor to the Earth Charter Initiative), Mirian Vilela (Executive Director Earth Charter Initiative Secretariat), Alide Roerink (Senior Advisor to the Earth Charter Initiative, NCDO)

Editorial Advisory Group: Joan Anderson (Senior Advisor Earth Charter Initiative), Rick Clugston (Earth Charter Steering Committee), Ruud Lubbers (Earth Charter Commissioner), Mohit Mukherjee (Education Program Manager, Earth Charter Initiative), Steven C. Rockefeller (Earth Charter Commissioner), Michael Slaby (Coordinator Earth Charter Youth Initiative)

Design: Frank Langedijk BNO, Almere, The Netherlands
Translation: Karin Noë, Gerlof Abels, Henk Alberts en Kees van den Heuvel
Editing: Elise Spanjaard for Deul & Spanjaard, Groningen, The Netherlands
Printing: T&P Far East Productions, Soest, The Netherlands

*The publisher wishes to extend its gratitude to the following organisations for making the first edition of this book possible: Earth Charter Secretariat (Costa Rica), Plan Nederland (The Netherlands), CRLE (The Center for Respect of Life and Environment of The Humane Society of the United States, USA), WWF China, Soka Gakkai International (USA and Japan), Earth Council Alliance, USA, Fundacion Puma (Bolivia), Club of Budapest International (Germany), The Calvert Group (USA). Additional thanks to PLAN Nederland for supplying most of the photographs.*

The Earth Charter Initiative is a global movement that promotes the understanding and implementation of the values and principles for sustainable development that are outlined in the Earth Charter. The Initiative involves organizations, groups, and individuals worldwide. The Earth Charter Initiative International Secretariat coordinates major programmes and global undertakings. It develops educational and training materials, facilitates workshops, and seeks international recognition for the Earth Charter (www.earthcharter.org).

This book is initiated and financially supported by NCDO (National Committee for International Cooperation and Sustainable Development), Amsterdam, The Netherlands

# Table of Contents

# Part II. Ecological Integrity 63

# Part III. Social and Economic Justice 81

## Part IV. Democracy, Nonviolence, and Peace   115

Mikhail Gorbachev, Russia. *Preface*

# The Third Pillar of Sustainable Development

**Mikhail Gorbachev** initiated the process of change in the Soviet Union. He put in place *perestroika*, the fundamental transformation of the nation and society. *Glasnost*, or openness, became *perestroika's* driving force. A big shift in international affairs was effected. The new thinking associated with the name of Gorbachev contributed to a fundamental change in the international environment and played a prominent role in ending the Cold War, stopping the arms race, and eradicating the threat of a nuclear war. The Congress of People's Deputies of the USSR, the first parliament in Soviet history, elected Gorbachev President in 1990. In recognition of his outstanding services as a great reformer and world political leader who greatly contributed to improving the very nature of world development, Mikhail Gorbachev was awarded the Nobel Peace Prize in 1990. Since 1992, he has been President of The Gorbachev Foundation. He is Chairman of the Board of Green Cross International – an international independent environmental organization with branches in more than twenty countries. He has authored seventeen books, and received forty-four honorary degrees. He is an Earth Charter Commissioner and has played a leadership role in the history of the Earth Charter.

The current millennium started with a recognition by the international community of the many critical situations it faces, the most appalling of which are addressed in the United Nations Millennium Declaration: hunger, poverty, gender inequality, child mortality, water crisis, and environmental decline. In more general terms, I believe that the world is confronted today with three major challenges which encompass all other problems: the challenge of security, including the risks associated with weapons of mass destruction and terrorism; the challenge of poverty and underdeveloped economies; and the challenge of environmental sustainability.

No national government, even that of a super power, no group of countries, even the richest ones, can meet these challenges alone. The deadly terrorist attacks in London in July 2005, came as the latest tragic reminder of this reality. We must and will fight terrorism, but one should not forget that we might lose this war if we do not eradicate its roots. The only answer is a universal coalition of informed, responsible, and active citizens. Hence the importance of initiatives like the Earth Charter which, from an idea shared by a handful of like-minded individuals, has developed into a mass movement supported by millions of people worldwide.

The book in front of you is not simply another activity report that any organization regularly compiles – far more than five years of work lie behind it. Movements like the Earth Charter Initiative do not come to life spontaneously or out of the blue. The fact of their creation is preceded by a long prenatal period during which the people concerned come to understand their needs, formulate their demands, organize themselves, and get ready for action. In this sense, the book *The Earth Charter in Action: Toward a Sustainable World* is a testimony to the process of all humanity becoming mature, aware of the dangers it faces, and of the responsibilities it will inevitably have to assume vis-à-vis future generations if it continues to treat the environment as "business as usual."

The subjects dealt with and opinions expressed in the book are as varied and complex as our reality itself, and range from more global concepts like democracy, nonviolence, and peace to very practical issues of youth employment and gender equality. Another very impressive feature revealed by the book is the multitude of purposes for which Earth Charter can be used: promotion of equitable employment, citizen participation in environmental and educational programs, creating global dialogue on sustainable development, working with ex-combatants from war-torn regions, and even local campaigns against genetically modified organisms. This list can be continued.

One of the main themes of the Earth Charter, and of the book, the theme particularly dear to me as Founding President of Green Cross International, is ecological integrity and our common responsibility for its preservation. I was not born an ecologist, but the environment has always meant a lot to me. I grew up in a village and perceived the dying of rivers and land erosion as personal pain. Right after coming to power in the Soviet

Union, I had to deal with a huge project of reversing the flow of the rivers from North to South. If not stopped, it would have resulted in a tremendous ecological disaster. I thought this was a tough school. Yet, I still had Chernobyl to face…. This catastrophe of planetary scale shook the world and showed, in the most harsh form, that nature does not forgive human mistakes.

The Earth Charter is an unusual document since it reflects a new, universally-shared level of understanding of the interdependence between humans and nature. It also corresponds to the stage of globalization at which we find ourselves.

Coming back to the three challenges I mentioned earlier, two global documents are called to help the human community to cope with them. The first pillar is the Charter of the United Nations, which regulates the relations among states and thus sets the rules for their behavior in order to secure peace and stability. The second pillar is the Universal Declaration of Human Rights, which regulates the relations between states and individuals, and guarantees to all citizens a set of rights which their respective governments should provide. The importance of these two documents cannot be overestimated. But it has become obvious that another document is missing, one which would regulate the relations among states, individuals, and nature by defining the human duties towards the environment.

In my opinion, the Earth Charter should fill this void, acquire equal status, and become the third pillar supporting the peaceful development of the modern world. The process of its endorsement has already begun – it is endorsed by a growing number of local and national governments, the United Nations Educational, Scientific and Cultural Organization (UNESCO), and many non governmental organizations. However, we founders and supporters should consider our mission accomplished only when the Earth Charter is universally adopted by the international community. ●

Maurice F. Strong, Canada. *Preface*

# A People's Earth Charter

**Maurice F. Strong** was born and educated in Canada. He has been working at senior levels for over thirty years in business, government, and international organizations. Mr. Strong has long-standing family, businesses, and official ties with China, including being the founder and first Co-Chair of the Canada-China Business Council. His current appointments include: Under Secretary General and Special Advisor to the Secretary General of the United Nations; President of the Council of the University for Peace; Advisor on international matters, State Environmental Protection Agency of China; and Founding Chairman Emeritus of the Earth Council Alliance. Mr. Strong is a Member of the Queen's Privy Council for Canada. Honours received include Companion of the Order of Canada, The Swedish Royal Order of the Polar Star, the Brazilian National Order of the Southern Cross, Tyler Environmental Prize, and the Blue Planet Prize. He has been awarded fifty-three honorary doctorate degrees. He is an Earth Charter Commissioner and has an historical role in its development.

The launching of the Earth Charter in the presence of Her Majesty, Queen Beatrix of The Netherlands, in The Hague in June 2000 was a critical benchmark in the worldwide people's movement to take up a challenge which governments were not ready to undertake at the Earth Summit in Rio de Janeiro in 1992. In the five years since its launching, the Earth Charter Initiative has developed a growing constituency of people throughout the world devoted to using the principles of the Earth Charter as a guide to their own actions.

The Earth Charter was born out of the deepening concern and awareness that, despite the progress made both in our understanding of the risks to the human future acknowledged at Stockholm in 1972 and the major increases in our capacity to manage these risks successfully by the 1980s, the world community was still proceeding on a continuing development pathway that was not sustainable. Why, then, if we know so much more about the nature and extent of the problems we face, and if we clearly have the capacity to implement the measures

required to make the transition to sustainable development, are we still not doing it on the scale required? Implementation depends on motivation, and the motivation of people is the source of the political will of their governments.

It became evident that world leaders at the Earth Summit in Rio de Janeiro in 1992 were not sufficiently compelled by the motivation of their people to accept my proposal, building on the recommendation of the Bruntland Commission and extensive consultations with others, to begin negotiation of an Earth Charter as a statement of principles designed to guide the behaviour of people and nations towards Earth and each other.

After the Earth Summit, a group of concerned people undertook a process designed to produce a people's Earth Charter to manifest the commitment of people to a set of principles designed to ensure the security and sustainability of life on Earth. On the initiative of Ruud Lubbers, then Prime Minister of The Netherlands, Mikhail Gorbechev joined in forming a small and widely-representative group to guide this process. Led by Professor Steven C. Rockefeller, extensive and inclusive consultations took place throughout the world which produced broad consensus on the drafting of an Earth Charter incorporating the fundamental moral and ethical principles essential to a sustainable

future. Agreement on it was reached at United Nations Educational, Science, and Cultural Organization headquarters in Paris in May 2000, followed by the formal launching in The Hague.

The Earth Charter has provided the impetus for a worldwide movement that has been gaining momentum in the past five years. It involves literally thousands of organizations ranging from the very local to those that are national in character, like the US Conference of Mayors, and major international organizations like the World Conservation Union (IUCN). Each of these commitments to the Earth Charter, together with those of countless individuals throughout the world, have been recorded through a small Earth Charter Initiative International Secretariat under the inspired and devoted leadership of Mirian Vilela.

These actions have produced an increasingly influential constituency for the Earth Charter that includes many world leaders. While no attempt has yet been made to obtain formal recognition of the Earth Charter by the United Nations, it is receiving growing recognition and support from United Nations members and representatives of other international organizations. It is also being included in the curricula of schools and universities, as well as the programs of a wide variety of youth organizations. Young people, particularly, have embraced the Earth Charter as an essential road map to the kind of future to which they aspire.

This timely book tells the story of the actions that have transformed the Earth Charter into a global movement which continues, and must continue to grow, as a primary source of the devotion and determination of people everywhere to ensure that our Earth remains a secure and habitable home for all people and those other forms of life with which we share it. As this book demonstrates, we have made immensely encouraging progress during the past five years. But, until the majority of people and organizations everywhere base their motivations on the principles enshrined in the Earth Charter, it will remain unfinished business. ●

Wangari Maathai, Kenya. *Foreword*

# Abandon Apathy and Be Moved to Action

**Wangari Muta Maathai** was the first woman in East and Central Africa to earn a doctoral degree. Professor Maathai was active in the National Council of Women of Kenya from 1976-1987. Here she introduced the idea of planting trees and developed the idea into a broad-based, grassroots organization called the Green Belt Movement launched in 1977; they have planted more than thirty million trees across Kenya. In 2002, Dr. Maathai was elected to Kenya's Parliament with an overwhelming ninety-eight percent of the vote. She is Assistant Minister for Environment and Natural Resources. Wangari Maathai is internationally recognized for her persistent struggle for democracy, human rights, and environmental conservation. In 2004, she was awarded the Nobel Peace Prize. She is an Earth Charter Commissioner and spokesperson.

When I look at the Earth Charter and reflect on it, I pick out several words. Then, if I take those words and I scan the horizon of my life, I can almost see the thousands and thousands of words that Steven C. Rockefeller must have heard, and the Earth Charter Commission must have heard, in order to come up with the very few words in the Earth Charter.

So as to make these words meaningful, we need to reflect on them. For example, when we pick the word "just," we want a just world. Can we think of all the injustices that we have on this planet, whether they are injustices against our own species, against one and another, or against the other forms of life? And, if we start with our own neighborhood, and go as far as we can before we get back to our place, we would see all the injustices that necessitate that word "just." I am sure that many communities and many individuals wrote letters to the Commission to say: you must include the word "just"—because we need justice. We need equitable distribution of our resources.

I look at the word "sustainable." I look at the word "peaceful." I look at the words "global interdependence." These words make me feel that we are truly interdependent. Do we use these words because they are beautiful words that are used often, or

do we truly *feel* interdependent? Do we really feel that we need the people in the South? Do we really feel that we need the biological diversity in the South? Do we really feel that we need the diversity of cultures in other parts of the world? Or are we only concerned about the cultures that we know? Are we only going to tolerate the cultures that we know and not hear about other rather simple, primitive cultures that we see in the films and on television?

I look at the term "shared responsibility." Is there really anything to be shared like "responsibility?" The question is whether we really feel that it is our concern when some people are dying of hunger in some parts of the world. Do we have a concern when we hear that countries are indebted to the point that they cannot provide their citizens with the basic necessities because they have to pay debts many times over what they borrowed? Is this fair trade?

I look at the words "human family" and I think sometimes we feel it is necessary to protect the butterflies, and it is necessary to protect the yet-undiscovered species in the Amazon, Congo, and other tropical forests, but we are not concerned about the diversity within the human family. I wonder whether we really know what the words "human family" mean. Is it my own family, my own nation, my own region?

So I am reflecting, and as you can see; there is not enough time for us to reflect on everything. There are enormously thought-provoking words in this document. What we should do, instead of just reading through, is to reflect on what the words mean so that we can be moved to action. In other parts of the world and in my own life, I love to do this because I can talk, I can reflect, and at the end, I can go home, dig a hole, and plant a tree.

As you will see from the stories in this book, many have reflected on words and principles in the Earth Charter so that they could be moved to action of many kinds. I encourage you to do the same—to find the words in the Earth Charter that speak to you and to give them meaning by reflecting on them. Then, allow yourself to abandon apathy and be moved to action! ●

The Earth Charter in Action

# Making the World One

**Peter Blaze Corcoran** is Professor of Environmental Studies and Environmental Education at Florida Gulf Coast University, where he serves as Director of the Center for Environmental and Sustainability Education. He has held academic posts at College of the Atlantic, Swarthmore College, and Bates College in the States. He has also been a visiting professor in Australia and The Netherlands. He works extensively in international environmental education with special interest in the South Pacific Island Nations. He is among the founders of the Global Higher Education for Sustainability Partnership and has recently conducted their consultations with stakeholders in tertiary education in many regions of the world. He is Past President of North American Association for Environmental Education. He serves as Senior Fellow in Education for Sustainability at University Leaders for a Sustainable Future in Washington, DC, and is Senior Advisor to the Earth Charter Initiative in San Jose, Costa Rica. His most recent book is *Higher Education and the Challenge of Sustainability: Contestation, Critique, Practice, and Promise* published in The Netherlands by Kluwer Academic Press in 2004.

*The Earth is one but the world is not. We all depend on one biosphere for sustaining our lives. Yet each community, each country, strives for survival and prosperity with little regard for its impact on others. Some consume the Earth's resources at a rate that would leave little for future generations. Others, many more in number, consume far too little and live with the prospect of hunger, squalor, disease, and early death.*
*Our Common Future*, 1987, p. 27

It has been a generation since the World Commission on Environment and Development famously introduced the concept of an integration of environment and development that is sustainable, "to ensure that it meets the needs of the present without compromising the ability of future generations to meet their own needs."[1] This concept, both brilliant and problematic, has framed a great debate of the turn of the millennium. How, and if, we will find a path to sustainability has become the most important narrative of our time.

What kind of world we will leave for the young, and what values will we transfer to them have become epic questions. The tragic truth pointed out by the Brundtland Commission is well-known but often ignored.

> We borrow environmental capital from future generations with no intention or prospect of repaying….We act as we do because we can get away with it: future generations do not vote they have no political or financial power; they cannot challenge our decisions. But the results of the present profligacy are rapidly closing the options for future generations. (p. 8)

Indeed, sustainability is a diminishing prospect. The gloomy and alarming forecasts for the future of life on Earth as we have known it create a great sense of urgency for action. Yet, almost everywhere we see the failure of governmental and intergovernmental institutions to take effective action. In the case of my own powerful USA government, we see a comprehensive policy of *not* taking action on the most serious problems, such as anthropogenic climate change. Indeed, this policy goes so far as to alter the conclusions of the science that show how serious the problems are. Most dangerously, this policy includes the rejection of all international agreements that might lead to effective action toward a sustainable world.

In the face of such urgency and such governmental ineffectiveness and, even, intransigence, what are we to do? Surely, as the indigenous peoples have taught us, we have an ethical responsibility not to foreclose future access to the beauty and bounty of Earth. We must reach across generations to acknowledge the profound inequity and irreversible loss of opportunity this represents. Neither ought we to condemn them, or ourselves, to a diminished future. Indeed, I believe we have an intergenerational responsibility to provide for sustainable livelihoods. We must secure, by our actions, a hopeful future for the fifty percent of the world population that is under the age of twenty-five.

It is becoming well-established that we can meet the basic needs of all and surely we could find satisfying and sustainable employment for the rising generations in doing so. The Millennium Development Goals' process is showing us the way to alleviate the suffering of the billion of our brothers and sisters who live in extreme poverty. But, are we *willing* to do so? By what thinking and what policy might we move toward a sustainable world?

As early as 1987, the Brundtland Commission wisely saw the need for "… a new charter to guide state behavior in the transition to sustainable development" (p. 332). This charter, of course, became the Earth Charter and it became a guide to much more than the behavior of states. As you will see in this book, for some it became a guide for an ethical life. For others, it became a values framework for business or public policy. For still others, it became a covenant for caring for Earth – and for others.

The Earth Charter is an inclusive, ethical vision that can guide action of all kinds toward a sustainable world in wich we recognize our mutual destiny and responsibility. It can show the way toward a world that is one, even as the Earth is one.

This book shows how people have built consensus on shared values for a better world and are taking action on this hopeful vision. For hope is not a given; it remains to be constructed. The Earth Charter is an "ark of hope"; it is a vessel for our hopes for a better world. It helps us to know what a just, peaceful, and sustainable world might look like.

I am convinced that we need such a hopeful vision of a sustainable world. The Earth Charter principles result from a successful process of building consensus on values that are widely shared. These core values, so clearly articulated in the Earth Charter principles, give us much to go on as we work toward bringing a sustainable world into being. They are substantive and specific. Earth Charter principles articulate common ethical values that are compatible with many indigenous beliefs, worldviews, religions, and secular philosophies. They help us interpret our beliefs in light of the perilous trends of our current unsustainable development path. They express these values as a global, civic ethic of specific rights and responsibilities. In my experience, by articulating common concerns and common values, the Earth Charter provides a righteous vision. By being part of a participatory, inspiring process, it gives us hope that the vision is viable. By specifically articulating a vision of sustainable development, it provides a path forward to achieve it. The Earth Charter is a guide to such a path and an inspiration to action.

It is easy to talk about the crises of social injustice and poverty, of violent conflict, and of environmental disasters that create such suffering for all forms of life. The world is in agony and, as we improvidently exceed its carrying capacity, so is Earth. This book captures the stories of those who are doing something about these crises. It demonstrates the rich diversity of uses of the Earth Charter and points toward many future possibilities for its greater use.

Thematic and descriptive essays from around the world tell of action informed by the Earth Charter and demonstrate its utility in diverse cultural contexts. They show its promise in working across the divide between the northern and southern hemispheres, across the faith traditions, the nations, and the generations.

Each Part of the Earth Charter, including the Preamble and The Way Forward, is given in full text, presented in a separate color, and is introduced by an extended essay on the overarching themes of that Part. Then, each of the sixteen main Principles is spoken to in either a thematic essay on its content or in a descriptive essay on a project related to the substance of that Principle.

The writers include the well-known whose action within an ethical framework has been enhanced by their work on the Earth Charter. The writers also include those little-known outside their circles whose heroic fortitude in putting the Earth Charter in action is often without recognition but which has been of critical importance. There are sixty-two essays by seventy-four contributors. They are from thirty-two nations and represent a wide diversity of geographies, cultures, and traditions. Several of the essays are by young people taking part in the great adventure of putting their high hopes and aspirations for a better world into action as inspired by the Earth Charter. Through these writers, taken together, we see that this is a people's movement – even as the Earth Charter is a people's treaty.

It is my desire that this book celebrates the ways in which the Earth Charter has been used. I also trust that it shows the efficacy of the Earth Charter in international law, religion, diplomacy, education, business, public policy, and many other fields – and that it points the way toward increasing usefulness.

Finally, it is my hope that you, the reader, will add your creative imagination to this endeavor of putting the Earth Charter into action – that *you* will live the Earth Charter, and thereby, join in the process of defining it as a living document. ●

**Note**

1   World Commission on Environment and Development. (1987). *Our Common Future* (p. 8). Oxford: Oxford UP. The Commission was chaired by Gro Harlem Brundtland and is informally known as the Brundtland Commission.

Mirian Vilela, Brazil and Peter Blaze Corcoran, USA. *History and Provenance of the Earth Charter*

# Building Consensus on Shared Values

**Mirian Vilela** is Executive Director of the Earth Charter Initiative. She has been working with the Initiative since early 1996. She coordinated the international process of consultation with national Earth Charter Committees, organized and led numerous workshops, participated in several international seminars, set up an international network of organizations and individuals who contributed to the consultation process. Prior to her work with the Earth Charter, Mirian worked for the United Nations Conference on Environment and Development (UNCED) for two years in preparation of the 1992 UN Earth Summit. She moved from Geneva to Costa Rica in 1993 to join in the establishment of the Earth Council. Mirian is from Brazil and she holds a Master Degree in Public Administration from the Kennedy School of Government at Harvard University, where she was an Edward Mason Fellow.

*Biographical note of Peter Blaze Corcoran on page 15.*

The decade of the 1990s was characterized by the increasingly important role of civil society in international policy-making processes, a growing understanding that issues can no longer be resolved in an isolated manner, and the growing spirit of interdependence and collaboration at all levels to ensure the common good. In this essay, we describe the widely-participatory, global process of building consensus on shared values that is the history and provenance of the Earth Charter.

The 1992 Rio Earth Summit, the end of the cold war, and the progress of communication technology were key elements that marked the beginning of this new era. The Earth Summit accredited an unprecedented number of non-state actors. Some 2,400 representatives of non-governmental organizations (NGOs) and more than 8,000 journalists attended the official event, and 17,000 people attended the parallel NGO Forum. Beginning with that trend, widespread participation of non-state actors in international affairs has continued to grow over the years. The internet has also enabled groups located in different parts of the world to exchange knowledge and join efforts

making their movements stronger. A unique, innovative outcome of the 2002 Johannesburg World Summit on Sustainable Development was the launch of partnerships among actors in different fields.

Given this general understanding that the United Nations (UN) and governments can no longer deal with the world problems alone, the value of collaborative efforts has been reinforced as has the role civil society can play. Furthermore, the concept of sustainability involves systemic thinking for bringing together the environmental, social, political, and economic dimensions of policy-making. This means that multiple ways of looking at global governance are necessary and imminent.

In this context, the Earth Charter Initiative has emerged as a collaborative effort and as an attempt to offer a vision of global ethics to guide society in this new period of history. It is part of the worldwide movement which seeks to identify common goals and shared values that transcend cultural, religious, and national boundaries. For over a decade, diverse groups and individuals from throughout the world have been inspired and motivated in the process of drafting the Earth Charter and using it. What could have ignited the interest, enthusiasm, and commitment from people from so many walks of life and different cultural and religious backgrounds to be involved in this process?

We believe it is the discomfort many people have with the current state of the world and their search for an alternative vision of development that ensures a better future for all. Many want to change the way we relate to each other and to the larger living world. Individuals and groups with different concerns such as water, desertification, health care, poverty, human rights, civil society participation, and environmental protection, more and more see the Earth Charter as a meaningful instrument that speaks to their concerns and helps connect to a larger collaborative good. Diverse groups – from indigenous peoples to UN officials, from grassroots activists to scientists, from attorneys to religious and spiritual leaders – have become passionately engaged in the shared ethical vision of the Earth Charter.

The Earth Charter is the result of a worldwide participatory process of consultation and drafting. As such, it is a synthesis of values, principles, and aspirations that are widely shared by a growing number of people and organizations all around the world. As a movement, it is a continuing process that seeks social transformation by incorporating the Earth Charter vision in many areas of activities.

The role and the significance of the Earth Charter can be better understood within the larger continuous efforts of the United Nations to identify the priorities to ensure a safe world. When the UN was founded in 1945, the world had many challenges to address in post-World War II circumstances. Thus, three major goals were identified for the UN – to ensure peace and world security, to secure human rights, and to foster cooperation for social and economic development. It was only in 1972, as the result of the Stockholm Conference on the Human Environment, that environment protection was considered as the fourth main preoccupation of the United Nations. Furthermore, it was not only until the 1980s that the concept of sustainable development emerged, raising the need to address these various preoccupations with an integrated approach and justifying the need for a new charter.

Much of the development of the Earth Charter derived from the 1987 World Commission on Environment and Development report *Our Common Future*. This report called for the need for "a new charter to guide state behaviour in the transition to sustainable development" and also stated that the charter "should prescribe new norms for state and interstate behaviour needed to maintain livelihoods and life on our shared planet" (p. 332).[1]

The idea of developing an Earth Charter was then included as part of the preparatory process for United Nations Conference on Environment and Development (UNCED) – the Rio Earth Summit. In 1990 and 1991, several preparatory meetings for the conference took place at the international and national levels, which identified elements for such a charter. This effort sought to develop, through intergovernmental negotiation, a charter which was to provide the ethical foundation upon which Agenda 21 and the other UNCED agreements were to be based. The possibility of such an ethical foundation generated significant enthusiasm, which led a number of governments and non governmental organizations to submit recommendations and proposals on this subject.

However, a few months before the actual Summit, at the fourth and last Preparatory Committee (PrepCom) for the conference, it was clear that intergovernmental agreement could not be reached, and the Earth Charter was removed from the agenda for the Summit. It was decided to write instead what became the Rio Declaration on Environment and Development. Nevertheless, during the 1992 NGO Global Forum, held in parallel to the Summit, NGOs from nineteen countries negotiated and drafted an Earth Charter building on the work done in the preparatory process. This Earth Charter was one of the forty-six non governmental treaties of the NGO Global Forum in Rio de Janeiro. The individuals involved in this are pioneers of the Earth Charter Initiative.[2]

In the closing statement of the Earth Summit, Secretary General Maurice F. Strong said, "We have a profoundly important Declaration, but it must continue to evolve towards what many of us hope will be an Earth Charter that could be finally sanctioned on the fiftieth anniversary of the United Nations in 1995."

In April 1994, the idea was then taken up by Strong, Chairman of the Earth Council, and Mikhail Gorbachev, President of Green Cross International, when a new Earth Charter initiative was launched with support from Queen Beatrix, Prime Minister Ruud Lubbers, and the government of The Netherlands. A management committee was formed to guide the initial phase of the project, and Ambassador Mohammed Sahnoun of Algeria, the first Executive Director of the Initiative, ran the project coordinating office from The Hague.

Therefore, because of the failure in intergovernmental negotiations in the 1992 process, an opportunity for broader involvement of civil society was created through this new project. This also enabled the drafting process to benefit from thoughtful progress in the international community and from the conceptual agreements reached at the UN Summits held over the decade of the 1990s.

This phase of the Earth Charter consultation process began with an international workshop held at the Peace Palace in The Hague in May 1995. This event brought together over seventy participants from thirty countries on all continents and a wide range of cultures and faiths. The workshop served to define the needs, basic elements, and the process of how the Earth Charter should be drawn up. From this first workshop on the basic elements for an Earth Charter came the notion of common, but differentiated, responsibility of all states and individuals; the right of every person to a healthy environment; and the strengthening of people's participation in decision-making.

During 1995 and 1996, extensive research was conducted in the fields of international law, science, religion, ethics, environmental conservation, and sustainable development in preparation for the drafting of the Earth Charter. In 1996, a compilation of approximately fifty international law instruments entitled *Principles of Environmental Conservation and Sustainable Development: Summary and Survey* was prepared by Steven C. Rockefeller, who was then invited to chair the drafting process. This manuscript was widely distributed in order to gather feedback in this initial phase of the consultation process. Organizations were asked to submit their recommendations by early 1997 in preparation to the Rio Forum+5, a forum organized by the Earth Council as an independent civil society review of the progress of implementation of the Earth Summit agreements. The Rio+5

The Earth Charter in Action

Forum was held in March 1997 in Rio de Janeiro and drew over 500 representatives of NGOs and some governments. The occasion was an extraordinary platform to start a dialogue with youth, faith, women's groups, and indigenous peoples to assemble their concerns and suggestions on the Earth Charter.

The Earth Charter Commission was formed in early 1997 to oversee the ongoing consultation and drafting of the Charter. The Earth Council, under the leadership of Maximo Kalaw, Jr. of the Philippines, functioned as the Secretariat for the Commission. The first meeting of the Commission took place during the Rio+5 Forum, and on 18 March 1997, at the last day of the event, the Earth Charter Benchmark Draft was publicly issued. The benchmark draft signaled the achievement of a significant milestone, while at the same time it acknowledged that the drafting process needed to continue. The Commission called for ongoing international consultations regarding the text of the document.

Subsequently, numerous meetings and consultations took place to identify the shared values and principles that should be part of such a document and to offer comments on the drafts of the Earth Charter. These consultations were held at the national, regional, and global level, as well as with some specific interest groups. Recommendations and comments generated by these consultations were forwarded to a drafting committee created by the Earth Charter Commission. This exercise was valuable, not only to offer suggestions for the final draft of the Charter, but it was important to engage people in a process of reflection and consensus-building on Earth Charter themes. Thus, the exercise was generating local impacts and contributing to an international effort. We see the Earth Charter consultations as a worldwide, participatory process of building consensus and shared values. Special consultations were held with expert groups in international law, faith traditions, contemporary science, women issues, and education.

Just one example of such involvement is that of indigenous peoples. The Indigenous People's Program of the Earth Council, with the collaboration of partner institutions, made significant efforts to engage the wisdom of indigenous peoples in the consultation process. First, in May 1996, a meeting in Costa Rica brought together indigenous peoples from throughout the Americas. A compilation of suggestions stressed that the Earth Charter should include concepts expressing the values of many different peoples and cultures.

In 1997, Beatriz Schulthess, a member of the Indigenous Peoples Spiritual Consultative Council participated in the meeting of Earth Charter Drafting Committee in order to voice the concerns of those consulted. There was also an opportunity to dialogue during Rio+5 Forum, when a group of indigenous representatives shared their views about the Earth Charter. Further contributions were made through a number of workshops. Significant interest was generated among indigenous groups from Latin America, such that Earth Charter National Committees in El Sal-

vador and Panama were led by indigenous peoples groups.

In addition, the Inuit Circumpolar Conference (ICC) became deeply involved in the debate concerning the wording of the Earth Charter text; in particular with regard to Principle 7 of Benchmark Draft II, "Treat all living beings with compassion." This was because of the interpretation of the word "compassion." Compassion for animals is a very important notion in many religious traditions, but it was unacceptable among the indigenous hunting cultures as related to animals. After significant deliberation, the notion of "respect and consideration" in relation to animals was accepted by all.

The Earth Charter Consultation also benefited from comments of well-known indigenous representatives such as Oren Lyons, Faith Keeper of the Onondaga Council of Chiefs of the Six Nations Iroquois Confederacy; and Henriette Rasmussen, of the Inuit people; and Pauline Tangiora, of the Maori from Aotearoa (New Zealand).

After consulting with such different groups, all involved in the drafting process agreed with recommendations received that the Earth Charter should give special recognition to indigenous peoples, but the question was related to the wording and the location of such principle. The reference to indigenous cultures appears in the final text of the Earth Charter as Principle 12, "Uphold the right of all, without discrimination, to a natural and social environment supportive of human dignity, bodily health, and spiritual well-being, with special attention to the rights of indigenous peoples and minorities." In addition, as a result of this process, the document is infused with indigenous wisdom.

The IUCN Commission on Environmental Law was closely involved throughout the consultation and drafting process. Among many other occasions was a consultation held in June 1999 with the Working Group on Ethics and Jurisprudence of the IUCN Commission on Environmental Law, where inputs were offered, as well as legal advice in the drafting of the Earth Charter. International lawyers from ten different countries, representing Africa, Asia, Australia, Europe, and the Americas attended the meeting and contributed to the discussions. As a result of this effort, the Earth Charter drafting benefited from the highest standards of content originating in international law.

Forty-two national Earth Charter committees were established between 1997 and 2000 in all regions of the world and numerous consultations were held. The levels of commitment ranged from fully operational national committees, as in Australia, Mexico or the United States which were successful in encouraging broad-based participation and involvement in different sectors and in regions within those countries, to a single consultation held in some nations.

Three regional meetings also took place in the Americas; Central Asia; and Africa and the Middle East. In December 1998, the Earth Charter Continental Conference of the Americas was held in Brazil. The conference brought together over one hundred delegates from twenty-two countries to dialogue about the Earth Charter. On the final day of the conference, a Latin American and Caribbean Earth Charter Draft Document was issued. The intention was that it would serve as a basis for continued discussion, debate, and revision in the international drafting process. In June 1999, approximately thirty participants from Kazakhstan, Kyrgyzstan, Tajikistan, Turkmenistan, and Uzbekistan, representing National Councils for Sustainable Development, NGOs, governments, academia, and the media, were brought together to learn more about the Earth Charter and comment on it. Participants defined some strategies for implementing Earth Charter values and principles and integrating them into National Sustainable Plans in Central Asia. Twenty participants from various countries of Africa and the Middle East met in December 1999 in Capetown, South Africa, to add significant value and perspectives to the Earth Charter consultation. The three-day dialogue with members of the Earth Charter Drafting Committee provided an opportunity for groups in the region to contribute to the drafting process. Issues regarding gender equality, compassion for animals, indigenous peoples, and respect for cultural traditions, among others were discussed. Participants represented Kenya, South Africa, Zimbabwe, Burkina Faso, Mauritius, Senegal, Niger, Ghana, and Jordan.

In addition, three online conferences on the Earth Charter were held in 1999. Among them, a forum held in October 1999 was designed to facilitate discussion on the content and structure of the Earth Charter Benchmark Draft II. It involved approximately seventy-four representatives of Earth Charter national committees and affiliated groups as well as participants of the Earth Charter Drafting Committee. Two internet-based forums on "Global Ethics, Sustainable Development, and the Earth Charter" were held to encourage dialogue between university students and professors, and to engage different constituencies more deeply on the concept of an Earth Charter. The first of these conferences was conducted in English in April 1999 and involved individuals from over 500 colleges, universities, and organizations from seventy-three different countries. The second one was held in Spanish and Portuguese in November 1999 and gathered individuals from over 250 colleges, universities, and organizations from forty countries.

All these efforts proved extremely valuable in highlighting areas of consensus, as well as areas of conflict, in relation to the structure and phrasing of the Benchmark Drafts. The contributions gathered in the consultation process enabled extensive revisions on the different drafts of the Charter.

The history of all of these consultations – the story of the Earth Charter – is a story of people. Two very special moments of this consultation process are marked in the memory of those who had the privilege to be there. The first one was during the closing of the December 1998 Earth Charter Conference of the Americas held in Mato Grosso, Brazil. To conclude the conference, participants were taken to a National Park located outside of Cuiabá called Salgadeira (Chapada Dos Guimaraes). Participants were invited to be part of a mobilization effort involving four thousand students wearing Earth Charter shirts, hand-in-hand forming a human chain of over three and a half kilometers in a symbolic embracing of the Earth. Following that, a striking Earth Charter monument was inaugurated. The monument, by artist Jonas Correa, presents the Earth being sustained by the trunk of a tree. In it, five children representing five continents surround the tree holding hands to symbolize protection and security of the planet. It was a moving and unforgettable experience for all participants. The second moment was later, on an evening in December 1999 during the World Parliament of Religions at the Arena of Good Hope in Cape Town, South Africa. The Arena of Good Hope was overflowing with more than five thousand people. Nelson Mandela entered in the room and the audience could not stop clapping; great emotion was in everybody's heart in the presence of such a significant leader of historical social change in his country. In the midst of this very moving moment, the Earth Charter was presented to the conference participants and to Nelson Mandela as a gift of their service.

Three formal International Earth Charter Drafting Committee meetings took place to review the results of these consultation processes, to address key issues identified during the consultation, and to prepare a revision of the draft. These drafting meetings brought together a diversity of scientists, international lawyers, ethicists, and NGO activists representing all regions of the world. Discussions on these meetings were especially important in shaping the document. These meetings were held in 1997, 1999, and 2000.[3]

The length, structure, logical arrangement of principles, and language style were carefully examined at the drafting meetings. Throughout the process, there was a debate about the length. Many believed that a substantial document was essential and that a brief document of a page or so would not fulfill the expectations of many, thus it would be difficult to gain widespread support. Others wanted a short Earth Charter with ten brief principles to be easy to use and circulated. It was concluded that a brief Charter tended to be general, and the generalities often did not address the complexity of the problems from the point of view of many groups. The Drafting Committee opted for a layered document and divided the Charter into four parts. Considering the many concerns that emerged in the consultation process, it was clear that the main principles should be organized in multiple layers of themes, accompanied by supporting principles, in order to be inclusive.

As a result of the worldwide consultation and drafting process, which involved thousands of individuals and hundreds of groups in various parts of the world, the Earth Charter Commission issued a final version of the Earth Charter after their meeting on 12-14 March 2000 at the UNESCO headquarters in Paris. A consensus of shared values had been reached. The official launching of the Earth Charter took place at the Peace Palace in The Hague on 29 June 2000, when a new phase in the Initiative began.

Upon adoption of the final document, the Earth Charter Commission recommended changes in the structure of the Earth Charter Initiative to adapt to its new phase. The main decision was that the Initiative should no longer function under the joint guidance of the Earth Council and Green Cross International, but was to be overseen by the Steering Committee designated by the Commission itself. The Earth Charter International Secretariat, located in Costa Rica, was given the mandate of promoting the Earth Charter widely and to continue serving as a facilitator and catalyst for Earth Charter activities taking place throughout the world.

One of the first tasks of the Secretariat was to seek support for the Earth Charter. Endorsements of the Earth Charter have come from all continents; they tell us that the Earth Charter message and plea for change is heard and shared. This building of support worldwide is reinforcing the purpose and aims of this movement. Endorsement of the Earth Charter is defined as signifying commitment to the spirit and aims of the document and an intention to use the Earth Charter in appropriate ways, given the situation of the individual or group. To date, the Earth Charter has been formally endorsed by over two thousand organizations worldwide[4]. Many of them have membership of thousands or even millions. Among these groups are national and international organizations, educational institutions, private sector entities, religious groups, and nearly four hundred towns and cities. A significant, recent endorsement was from the World Conservation Union (IUCN) in 2004.

Earth Charter events were organized by the Secretariat at all the PrepComs leading up to the 2002 World Summit on Sustainable Development. At the last plenary session of PrepCom IV held in Bali, Indonesia, a number of governments expressed their support for including a reference in the Summit Political Declaration acknowledging the Earth Charter. This was recorded in the Chair's summary of the PrepCom. Later, at Johannesburg, the Earth Charter received acknowledgment from governments of Costa Rica, the Dominican Republic, Mexico, Honduras, Bolivia, Niger, The Netherlands, Romania, Spain, Jamaica, and Jordan. It had a reference in the opening speech of President Mbeki, in a number of addresses of heads of state, and in the Draft Political Declaration of Johannesburg. Unfortunately, as a result, last-minute, non-public objections from certain governments, reference to the Earth Charter was deleted from the final version. This happened despite the fact that the Earth Charter was also recognized in a number of documents set forth in preparatory meetings for the Summit, including the UN regional roundta-

bles, the Latin American and Caribbean Ministerial Initiative for Sustainable Development, and the report of the Secretary General's High Level Advisory Panel.

In the year 2000, the Secretariat put in place a programme to promote the educational uses of the Earth Charter and to develop educational resources that would help undertake this task. An International Education Advisory Committee was formed in 2001 to assist the development of a strategic plan and overall advise the programme activities. Two on-line forums on education and the Earth Charter were held; the first one was held in 2001 with the aims of articulating an educational philosophy to underpin the educational use of the Earth Charter and identifying strategic educational opportunities, priorities, and partnerships. The second forum, held in December 2003, responded to the need to further the discussions and to advance the education programme's activities. Considering the requests and the need for teaching materials to help educators use the Earth Charter in their practice, an Earth Charter Education Guidebook for teachers in primary and secondary schools has been developed.

Over the past five years, the Earth Charter has been endorsed and utilized by an increasing number of schools and institutions of higher education. A noted achievement was the adoption of a resolution in support of the Earth Charter at the UNESCO General Conference held in October 2003. The resolution recognizes the Earth Charter as an important ethical framework for sustainable development and affirmed member states' intention "to utilize the Earth Charter as an educational instrument, particularly in the framework of the United Nations Decade for Education for Sustainable Development." Moreover, in the Draft UNESCO Implementation Scheme for the Decade, the Earth Charter is recommended to be put in action.

The Earth Charter International Secretariat has also emphasized work with the Earth Charter at the local community level. Work with local communities has been done with the support of key organizations such as the Earth Charter Community

Summits, Local Governments for Sustainability (ICLEI), Fundacion Deyna and ForoSoria 21 in Spain, Global Community Initiatives (GCI), and the World Resources Institute (WRI). Cities such as Joondalup, Australia, and Toronto, Canada, have utilized the Earth Charter as a tool in their planning. The City of San Jose, Costa Rica, used the Earth Charter vision to undertake a project to train all their staff with regard to sustainability principles.

An important example of local community work is that of Jan Roberts and the Institute for Ethics and Meaning in Tampa, Florida, USA. Earth Charter Community Summits are held annually as grassroots efforts to bring people together to be inspired to make the Earth Charter's principles a reality in their lives and communities. Local summit organizers are volunteers who simply want to bring the Earth Charter to their home towns. The number of cities holding simultaneous gatherings on this topic has ranged from twelve to thirty-three over the past four years.

In late 2003, an Earth Charter Partnership for Sustainable Communities consisting of the World Resources Institute, the Earth Charter Initiative, and Global Community Initiatives was formed to further the development of necessary tools to help local communities use the Earth Charter. An Earth Charter Community Action Tool (EarthCAT) has been developed to provide communities with a guide to develop goals, targets, and strategies to implement sustainable practices and to measure their progress using indicators and reporting systems.

Building consensus on shared values has been a long, thoughtful, and richly human process. The Earth Charter Initiative is a civil society movement working toward a just, peaceful, and sustainable world. Even though much progress has been made, the Earth Charter Initiative now faces the challenge of making the Earth Charter an effective instrument of global governance, and international law, as well as grounding it in peoples' daily lives. The success of this initiative depends upon the cooperation and mutual support of involved groups – and the ongoing enthusiasm of individuals for putting the Earth Charter into action. ●

**Notes**

1    World Commission on Environment and Development. (1987). *Our Common Future* (p. 332). Oxford: Oxford UP. The Commission was chaired by Gro Harlem Brundtland and is informally known as the Brundtland Commission.
2    Among them we would like to mention Peter Adriance, who led much of this effort in his capacity as secretary and co-chair of the Citizens Network Working Group on Ethics, Environment and Development; Rick Clugston; Moacir Gadotti; Moema Vizzer; Prue Taylor; and Klaus Bosselmann. All are still involved in the Earth Charter Initiative.
3    A small and informal drafting meeting also took place in early 1998.
4    See www.earthcharter.org for further information on endorsements.

# Preamble

# Preamble

We stand at a critical moment in Earth's history, a time when humanity must choose its future. As the world becomes increasingly interdependent and fragile, the future at once holds great peril and great promise. To move forward we must recognize that in the midst of a magnificent diversity of cultures and life forms we are one human family and one Earth community with a common destiny. We must join together to bring forth a sustainable global society founded on respect for nature, universal human rights, economic justice, and a culture of peace. Towards this end, it is imperative that we, the peoples of Earth, declare our responsibility to one another, to the greater community of life, and to future generations.

## Earth, Our Home

Humanity is part of a vast evolving universe. Earth, our home, is alive with a unique community of life. The forces of nature make existence a demanding and uncertain adventure, but Earth has provided the conditions essential to life's evolution. The resilience of the community of life and the well-being of humanity depend upon preserving a healthy biosphere with all its ecological systems, a rich variety of plants and animals, fertile soils, pure waters, and clean air. The global environment with its finite resources is a common concern of all peoples. The protection of Earth's vitality, diversity, and beauty is a sacred trust.

## The Global Situation

The dominant patterns of production and consumption are causing environmental devastation, the depletion of resources, and a massive extinction of species. Communities are being undermined. The benefits of development are not shared equitably and the gap between rich and poor is widening. Injustice, poverty, ignorance, and violent conflict are widespread and the cause of great suffering. An unprecedented rise in human population has overburdened ecological and social systems. The foundations of global security are threatened. These trends are perilous—but not inevitable.

## The Challenges Ahead

The choice is ours: form a global partnership to care for Earth and one another or risk the destruction of ourselves and the diversity of life. Fundamental changes are needed in our values, institutions, and ways of living. We must realize that when basic needs have been met, human development is primarily about being more, not having more. We have the knowledge and technology to provide for all and to reduce our impacts on the environment. The emergence of a global civil society is creating new opportunities to build a democratic and humane world. Our environmental, economic, political, social, and spiritual challenges are interconnected, and together we can forge inclusive solutions.

## Universal Responsibility

To realize these aspirations, we must decide to live with a sense of universal responsibility, identifying ourselves with the whole Earth community as well as our local communities. We are at once citizens of different nations and of one world in which the local and global are linked. Everyone shares responsibility for the present and future well-being of the human family and the larger living world. The spirit of human solidarity and kinship with all life is strengthened when we live with reverence for the mystery of being, gratitude for the gift of life, and humility regarding the human place in nature.

We urgently need a shared vision of basic values to provide an ethical foundation for the emerging world community. Therefore, together in hope we affirm the following interdependent principles for a sustainable way of life as a common standard by which the conduct of all individuals, organizations, businesses, governments, and transnational institutions is to be guided and assessed.

*The text of the Earth Charter continues with Part I on page 42.*

# Humanity is Part of a Vast Evolving Universe

**Mary Evelyn Tucker** is a Professor of Religion at Bucknell University in Pennsylvania where she teaches courses in Asian religions and religion and ecology. With John Grim, she organized a series of conferences on World Religions and Ecology at Harvard University; they are series editors for the ten volumes from the conferences (Harvard University Press). She is the author of *Worldly Wonder: Religions Enter Their Ecological Phase* (Open Court Press, 2003) and *Moral and Spiritual Cultivation in Japanese Neo-Confucianism* (SUNY 1989). She co-edited *Worldviews and Ecology* (Orbis, 1994), *Buddhism and Ecology* (Harvard, 1997), *Confucianism and Ecology* (Harvard, 1998), and *Hinduism and Ecology* (Harvard, 2000) and *When Worlds Converge* (Open Court, 2002). Mary Evelyn is a member of the Interfaith Partnership for the Environment at the United Nations Environment Programme (UNEP) and served as a member of the International Earth Charter Drafting Committee from 1997-2000.

*The twentieth century will be chiefly remembered by future generations not as an era of political conflicts or technical innovations but as an age in which human society dared to think of the welfare of the whole human race as a practical objective.*
Arnold Toynbee

This is a powerful statement from one of the leading historians of world history. Indeed, the Earth Charter, completed at the end of the twentieth century, represents a fulfillment of this prediction by Toynbee. However, the Charter expands Toynbee's statement to suggest that the twenty-first century will be remembered by this extension of our moral concerns not only to humans, but to other species and ecosystems as well. From social justice to ecojustice, the movement of human care is part of ever widening concentric circles. This is what the Earth Charter embodies as an aspiration and as a movement. Indeed, the twenty-first century may be remembered as the century in which humans laid the foundations for the well-being of the planet as a whole by embracing the Earth community. The future of life may depend on the largeness of our embrace, for we are now challenged as never before to build a multi-form, planetary civilization inclusive of both cultural and biological diversity.

In this context, the particular challenge of the Earth Charter is for us to identify the kind of vision, values, and ethics that will help spark the transformation toward creating such a planetary civilization. A sustainable future requires not just managerial or legislative approaches, as important as these may be, but also a sustaining vision of that future. This vision needs to evoke depths of empathy, compassion, and sacrifice that have the welfare of future generations in mind. We are called, for the first time in history, to a new intergenerational consciousness and conscience – and this extends to the entire Earth community.

As the Preamble to the Charter notes, this is a task of considerable urgency. As the world becomes warmer, as hurricanes increase, as species go extinct, as air and water pollution spreads, and as resource wars heat up, there is a disturbing sense among many environmentalists and ordinary citizens that the clock is ticking towards major disasters ahead. The looming environmental crisis, with its massive scale and increasing complexity, clearly defies easy solutions. Moreover, the heightened frenzy of the global war on terrorism creates blindness toward the widespread terror humans have unleashed on the planet – on its ecosystems on land and in the oceans and on all the species they contain. Blindness is combined with enormous apathy or denial from various quarters regarding the scale of the problems we are facing. This is especially true of those living within the confines of high consumer societies.

In this context of the global environmental crisis, the critical nature of our historical moment is described by Mihaly Csikszentmihalyi in his book *The Evolving Self* (HarperCollins, 1993). He highlights the enormous responsibility of our species that describes the impetus behind the Preamble of the Earth Charter:

The time of innocence…is now past. It is no longer possible for mankind to blunder about self-indulgently. Our species has become too powerful to be led by instincts alone. Birds and lemmings cannot do much damage except to themselves, whereas we can destroy the entire matrix of life on the planet. The awesome powers we have stumbled into require a commensurate responsibility. As we become aware of the motives that shape our actions, as our place in the chain of evolution becomes clearer, we must find a meaningful and binding plan that will protect us and the rest of life from the consequences of what we have wrought. (p. 18)

He goes on to acknowledge, as does the Preamble, that the emerging consciousness of ourselves as a planetary species sharing in life's future is vital:

> The only value that all human beings can readily share is the continuation of life on earth. In this one goal all individual self-interests are united. Unless such a species identity takes precedence over the more particular identities of faith, nation, family, or person, it will be difficult to agree on the course that must be taken to guarantee our future….. (p. 19)

To create such a species identity is precisely the challenge of ourselves as individuals as well as ourselves as an Earth community. As the Preamble states: "To move forward we must recognize that in the midst of a magnificent diversity of cultures and life forms we are one human family and one Earth community with a common destiny" (paragraph one).

The Preamble notes that we can risk "the destruction of ourselves and the diversity of life" (paragraph four), if we don't embrace this larger species identity. Csikszentmihalyi recognizes that the future of evolution is at stake if we should fail. He writes:

> It is for this reason that the fate of humanity in the next millennium depends so closely on the kind of selves we will succeed in creating. Evolution is by no means guaranteed. We have a chance of being part of it only as long as we understand our place in that gigantic field of force we call nature. (p.25)

As Csikszentmihalyi suggests, one of the crucial areas we need to explore is the depth of our evolving selves that are part of the larger matrix of life. We can have a certain measure of confidence that we will find the next season of our evolution as humans as we come to "understand our place within that vast field of force we call nature."

The Preamble of the Earth Charter points toward finding our way forward as citizens of Earth dependent on the forces of nature. It suggests that we need to rediscover the intertwined coding of ourselves as bio-cultural beings – filled with the mixed heritage of biological survival and cultural creativity. Such is the imperative of our evolution as a species that calls for a new "cultural coding" resonant with, but distinguished from,

the genetic coding of evolution itself. We can see ourselves now as imprinted with nature's complex coding and entwined within nature's rhythms. At the same time, our cultural coding needs to be brought into alignment with the forces and limits of nature. This calls for new forms of education, religion, politics, and economics for a sustainable future.

There are many indications that these forms are emerging and that we are evolving into our next phase as humans. With sustainable technologies and design, with ecological economics and politics, with environmental education and ethics, we are learning how to assist evolution and to participate in the myriad processes of universe powers. If human decisions have swamped natural selection because of our planetary power as a species, we can learn how to become aligned again with evolutionary flourishing. In what we protect, in what we build, in what we eat, in what we cherish, we will find the animating principles of universe evolution that also ground culture and guide humans in our creation of communities. We will become partners with evolutionary processes. This is what the Preamble calls for – the choice to "form a global partnership to care for Earth and one another" (paragraph four).

To form such a partnership we will have to draw on the comprehensive framework of evolution of the universe, of Earth, and of the human. This evolutionary perspective provides an expansive context to articulate empowering frameworks of values and virtues for individuals and communities. The enlarged worldview of evolution affords a means of activating a comprehensive set of values and ethics that will point the way toward partnering with evolution.

Such is the large-scale context that the Preamble offers. It states: "Humanity is part of a vast evolving universe. Earth, our home, is alive with a unique community of life. The forces of nature make existence a demanding and uncertain adventure, but Earth has provided the conditions essential to life's evolution" (paragraph two). The Preamble thus affirms that the physical, chemical, and biological conditions for life are in delicate interaction over time to bring forth and sustain life. Our response to this awesome process is responsibility for its continuity and thus to become a life-enhancing species.

The significance of this evolutionary perspective in the Preamble should be underscored as it marks a watershed in our rethinking ethics within such a vast framework. The implications of the story of evolution that we are beginning to absorb are manifold. They include a new sense of *orientation*, *belonging*, and *vitality*. The universe story gives us an orientation toward the vastness of time and space that evokes wonder and awe. We begin to see into the macrophase of our own being as we embrace 13.7 billion years of universe unfolding through stars, galaxies, planets, and life forms. We recognize that the chemical components of our bodies came out of the formation of stars. We are stardust come to light in human form.

Along with such expansive orientation, we are given a deepened sense of belonging to the universe and to the Earth. We are grounded and connected to the planet as we share in our dependence on the elements of air, water, and soil for our survival. The universe story thus decenters humans amidst the vastness of the universe and recenters humans as part of, not apart from, the great community of life. In particular, it highlights our role as a species among other species, all radically dependent on the Earth for our well-being. We are recognizing anew that we belong to the Earth community.

This perspective gives us a reinvigorated vitality for caring for and participating in Earth processes. Our partnering with evolution becomes an expression of our comprehensive compassion for all life – human and "more than human."[1] To encourage the future flourishing of life is the destiny of humans as they participate in what the Chinese Confucians have called, "the transforming and nourishing powers of Heaven and Earth."[2] The zest for life is what will carry us forward as we align ourselves with these cosmological powers. With such alignment we are able to create new forms of human-Earth relations that have expression in diverse fields of education, religion, government, economics, medicine, law, technology, and design.

Within the framework of the universe story, we are beginning to acknowledge that our common ground is the common ground of the Earth itself. Survival of species and the planet depends on this. Adaptation for survival is necessary for all species and thus is especially crucial now for humans. This adaptation will be less biological than cultural. It involves a shift in vision and values from a western Enlightenment mentality emphasizing radical individualism to an Earth community mentality of a shared future.

This shift will require an expansion of ethics such as the Charter embodies and the Preamble outlines. The Enlightenment values of "life, liberty, and the pursuit of happiness" are reframed in the Preamble, not just to suit the human person and individual property rights, but to include the larger Earth community. Moving from anthropocentric values to bio-centered values is the challenge that the Preamble sets forth.

Thus, in designating "life" as an important value, the Preamble uses the term to include all life - other species and ecosystems, as well as people at a distance, and future generations. Up to now, as Thomas Berry has observed, we have developed ethics in the human community regarding life to address the problems of homicide and suicide and even genocide, but not biocide, ecocide, or geocide. This is what the Preamble represents – a comprehensive ethical response to avert potential geocide. It shifts us from viewing nature simply as a resource for human use to nature as source of life. In short, the Preamble moves us from viewing Earth as commodity to Earth as a "community of life."

"Liberty" is seen in the Preamble as not simply a matter of individual rights, but as including human responsibilities to the larger whole. It urges the peoples of the Earth to "declare our responsibility to one another, to the greater community of life, and to future generations" (paragraph one). Thus, the Preamble calls us from personal freedom to communitarian care. From celebrating radical individualism, we move toward "kinship with all life." The Preamble highlights this in the call for "Universal Responsibility" that ranges from local issues to global concerns.

With regard to the "pursuit of happiness," the Preamble moves us from individual acquisition and consumption to the great work of contributing to transforming human-Earth relations. It highlights the notion that "when basic needs have been met, human development is primarily about being more, not having more" (paragraph four). It calls us from private property as an exclusive right to embracing the public trust of land and water and air for future generations. The Preamble states: "The protection of Earth's vitality, diversity, and beauty is a sacred trust" (paragraph two).

Such an expanded framework beyond Enlightenment values provides a context for humans to see inter-linked problems along with interconnected solutions. This is what the Preamble of the Earth Charter aims to do as it delineates a simple, but viable, blueprint for a sustainable future. It highlights the inter-related issues of environment, justice, and peace as at the heart of our global challenges. Against the comprehensive background of evolution in the Preamble, the main body of the Charter outlines an integrated set of ethics and practices to address these three interrelated issues. It aims to address the sometimes competing areas of environment and development.

The Charter recognizes that the future of life is impossible without ecological integrity. Life and all economic development depend on the health of the biosphere. Thus, the preservation of ecosystems and biodiversity are essential along with the careful use of nonrenewable resources and the exploration of renewable sources of energy.

To do this effectively demands social and economic equity and empowerment. The widening gaps between the rich and the poor in the developed and developing world are a cause for social unrest and can breed resentment and terrorism. How to close these gaps is of utmost importance. Poverty and environmental issues are closely linked in this framework. How to manage economic development for the improvement of standards of living without permanently degrading the environment is the challenge.

A third point in the main body of the Charter is democracy, nonviolence, and peace. It is almost impossible to achieve the goals of a healthy environment and equitable societies without democratic institutions and legal structures that encourage participation and transparency. The aspirations of millions to live in democratic societies without human rights abuses is demonstrable throughout the world. Moreover, it is becoming increasingly clear that peace among nations will not be achievable without addressing both environmental and social issues. Thus, the Charter sees the importance of an empowering framework that identifies an integrated set of ethics linking healthy environment, principles of justice, and institutions of democracy.

The empowering spirit of the Earth Charter is linked to its sense of historic challenge, in the Preamble, namely that: "The foundations of global security are threatened" (paragraph three). However, it observes: "These trends are perilous but not inevitable" (paragraph three) and goes on to suggest that: "The choice is ours: form a global partnership to care for Earth and one another or risk the destruction of ourselves and the diversity of life" (paragraph four).

The Charter concludes with a similarly cautiously optimistic tone saying, "As never before in history, common destiny beckons us to seek a new beginning" (The Way Forward, paragraph one). It notes that "This requires a change of mind and heart" – of vision and values (The Way Forward, paragraph two). The Charter, then, exemplifies an important trend toward an integrative global ethics. It highlights the importance of our moment in human history. It provides an empowering context of values and practices that will steer the human community forward toward the enhancement, not the diminishment, of life. Further reflection of the Earth Charter in political gatherings, religious groups, academic settings, and environmental organizations is already beginning to foster a more unified basis for thought and action.

The Earth Charter, then, embodies the hope for expanded vision and inspiring values for the larger Earth community as it seeks to build common ground for a sustainable future. The comprehensive framework of the story of evolution in the Preamble provides animating principles of orientation to the universe, belonging to the Earth community, and vitality in relation to life processes. These principles forge the bonds of human-Earth relations, thus sustaining the demands of relationality and restoring the wellsprings of zest. Within this comprehensive vision of interconnections set forth in the Preamble, a new set of global ethics emerges in the principles of the Charter. This Charter becomes an empowering framework to inspire engagement in and participation with mutually enhancing human-Earth relations. For humans to imagine and activate these relations is to bring into being the emerging contours of the future of the evolutionary process itself. ●

**Notes**

1    To use David Abram's phrase
2    *The Doctrine of the Mean*, Confucius

Parvez Hassan, Pakistan. A thematic essay on the historical context and significance of the Earth Charter

# Earth Charter: An Ethical Lodestar and Moral Force

**Parvez Hassan**, a former Chairman (1990-1996) of the Commission on Environmental Law of IUCN – The World Conservation Union, participated in the drafting of the Earth Charter and was a keynote speaker at its launch. Earlier, he had led the drafting of the IUCN Draft Covenant on Environment and Development, 1995. Dr. Hassan facilitated the recognition in the Earth Charter of the need to support the implementation of its principles with "an internationally legally binding instrument on environment and development". Through his membership of the Eminent Persons Fora established in preparation for the World Summit on Sustainable Development in 2002, in both the Central Asia and Asia Pacific Regions, Dr. Hassan has continued to promote the adoption of the Earth Charter principles as a central plank of the development agenda.

We all came away from the launch of the Earth Charter in June 2000 with an unmistakable feeling that here was a vision that, over time, would anchor human dignity and humanity's interdependent relationship to Earth and the universe. There are, after all, many examples where inspirational documents have changed the course of civilization: the Magna Carta, the American Declaration of Independence, the French Declaration of the Rights of Man and of the Citizen, and the Universal Declaration of Human Rights, all stirred human imagination and changed the quality of life of peoples all over the globe.

Five years later, our optimism has proved well-founded: the Earth Charter is on course to become one of the most inspirational documents of this century, joining ranks with the Universal Declaration of Human Rights of the past century, which strove for the worldwide recognition of values previously upheld in national settings. However, in promoting the Earth Charter as the conscience of the world, we can draw a valuable lesson from the experience of the Universal Declaration, which was not legally binding on states, and which needed the aid of hard law treaties to create an effective international bill of rights.

After the devastation and misery wrought by World War II, human rights emerged as one of the dominant themes of international relations for the next several decades. In the midst of our current ecological predicament, caring for Earth has become a matter of equally compelling priority. This change of focus has gone hand in hand with a realization that the primacy of economic growth cannot be the dominant ideology for the new century as it was for the old.[1] In an open letter to heads of states of American nations, a distinguished group of Western Hemisphere leaders noted:

> ...there is much reason to believe, based on past experience and current trends, that unless major complimentary initiatives are undertaken to bring environmental, economic, and social objectives together in the new synthesis called sustainable development, liberalizing trade and economic growth could lead to short-term gains and long-term disaster. More than anything else, the Compact for a New World must be a compact for sustainable development.[2]

There is, at the dawn of a new century, an unprecedented ecological crisis at hand: we live in a world where national, religious, and ethnic fault lines dominate the landscape; where the gap between rich and poor continues to inexorably widen; where the global natural resources are being exploited without regard to their future needs; where a significant part of the over six billion global population is living in abject poverty without access to clean water and sanitation facilities; and where terrorist groups turn modern technology to their ruthless designs. There is a palpable need, as at no other time in history, to forge a global ethic for building a just, sustainable, and peaceful world in the twenty-first century. This is recognized in the Preamble to the Earth Charter, which states, "We urgently need a shared vision of basic values to provide an ethical foundation for the emerging world community" (paragraph six).

As Maurice Strong has cautioned, scientific, legal, or economic resources can only take us so far without a fundamental change in orientation:

Economic change is imperative, indeed critical. But, in the final analysis, economic factors, like other aspects of human behavior, are deeply rooted in the human, cultural, spiritual, social and ethical values which are the fundamental sources of motivation of the behavior of people and nations. Technocratic measures can facilitate, but not motivate solutions to the basic issues that will face the Earth Summit. The practical solutions we devise, the concrete measures we propose will be of little effect if they are not accompanied by a deep and profound stirring of the human spirit.[3]

As an ethical lodestar and motivational tool, the Earth Charter succeeds magnificently across many dimensions. By integrating ecological concerns with mankind's historic quest for social justice, democracy, and peace, it creates a successful environmental ethic which will resonate well beyond the constituency of environmental activists. Having gone through the most participatory consultation process of any document in history, its call for global responsibility has an unshakeable legitimacy.

There is no doubt that the Earth Charter will have tremendous utility as a pedagogical tool for the next generation and as a values framework for businesses, communities, and nations alike. In the tradition of some of the great historical texts, it is a pithy document (no more than 2,400 words), but one which contains the wisdom needed to learn to live off nature's income, not capital.

Without undermining its tremendous moral force[4], there is a need to carry the energy behind this landmark document into a hard law treaty creating binding obligations on state and non-state actors. This is one of the areas of cooperation being pursued by IUCN, the World Conservation Union (formerly International Union for the Conservation of Nature and Natural Resources) in association with the Earth Charter initiative in which I have been closely involved. In explaining our attempts to forge a global treaty, I often draw an analogy with the Universal Declaration of Human Rights, which was proclaimed in 1948. In the field of human rights, the Universal Declaration was the foundation on which the edifice of human dignity was built through one building block after another: the Rights of the Child, the Rights of Women, the Covenant on Civil and Political Rights and the Covenant on Economic, Social and Cultural Rights and several others. However, it needs to be appreciated that as a resolution of the UN General Assembly, in spite of its moral force, the Universal Declaration was not legally binding on states. It was, therefore, necessary to adopt, in 1966, eighteen years after the Universal Declaration, the International Covenant on Civil and Political Rights and the International Covenant on Economic, Social and Cultural Rights and the related Optional Protocol. These transformed the international protection of human rights into binding treaty commitments.

But I hope that it does not take the international community eighteen years to transform the principles of the Earth Charter into binding obligations of states and societies. IUCN has tried to accelerate and jump-start the process beyond the Earth Charter by proposing a comprehensive draft Covenant on Environment and Development[5] to follow and supplement the Earth Charter[6]. It is only when the lofty principles of the Earth Charter become binding legal obligations and are implemented by people all over the world, will the Earth Charter have achieved its full potential. International environmental law would then have entered a new phase of universal recognition.

In a speech to the United States Congress in 1941, President Roosevelt bravely looked forward to a world where "four freedoms" were celebrated:

> In the future days, which we seek to make secure, we look forward to a world founded upon four essential human freedoms. The first is freedom of speech and expression-everywhere in the world. The second is freedom of every person to worship God in his own way-everywhere in the world. The third is freedom from want-which, translated into world terms, means economic understandings which will secure to every nation a healthy, peaceful life for its inhabitants-everywhere in the world. The fourth is freedom from fear-which translated into world terms, means a worldwide reduction of armaments to such a point and in such a thorough fashion that no nation will be in a position to commit an act of aggression against any neighbor-anywhere in the world.[7]

The Earth Charter is a no less ambitious statement of lofty concepts as it builds on the essential human freedoms of expression, worship, dignity, and security and adds the crucial freedom to live in a world which is in harmony with nature. It provides a richness of content that is impressive in its sheer breadth. This is reflected in the basic shell of the four foundational Parts: I. Respect and Care for the Community of Life; II. Ecological Integrity; III. Social and Economic Justice; and IV. Democracy, Non Violence, and Peace, which are in turn supported by several subsidiary principles. Given its provenance, it has justly been called "[t]he most sophisticated and participatory effort to date to frame values and principles for a sustainable future."[8]

Since its launch, the Earth Charter has attracted a growing constituency in Asia. When the global community was preparing for the decennial World Summit on Sustainable Development (WSSD) in Johannesburg in 2002, the preparatory work involved the convening of "Eminent Persons" in each geographical region. The Eminent Persons Forum held in Bishkek, Kyrgyzstan, recommended the importance of the Earth Charter to the global community in its report in 2001:

> Governments need to give serious consideration to launching a process leading to elaboration of an overarch-

ing international treaty on sustainable development that will provide an "umbrella" to more specialized treaties and instruments dealing with specific environmental, social and economic issues. This work could build on IUCN's Draft International Covenant on Environment and Development, and the Earth Charter.[9]

Similarly, the Asia Pacific Forum for Environment and Development (APFED) has continued to highlight the relevance of an ethics-based approach to sustainable development for the Asia Pacific region, using the Earth Charter as a foundational document:

> To initiate the shift along the sustainable development path toward the long-term vision, innovative policies should be articulated for the region. However, with recognition that achieving sustainability is not just a technical problem, but also based on people's mentality, such policies would be most effectively designed around provocative ethical principles such as those advocated by the Earth Charter.[10]

I was a part of both the efforts in Kyrgyzstan and in APFED and facilitated the acknowledgement of the Earth Charter in the Central and South Asian bloc and in Asia Pacific. Given the rapid economic transformation of Asia currently underway and projected in the new century, the reception given to the Earth Charter in this region is a most welcome indicator of a growing environmental consciousness and resolve. ●

**Notes**

1    According to historian J.R McNeill, the primacy of economic growth is "easily the most important idea of the twentieth century". McNeill, J.R. (2000). *Something new under the sun: An environmental history of the twentieth century world* (p. 33). New York: W.W Norton.
2    World Resources Institute. (1991). The New World Dialogue on Environment and Development in the Western Hemisphere, *Compact for a new world* (p. 1). Washington D.C.: Author.
3    Remarks delivered at the Preparatory Committee of the Earth Summit.
4    The Millennium Development Goals reinforce the moral impact of the principles of the Earth Charter; see Parvez Hassan, "The Earth Charter: Providing an Ethical Basis for Millennium Development Goals", presented at the Aberdeen conference, *Ibid*.
5    Hassan, P. (1994). The IUCN draft international covenant on environment and development: Background and prospects. In *A law for the environment-Essays in honour of Wolfgang E. Burhenne*. Gland: IUCN.
6    Hassan, P. (2000, June 30). The Earth Charter: The journey from the Hague 2000. Presented at the Official Launch of the Earth Charter at the Peace Palace, The Hague.
7    US Congress, *Hearings documents*, 77th Congress, 1st Session.
8    Speth, J.G. (2004). Red Sky at morning-America and the crisis of the global environment-A citizen's agenda for action (p. 193). New Haven: Yale University Press.
9    Johannesburg Summit. *Report of the regional roundtable for Central and South Asia*. p. 14.
10   Asia Pacific Forum for Environment and Development (APFED), *Paradigm shift towards sustainability for Asia and the Pacific-turning challenges into opportunities*. p. 75.

Hamza Ali Alamoosh, Jordan. A project descriptive essay on bridging Islamic and Christian cultures

# Black Iris: The Earth Charter as a Common Vision for Muslim and Christian Youth in Jordan

**Hamza Ali Alamoosh** participated in the Global Youth Reporters Program at the IUCN Congress in Amman in 2000. In the same year, he founded Jordan's first Environmental Students Conference. In 2003, Hamza joined the Earth Charter Youth Initiative. Since 2004, Hamza has been a member of the core-group that coordinates the network activities worldwide. On national level, Hamza played a vital role in the formulation of the National Youth Strategy. In 2004, Hamza had the honor of accompanying His Majesty King Abdullah II on an official visit to the USA. Since 2005, Hamza is a member of the Third Chamber, the Dutch Shadow Parliament established to raise awareness of the Dutch people on issues of international development and cooperation. He is also a member of the Technical Committee of Jordan Youth Parliament Institution which he hopes will stand as a voice and a legitimate representative of the young Jordanians.

Being centred in the Middle East, the largest area of conflict in the world, Jordan is surrounded by war and violence from East and West. The existence of many social, economic, and environmental difficulties is added to the burdens of poverty, pollution, leakage of water, and violent conflict. Over sixty percent of the population in Jordan – nearly three million people – are currently under the age of twenty-five.

Many of these are between sixteen and twenty-four. The high percentage of unemployment among young people and the feelings of depression induced by injustice and difficult life conditions have turned the Middle East into a very dangerous place. Such aspects of the global situation, described in the Preamble, are part of everyday life for Arab youth.

Despite these perilous trends, the threat of a "clash of civilization" does not hold true in the Jordanian context. On the contrary, Jordan's rich and diverse religious history can be considered a model for harmony among religions, especially between Christians and Muslims. The land around the Jordan River valley and the Dead Sea plain is revered by Muslims, Christians, and Jews alike. Jesus, the Prince of Peace, was baptized in its river, very close to the city of Madaba. During the difficult times of the endless wars between the Roman and Persian empires, the Arab families stood by the early Christians and protected them.
Since then, Christianity has been deeply rooted in Jordan's society.

When Islam was introduced around six centuries later, its message was understood as a continuation of what the other sent Messenger had started, completing the universal call to justice, freedom, and care for nature and one's fellow human beings. Therefore, the people who adopted the new religion paid their full respect to Christianity. This is underlined by the new heritage findings which prove that no Christian sites were disturbed by the Muslims. All the churches and other holy sites are preserved. Thus, the old churches along with the historic mosques, tell a story about the common call towards universal brotherhood among all people. United Jordanian Muslims and Christians sacrificed much of their lives, energies, and efforts together to achieve these humanitarian principles, which currently are globally threatened by conflicts and mistrust. Jordan's history of tolerance, and its people's motivation towards building a just and sustainable life continued with the support shown for the Earth Charter, when it was endorsed by all ninety-nine municipalities under the leadership of Her Royal Highness Princess Basma bint Talal, the Earth Charter Commissioner from the Middle East and North Africa. This strong movement helps the individuals and organizations who are looking forward to implementing the Earth Charter, not for only its ethical framework, but for the vision it has for sustainability. The Black Iris is looking now to join the municipal councils in order to develop a wide partnership to disseminate the vision of the Earth Charter, and to get involved in their projects.

When the Earth Charter was introduced among Jordanian youth, it was not seen as a threat to their traditions or faiths. On the contrary, it was considered a new opportunity to reflect on our aspirations for a better world. Many young Jordanians saw that the Charter's inclusive, ethical vision is very much in line with the guiding values of our religious ancestors. Therefore, its call was easily accepted and widely respected by those who got its message.

As the harmony between Muslim and Christian Jordanians is still as alive and strong as ever, the story of the Black Iris Earth Charter Youth Group Jordan, which was created in 2003, is only another chapter added to the success story of fruitful interreligious cooperation in Jordan.
Named after the black iris of Jordan, a flower which is the national symbol for growth and renewal, Black Iris is a network of various Jordanian youth bodies, including both governmental and non-governmental entities, and focuses on the creation of synergy effects between them. Restructured in September 2004, Black Iris is now coordinated by a core group of seven youth leaders from different social, ethnic, and religious backgrounds affiliated with different youth organizations in Jordan. These seven Muslim and Christian youth are mainly students from different universities who disseminate the Earth Charter in their respective communities. They are working together to provide a common national platform for youth non governmental organizations to study the principles of the Earth Charter, and to encourage the creation of youth-led initiatives that foster youth participation in all levels of community life. Black Iris receives passionate support from Her Royal Highness Princess Basma bint Talal, who provides the group with the legal backing of her Princess Basma Youth Resource Centre, which is part of the Queen Zein Al Sharaf Institute for Development.

The network has already managed to spread the Earth Charter idea to important organs and projects. As an outcome of a national survey, the Higher Council of Youth in Jordan has set up nine main themes as youth concerns and issues, and in March 2005 the Jordanian King presented the Council's strategy on how to reach various youth-

oriented goals in a five-year perspective. As a result of Black Iris' work, the Earth Charter has been recognized as one of the international references in the Higher Council's youth and environment theme, and has been highlighted as one of the pioneer global calls for sustainable development. In addition, some group members have been able to foster discussions on youth participation guided by Earth Charter principles in the NGO called Jordan Forum for Youth and Culture, which is an umbrella organization for youth-based initiatives. The members of Black Iris also contribute articles to the Youth Section in the Jordanian newspaper *Alrai*, discussing topics such as international development issues, youth development issues, and democracy. In addition, the Black Iris members express their convictions in the Earth Charter by doing voluntary work, such as giving free lessons to orphans and non-privileged students at school and university levels; running exchange programs for including youth with physical and social barriers in different bodies of youth representation; protecting the local environment; and participating in youth forums, non-formal university activities, and international youth settings.

Being a young citizen in the Middle East

is truly not an easy thing, and a lot of young Jordanians believe that they are not living in the Middle East by accident. To most of them, it appears that they are here for the purpose of building a secure homeland in a peaceful region and of building a fair world. Exactly this goal, which forges both Christian and Muslim youth together, is reflected in the Earth Charter's inclusive, ethical vision of justice, sustainability, and peace. ●

# Universal and Differentiated Responsibility

**Abelardo Brenes** is Director of the Master of Arts in Peace Education at the University for Peace (UPEACE), a Treaty Organization created by the General Assembly of the United Nations in 1980 and based in Costa Rica. In 1989 he directed the Seeking the True Meaning of Peace Conference, which produced the Declaration of Human Responsibilities for Peace and Sustainable Development. This document was presented to the General Assembly that same year by the Government of Costa Rica. He joined the drafting committee of The Earth Charter in 1998. Currently he is a Senior Advisor to the Earth Charter Initiative. He has directed several projects in Central America in support of peace-building processes in the region. He is now working with educators in diverse contexts in exploring the educational potential of the Earth Charter.

The principle of universal responsibility, stated in paragraph five of the Preamble of the Earth Charter, is of fundamental importance in meeting the critical challenges of the twenty-first century. It provides a necessary complement to the Universal Declaration of Human Right's recognition of each person as a global citizen, worthy of equal respect and dignity on the part of the universal community of nations. From an ethical perspective, "universal responsibility" can be interpreted as having two key implications: each and every person is equally responsible to the whole Earth community, and the scope of our ethical responsibility impinges on our relationship to the Universe as a whole.

In Subprinciple 2.b, the Charter states as an imperative the principle of "differentiated responsibility": "Affirm that with increased freedom, knowledge, and power comes increased responsibility to promote the common good." How can responsibility be common yet differentiated? On face value, it seems contradictory. The intended meaning of responsibility seems to be different – capacity to respond – given that the subprinciple states that the basis of differentiation *is* freedom, knowledge, and power.

These two meanings are complementary and of equal importance within the rationale of the Earth Charter for it to have practical utility in a world confronting the current "global situation" (Preamble, paragraph three) and the "Challenges Ahead" (Preamble, paragraph four). They pose, however, distinct implications, particularly from political and educational points of view. In particular, the political dimension of differentiated responsibility poses the seemingly intractable problem of the transmutation of "power."

The case for differentiated responsibility could rest on a principle of trans-generational justice. It can be argued that those individuals and groups who have accumulated more power throughout history by exploiting Earth's resources and the fruits of human labor have a proportionate debt to present and future generations within the context of our common good. This line of argumentation would flow from paragraph three of the Preamble: "The benefits of development are not shared equitably and the gap between the rich and poor is widening." It does not seem that this argument by itself will suffice, however, unless we are willing to accept further wars and strife. If it is true that "legitimated avarice" is the driving force of global capitalism (Wood, 2004), then any serious attempt to obligate the powerful will increase the existing trend towards what Hammond (1998) has described as a "fortress world."

An alternative approach is enlightened self-interest, as insinuated in the Charter's Preamble: "The choice is ours: form a global partnership to care for Earth and one another or risk the destruction of ourselves and the diversity of life" (paragraph four). Security-based motivations have proven to be effective in changing diverse domains of human behavior. The fundamental problem with this approach, even if coupled with the "debt" principle, is that change tends to be the minimum required to overcome perceived risks and is often too late. "As the world becomes increasingly interdependent and fragile, the future at once holds great peril and great promise" (Preamble, paragraph one). This insight reflects our knowledge that problems of economic and social injustice, ecological (dis)integrity, absence of democracy, and violence are causally interrelated; and, their cumulative effect can lead to catastrophic changes. Security-oriented approaches will likely provide, at best, an illusion of safety for those who believe they are protected within their fortresses.

The development of human virtues and altruistic motivations is a third way for voluntarily taking on differentiated responsibility. This rationale is also found in the Earth Charter's Preamble: "Fundamental changes are needed in our values, institutions, and ways of living. We must realize that when basic needs have been met, human development is primarily about being more, not having more" (paragraph four). Principle 2 provides an imperative describing the kinds of virtues and skills that we must nurture to fulfill such a vision of human development: "Care for the community of life with understanding, compassion, and love". The challenge seems to be how to bring about such a profound cultural shift in the predominant models of human development oriented towards utilitarian and possessive individualism.

These three approaches are not mutually exclusive. My personal experience in educational work with the Earth Charter has led me to conclude that strategic combinations of these approaches, tailored to diverse educational target groups, are needed to effect change in conscientization and behavior within a universal/differentiated responsibility framework. The key problem is how to critically counter the globally hegemonic conception of power, as domination, to a new hegemony of power, as "understanding, compassion, and love" (Principle 2).

A starting point has been reflection on the relationship between freedom and responsibility. The dominant notion of freedom driving global capitalism is external freedom to accumulate wealth and power. As posited by Giddens (1991), in the external freedom dimension, "freedom from" oppression and exploitation provides the legitimate impetus for majorities of peoples towards emancipatory agendas for social justice. On the other hand, "freedom for" connotes the existential freedom enjoyed by emancipated peoples to define a life politics agenda that will give life a sense of mission. These two agendas can either be in conflict or can be harmonized. The key to what will be the final result is found in the inner dimension of freedom, as indicated in paragraph four of the Charter's Preamble: "We must realize that when basic needs have been met, human development is primarily about being more, not having more." The unanswered question, which to some degree is personal, is the meaning of "being more." We may agree, though, that the imperative of universal responsibility entails a notion of freedom from fears, compulsions, and other forms of alienation that are at the root of avarice and which impede the full flourishment of our human potential.

I have been engaged in diverse educational explorations based on the above reflections:

A substantive program carried out in Costa Rica throughout four years (1997-2001) based on universal and differentiated responsibility is described in Brenes (2004). It focused on a large, densely-populated, urban settlement with a reputation of being very violent. Educational interventions targeted community leaders, schools, and journalists, following an immersion approach (Evans, Evans & Kennedy, 2000). Changes included a reduction of violence in the community and a recognition in press reports and editorial analysis that the roots of the problems in the community were the common responsibility of the Costa Rican society and successive governments.

The M.A. in Peace Education at the University for Peace, which began in 2004, has provided an opportunity to explore diverse didactic approaches to the universal/differentiated responsibility issues. I am convinced that the rationale of the Preamble of the Earth Charter provides a promising guide for critical reflection and dialogue, and the result can be a commitment to its main body of principles. The opportunity to engage in dialogical processes of analysis of contemporary challenges in heterogeneous groups of students representing rich and poor regions, who also undertook immersion experiences of action-learning in poor urban settlements in San José, has offered insights into diverse reactions to such challenges. Whereas students from countries with similar problems could easily identify and transfer learning to their contexts, reactions from many of the students from wealthier nations illustrated the complexities and sensitivities involved in educating the non-poor to accept differentiated responsibility. Typical initial reactions of some students, who on surface level had manifested peace and justice-related values, have been: "I feel guilty, disempowered and there is nothing that I can personally do"; or "The challenges are so massive and the people in the wealthy countries are never going to change." In the longer run, our experience seems to indicate that a continuous process of immersion and action to foster "understanding, love, and compassion" for the oppressed, and those living in marginal environmental conditions, can gradually lead to significant changes.

The above experiences have confirmed that it is relevant which dimensions of the Charter's principles are given priority in both educational and policy contexts. When the priority is social and economic justice, particularly in heterogeneous groups such as the one characterized above, the result has been inter-group polarization and identity-related conflicts. When our approach towards universal responsibility is placed on an awareness of our place within the context of the history of our universe, and our potential life mission in the ongoing cosmogenesis, an awareness of our deeper unity ensues. Were we not all stardust created through the explosion of a super nova anteceding the Sun? This work has been aided by a permanent one mile long exhibit[1] of the evolution of Earth from a five-thousand million year perspective. The exhibit culminates with the first four principles from the Earth Charter and invites each viewer to ask, "where do we go from here?" This is then complemented with reflection on one's life project within the perspective that a key dimension of universal responsibility is defining a life mission within an awareness of how past evolutionary history is implicated in one's existence, and how one's life can determine the lives of future generations.

Work is presently being undertaken exploring the use of the Earth Charter to link formal education and community-based education using the Earth Charter Community Action Tool (EarthCat, 2005). Interestingly, participants in this process have identified "personal peace" as a fundamental starting dimension. Seen from a systemic point of view, this makes sense. If individuals in key leadership positions are motivated by values such as those central to the Charter, and live according to them with integrity, the implications for a community or organization to move accordingly are very high.

Experiences with the latter two approaches provide support for a pedagogical rationale for fostering universal and differentiated responsibility by framing inquiry within the Earth Charter's concept of peace: "Recognize that peace is the wholeness created by right relationships with oneself, other persons, other cultures, other life, Earth, and the larger whole of which all are a part" (Subprinciple 16.f). Reflecting deeply on this concept of peace and on the meaning of wholeness seems to tap into powerful aspirations within the human psyche to develop a cosmological sense of selfhood (see Naess, 1989; Harris, 1991) which provides the needed depth of commitment to the values and principles of the Earth Charter required for differentiated responsibility to flourish.

This inquiry can be linked to reflection on one's life project guided by the phrase "We must realize that when basic needs have been met, human development is primarily about being more, not having more" (Preamble, paragraph four). If one reflects on the relationship between "being more" and "being peace," a phrase introduced by Hanh (1987), within the framework of the Charter's concept of peace, this can stir the passion to plunge into the psychological substratum of universal and differentiated responsibility – that is to "Care for the community of life with understanding, compassion, and love" (Principle 2). It is believed in the Buddhist tradition of the five wisdoms that a person with a developed consciousness can simultaneously see the equality and the uniqueness of all things. Seen from this perspective, universal and differentiated responsibility are inseparable. ●

### Notes

1    *The walk thru time...From stardust to us*, originally produced by the Hewlett-Packard Company and later gifted to the Foundation for Global Community, in Palo Alto, California. They, in turn, authorized UPEACE to translate the exhibit into Spanish.

### References

Brenes, A. (2004). An integral model of peace education. In A.L. Wenden (Ed.), *Educating for a culture of social and ecological peace* (pp. 77-98). Albany: State University of New York Press.

Earth Charter Community Action Tool. Retrieved May 5, 2005, from http://www.earthcat.org/.

Evans, A. F., Evans, R.A. & Kennedy, W.B. (2000). *Pedagogies for the non-poor*. Eugene, OR: Wipf and Stock Publishers.

Giddens, A. (1991). Modernity and self-identity. *Self and society in the late modern age*. Stanford: Stanford University Press.

Hammond, A. (1998). *Which world?: Scenarios for the 21st century*. Washington DC/Covelo, California: Island Press/Shearwater Books.

Hanh, T.N. (1987). *Being peace*. Berkeley, CA: Parallax Press.

Harris, E. (1991). *Cosmos and anthropos: A philosophical interpretation of the anthropic cosmological principle*. New Jersey/London: Humanities Press International, Inc.

Naess, A. (1993). *Ecology, community and lifestyle: Outline of an ecosophy*. Cambridge: Cambridge University Press.

Wood, N. (2004). *Tyranny in America: Capitalism and national decay*. London: Verso.

# The Earth Charter Covenant

**Ron Engel** was a core member of the international drafting committee for The Earth Charter. Ron first became active in international work on behalf of global ethics in 1984 when he founded the Ethics Working Group (EWG) in IUCN (The World Conservation Union). Over the following decade the EWG grew into a network of several hundred persons from over sixty nations. As co-chair of the Ethics Specialist Group of the IUCN Commission on Environmental Law, Ron was able to exercise leadership in advancing the Earth Charter Resolution through the World Conservation Congress in Bangkok in 2004. Ron is currently Senior Research Consultant with the Center for Humans and Nature in New York and Chicago and Professor Emeritus at Meadville/Lombard Theological School of the University of Chicago.

On November 24, 2004, a large step was taken toward making the Earth Charter a covenant of the world community. The World Conservation Congress, representing over one hundred countries, meeting in Bangkok, Thailand, endorsed the Earth Charter and recognized it "as an ethical guide for IUCN policy." IUCN, an acronym for International Union for the Conservation of Nature and Natural Resources, also known as the World Conservation Union, has over 1,000 member organizations from some 140 countries, including 77 states, 114 government agencies, and 800-plus national and international non governmental organizations.

I had special reason to vote for the Earth Charter resolution on November 24. My granddaughter, Helene, was born that morning. A few days later, on the Buddhist festival of Loy Krathong, I sent a candle-lit boat of flowers out on the canals of Bangkok; and I again thought of Helene, and the thousands of flickering lights on the water became symbols of all our world's children. It was an occasion to renew my personal covenant with life, a covenant that finds expression in the Earth Charter.

We humans possess a unique and terrible freedom. We are free to choose the unconditional rights and obligations that will govern the relationships to which we are bound – the covenants of our personal and collective existence. But our freedom is ambiguous. Anxiety tempts us to choose narrow forms of commitment, or to deny the reality and responsibilities of covenant altogether. Hence are born the ideologies of superiority, exclusivity, and exceptionalism that wreak such havoc in the world.

History takes the course that it does by virtue of the covenants that men and women, communities, and nations choose to honor. History is a clash and contest of covenants, and genuine cooperation among human beings, especially among those of diverse cultures, is an immense moral and spiritual challenge.

The Earth Charter stands in a long line of covenantal thinking that holds our most fundamental covenant to be a covenant with the creativity of life – variously called a primordial bond, a covenant of creation, or a cosmic covenant. Once we affirm our own life, we affirm all that life entails – our emergence from, our dependence on, and our impact upon, the whole evolving community of life. Therefore, it is our responsibility to honor and obey the conditions for life's continued flourishing, including the universal moral imperative to respect and care for one another that is written into the fabric of being itself. When, in endorsing the Earth Charter, "We pledge to join the global partnership for a just, sustainable, and peaceful world and to work for the realization of the values and principles of the Earth Charter,[1]" this is the covenant we are affirming.

Global ethics may be defined as citizens engaged in critical conversation about the covenants by which we live. The aim of these conversations is to make the covenants of our civilization more responsive to the life-sustaining relationships of our existence, more inclusive in their membership, more respectful and caring of the integrities of their members, and more holistic in their grasp of the multiple moral concerns that must be met for communities to thrive.

It was out of such conversations that the Earth Charter was written; and it was because of such conversations, held over many years, that the IUCN World Conservation Congress was led to endorse the Earth Charter at Bangkok. It is the only organization with Observer status in the United Nations General Assembly providing expertise on the conservation of nature. Founded in 1948 to promote international cooperation on behalf of science-based conservation, it sponsored the consultations that resulted in such ground-breaking formulations of global ethics as The World Conservation Strategy (1980); The World Charter for Nature (adopted by United Nations General Assembly in 1982); Caring for the Earth (1991); and the Draft International Covenant on Environment and Development (Third Edition 2004).

To make the Earth Charter covenant a present and active reality in the lives of people, it is essential that the kinds of conversations held by the Earth Charter Commission and IUCN be held in as many of the world's communities as possible. The work of global ethics to advance the Earth Charter covenant has only begun, and the agenda of questions for discussion is long.

How can we reclaim the concept of "covenant" for the modern world? Two problems face us. On the one hand, covenant is often so closely associated with a particular religious tradition that it is inappropriate for public life. On the other hand, we are so accustomed to living by "contract," the notion that our obligations need extend only as far as our self-interest warrants, that the inevitable covenantal basis of social life is eclipsed. Yet, there is little hope that societies based on sectarian dogma, contract, or even an overlapping consensus on values, will ever have sufficient motivation to live in accord with Earth Charter principles.

Our present geopolitical situation removes all illusions that the Earth Charter is being carried forward by the tides of evolutionary advance to inevitable triumph. If "another world is possible,"[2] it will come because persons are grasped by the vision of the Earth Charter in the innermost core of their being and believe its principles are right and true in spite of the ravages of warfare, irrationality, oppression, betrayal, and death. This is the kind of covenant it will take to confront overweening power and engage in non-violent dissent. Is there a significant advance in human rights, environmental protection, economic justice, or peace that has not involved sacrifice by persons of principled commitment?

What are the sources of such covenantal faith? The Earth Charter answers: gratitude for the "gift" and "beauty" of life; "reverence for the mystery of being"; confidence that peace is right relationship to "the larger whole of which all are a part." We need conversations on global ethics that probe such spiritual depths if we are to find the understanding necessary for embracing a commitment as large as the Earth Charter covenant.

We have other questions to answer, practical ethical questions such as those that the World Conservation Union must now address as a result of its historic vote at Bangkok. What does it mean for the Earth Charter to be an "ethical guide for IUCN policy"? What does it mean for policy on climate change or for the new IUCN engagement with corporations and markets? What does it mean for biodiversity conservation and biotechnology, education, the elimination of poverty, population stabilization, and how we relate the "rights of the child" to ecological integrity?

I wish all my fellow American citizens could have been with me that evening in Bangkok. It might have broken down their fears of the rest of the world and opened them to a vision of global partnership. Many delegates representing American non governmental organizations at Bangkok took strong leadership roles at the Congress and supported the Earth Charter. Unfortunately, the seven United States Government delegates who were present voted against the Earth Charter resolution, as well as most other resolutions that involved international cooperation; and they declined to give any substantive reasons for their votes.

The Earth Charter includes a call to "the nations of the world" to "renew their commitment to the United Nations" and to "fulfill their obligations under existing international agreements." The present United States government has rejected this call and chosen instead the path of militarism. Yet, this is the country that hosted the United Nations and whose founding covenant, the Declaration of Independence, with its ringing affirmation of equal human rights and natural moral law, must be counted as one of the antecedents of the Earth Charter. American citizens have, not only a national responsibility, but a global moral responsibility to engage in prophetic global ethics and call our country back to its universalist covenantal traditions. Martin Luther King, Jr., faced with a similar dilemma at the time of the Vietnam War, called on Americans to reaffirm their commitment to non-violent global cooperation and the rule of law.

Global ethics is concerned not only for the comprehensive covenants of international and national life, but how these interlock with the covenants of our local communities. What is the meaning of the Earth Charter for the world's communities, especially the sprawling urban areas that are the primary drivers of economic globalization and inequality? What, for example, are its implications for a metropolitan region like Chicago where I live? This, in turn, requires asking what form of power and authority will best embody the principles of the Earth Charter locally, regionally, and globally.

The form of global governance envisioned by the Earth Charter is suggested by the Latin word for covenant, *foedus*, from which we derive the English word "federal." The form of power and authority that the Earth Charter covenant proposes for the world is a federal structure composed of equal confederates who freely bind themselves to one another in a common whole that retains their respective integrities. The communities of the world weave a complex global tapestry that combines autonomy and shared authority.

I had an opportunity in October 2005 to propose to the Chicago Earth Charter Community Summit that we hold consultations to write a "Chicago Charter" comparable to the consultations we held to write the Earth Charter. The challenge is to draft the covenant that this metropolitan region needs to make with itself if it is to create a just and sustainable life for its citizens, and, at the same time, fulfill its responsibilities to the rest of the world. The inspiration for the new covenant must come from the region itself, its unique geography, history and civic culture, and from the unique relationships it has to other specific places throughout the globe. One regional obligation we know we have is to stop polluting our aquifers. One global obligation we know we have is to treat the Great Lakes, the largest system of fresh water on the planet, as a sacred trust.

Lake Michigan is not the Mekong Delta, but all the waters of the planet flow together. The destinies of American and Thai children are not the same, but they are utterly interdependent. When I read the Earth Charter, I think of my covenant with Helene, and this land, and my family, and city and country, and with Thailand, and its land and people, and all the Earth. It makes a big difference in how I see the world and what I do with my life. ●

**Notes**

1    Earth Charter Endorsement Statement,
http://www.earthcharter.org/endorse/
2    The slogan of the World Social Forum

# Part I. Respect and Care for the Community of Life

Let our smiles touch one another!

## Principles

1.  Respect Earth and life in all its diversity.
    a.  Recognize that all beings are interdependent and every form of life has value regardless of its worth to human beings.
    b.  Affirm faith in the inherent dignity of all human beings and in the intellectual, artistic, ethical, and spiritual potential of humanity.

2.  Care for the community of life with understanding, compassion, and love.
    a.  Accept that with the right to own, manage, and use natural resources comes the duty to prevent environmental harm and to protect the rights of people.
    b.  Affirm that with increased freedom, knowledge, and power comes increased responsibility to promote the common good.

3.  Build democratic societies that are just, participatory, sustainable, and peaceful.
    a.  Ensure that communities at all levels guarantee human rights and fundamental freedoms and provide everyone an opportunity to realize his or her full potential.
    b.  Promote social and economic justice, enabling all to achieve a secure and meaningful livelihood that is ecologically responsible.

4.  Secure Earth's bounty and beauty for present and future generations.
    a.  Recognize that the freedom of action of each generation is qualified by the needs of future generations.
    b.  Transmit to future generations values, traditions, and institutions that support the long-term flourishing of Earth's human and ecological communities.

*The text of the Earth Charter continues with Part II on page 64.*

# Respect and Care for the Community of Life with Understanding, Compassion, and Love

**Leonardo Boff** is one of the founders of liberation theology and was for many years Professor of Systematic and Ecumenical Theology at the Franciscan Institute of Petropolis, in Rio de Janeiro. In 1984, as a result of his book *Church: Charisma and Power* he faced a doctrinal process imposed by the Congregation for the Doctrine of Faith in Rome. An "obsequious silence" was imposed on him and he was prohibited from writing and teaching. Later he was a Professor of Ethics and Philosophy of Religion at the State University of Rio de Janeiro. He is the author of more than sixty books in various areas of philosophy, theology, and ecology. These include among others: *Jesus Christ Liberator* (1972), *The Maternal Face of God* (1979), *Ecology: Earth's Scream, the Poors's Scream* (1995), *Learning How to Care: Human Ethics and Compassion for Earth* (2000), and *World Ethos: a Minimum Consensus among Human Beings* (2002). Currently, he follows grassroots organizations and speaks at conferences and courses on spirituality, ecology, ethics, and ecumenical theology in Brazil and abroad. He is a member of the Earth Charter Commission.

The Earth Charter represents an important contribution for a holistic and integrated vision of the social and environmental problems of humanity. Actually, it embodies the best and most established ecological intuitions, making them fertile in the elaboration of a new vision for the issues upon which spirituality and new ethics are based. However, it does not consider ecology as a technique to manage scarce natural resources but as a new paradigm to relate to nature, looking at "all interconnected beings" as forming an immense and complex system. The four great trends of the ecological discourse are assimilated in the following creative approaches: the environmental, the social, the profound, and the integral.

The *environmental* vision is enriched by inserting the environment in "the community of life." Earth itself is presented as "alive with a unique community of life" (Preamble, paragraph two), espousing Gaia's idea as a super, living organism. This idea gets more and more acceptance in the world scientific community.

The *social* ecology emerges in the themes: social and economic justice, democracy, non-violence, and peace.

The *profound* ecology appears when it refers to "the sense of universal responsibility," to the "spirit of human solidarity," to "the reverence for the mystery of being, gratitude for the gift of life, and humility regarding the human place in nature" (Preamble, paragraph 5).

Finally, the integral ecology is expressed defining human beings as a "part of a vast evolving universe" and that "Earth has provided the conditions essential to life's evolution" (Preamble, paragraph two).

Only a holistic vision allows us to see that "our environmental, economic, political, social, and spiritual challenges are *interconnected*, and together we can forge inclusive solutions." These solutions must be effectively inclusive, encompassing all aspects of the personal, social, and planetary human being, because the history of humankind is at a critical juncture, due to the fact that "the foundations of global security are threatened" (Preamble, paragraph three).

Humankind is forced to choose its future: "… form a global partnership to care for Earth and one another or risk the destruction of ourselves and the diversity of life" (Preamble, paragraph four).

Therefore, "fundamental changes are needed in our values, institutions, and ways of living" (Preamble, paragraph four) to guarantee our future. These changes derive from a new ethics, derived from a new point of view: the ethics of love, care, caution, solidarity, responsibility, and compassion.

If we had to summarize in one single phrase the great political, ethical, spiritual, and cultural proposition of the Earth Charter – a true liberating dream for humankind – I would say that this is "a sustainable life style" (Preamble, and passim). This sustainable lifestyle assumes the understanding that human beings and Earth have the same destiny, and they face the future together – not separately. They must either take care of one another and thus guarantee a common future, or both take the risk to perish.

A sustainable lifestyle is the one that allows Earth, with its beauty and integrity and its abundant but limited resources, to meet the current needs of all humankind in a way that will allow Earth to reproduce itself, to regenerate itself, and to continue its evolution as it has done for four and a half billion years, and thus also meet the needs of future generations. The current global lifestyle is absolutely unsustainable. If this lifestyle persists, it may take us to the same destiny as the dinosaurs.

Never in history has humankind confronted such a grave challenge. To respond to this challenge, we must change with urgency. Otherwise, we are running into disaster. Here lies the importance of the Earth Charter, which awakens all of us to this dramatic life or death situation. At the same time, it raises hope and trust since this is not a fatal situation. "Together in hope" (Preamble, paragraph six), we may be able to find liberating solutions, inspired by the four axes with its sixteen recommendations. As Mikhail Gorbachev expressed very well in his book *Perestroika* (1987): "This time there will be no Noah's Ark to save some few and allow all others to perish: ...we save ourselves together or together we all perish." If we turn the Earth Charter proposal into reality, we will have a future and will witness the birth of a new human civilization now unified in the same common house.

Wisely, the Earth Charter does not rest its central tenet on sustainable development, per se, as one would expect, because sustainable development dominates in the official documents of governments and international organizations. Rather, the Earth Charter places its central focus on the community of life, in all its splendid diversity, since it is the most threatened reality. And, together with the community of life, the Earth Charter raises another issue, which is essentially connected with it: respect and care. Its first part is thus worded: *"Respect and Care for the Community of Life"* (Part I).

Why does it say "community of life" and not simply "life"? Because in accordance with Earth sciences and modern biology, all living beings - beginning with the first most original bacteria, which appeared 3.8 billion years ago, then going through to plants, animals, and human beings - basically carry the same genetic alphabet. All living beings carry the same twenty amino acids and the same four phosphate bases. Therefore, we are all relatives and brothers and sisters of one another. What really exists is not the environment but the community of life, in which all beings are inter-dependent and entangled in inter-retro-relationships, which guarantee biodiversity and sustainability for all, including the weakest ones.

As life and the community of life do not exist without the physical and chemical infrastructure which feeds them, and on which they depend, these elements must also be included in the understanding of life. From the initial and ever-present chaos, the entire universe worked to create life, order, and increasingly complex structures. Life itself appeared when matter, in an advanced stage of evolution, became more complex and organized itself from chaos. Thus, life was born as a cosmic imperative, as 1974 Nobel biology laureate, Christian de Duve, said. Life is thus a chapter in the history of the universe and of matter, which does not have anything to do with the "material," because it is an extremely condensed and stable energy and represents a field of innumerable interactions.

The human being is a sub-chapter in the chapter of life, a link in this vital chain and a unique member of the community of life. In the last centuries, he departed from it, placing himself above it, and many times against it, showing that he could play the role of Satan on Earth when he was actually called to be its guardian angel. As the Earth Charter says, the human being "has the right to own, manage, and use natural resources" but also has "the duty to prevent environmental harm" (Subprinciple 2.a).

Nowadays he feels the urge to return to the community of brothers and sisters and to assume his double role: on the one hand to feel part of the community of life, together with its other members; on the other hand, as the one who elevated himself above all and placed himself as a reference point of the community of life with the objective to creatively intervene in it, enabling the evolution process, and in a responsible way be the caretaker and guardian of all other living beings. This is his ethical mission, as worded in Genesis, which states that the human being was called to be "Eden's gardener" – the one who cares, protects, and completes, with his work and creativity, the Creator's work.

Like the community of life, the human being is similarly not defined individualistically, in the overwhelming way of a globalized dominant culture, but as a component of a community and a society. The type of community and society – the one most consistent with human nature and the one that derived from peoples' cultural experience and humankind's political thoughts – is democracy. The desire to participate and build together the common good, and to feel co-responsible for all that is of concern to all, is expressed in democracy. As such, the mandate to "build democratic societies that are just, participatory, sustainable, and peaceful" (Principle 3) is placed under Part I, Respect and Care for the Community of Life.

Let us now address two fundamental attitudes which are important to cultivate before the community of life: respect and care. First of all, respect means to recognize the other, and, secondly, to perceive its intrinsic value. Since the appearance of "Homo habilis," who invented tools about 2.3 million years ago, the human being began to intervene in nature. Following this intervention, lack of respect for nature, and denial of nature being altered, simply derived into the understanding of nature as something to be used.

This is the main weakness of anthropocentrism, which rules over all the world's cultures, except for indigenous cultures, which still live in a deep communion with the community of life.

Anthropocentrism wants us to believe that all beings only make sense as they bow to humans, who can dispose of them as they wish. Contrary to this point of view, there is the following argument: the great majority of living beings existed before the human being appeared. When 99.98% of Earth history was concluded, the human being appeared on the evolution stage. Thus, nature did not need human beings to organize its immense complexity and biodiversity. The correct approach would call for the human being to understand himself in communion with the community of life, as one link in the immense life network – a unique link because he is ethical and responsible.

Respect implies recognizing that other beings are older and, therefore, they deserve to exist and coexist together with us. By respecting them, we impose limits on our willpower and on our arrogance. Historically, this limit has always been disrespected. Edward O. Wilson, the well-known researcher of biodiversity, making an account of the relationship between human being's respect and disrespect of nature, concluded sadly:

> The human being transformed the Eden into a slaughterhouse and the occupied Paradise into a lost paradise. To this date, he has been performing the role of a planetary assassin, only concerned with his own short-term survival; we have already sacrificed a large portion of the biosphere; from totemism or science, conservation ethics, in the form of taboos, has always arrived too late. (*The Future of Life* (2002), p. 121)

Today, we are at a point of no return. We must rescue an attitude of respect as a limit to our destructive capacity and as a condition to preserve nature and our survival.

Secondly, respect implies the recognition that other living beings have a value. From a religious point of view, each living being has a worth for itself, because it exists, and, therefore, it expresses something of the Being and comes from that original source of energy and virtues from which all beings originate and to which they will return (quantic vacuum), as expressed by the Creator. As a result, value belongs to the kingdom of excellencies. Each being, in particular the living ones, carries this excellence "regardless of its worth to human beings," as the Charter clearly states (Subprinciple 1.a). Understanding that beings have value, we develop the feeling of reverence and veneration. In the East, Buddha and all Hinduism, and in the West, Saint Francis, A. Schopenhauer, and Albert Schweitzer developed an ethics founded on respect and reverence, affirming that all that exists deserves to exist, that all that lives deserves to live. The guiding principle of this ethic of respect and veneration (*ehrfurcht, verehrung*) was defined by Albert Schweitzer: "Good is all that preserves and considers all beings, in particular the living beings, and within them, the weakest ones; evil is all that damages, diminishes and eliminates beings." And he added: "Ethics is the unlimited reverence and responsibility for all that that exists and lives."

Let us now reflect on the second attitude in approaching community of life: care with understanding, compassion, and love. It has a long tradition in the West, beginning with the well- known fable, number 220, of the philosopher-slave Hyginus (43 BC-17 AD) during the rule of Caesar Augustus that deserved a detailed philosophic comment by Martin Heidegger in *Being and Time* (pp. 39-44). From this fable, we learn that care is not only an attitude and a fundamental virtue among others, but it belongs to the real essence of the human being. Care is that *a priori* condition which allows a conscious, rational, and free being to exist. Only with care, in the act of living, can he shape his existence in the world together with others toward the future. Thinking in a cosmological manner, if there weren't careful synergy with all the Universe's energies, life and conscience would not have come into being and we would not be here to talk about all of this today.

Care is really the guiding principle, which forestalls all behaviors. All that we do with care is well done. What we do carelessly may be destructive. The debased state of Earth and the perverse quality of life around the world are essentially due to human beings' lack of care. As the psychoanalyst Rollo May said:

> In the currently confusing events between rationalists and technicians, we are forgetting the human being [we lose sight of the human being]. We must humbly return to simple care. It is the myth of care, and only care, which will allow us to resist cynicism and apathy which are the psychological malaises of our times. (*Love and Will*, (1969), p. 338)

The same idea was vehemently presented by the World Conservation Union (IUCN), United Nations Environment Programme (UNEP), and by the World Wildlife Fund (WWF), which in 1991 together published a book with practical recommendations on ecology that carried a programmatic title "Caring for Earth: A Strategy of Sustainable Living." The issue of care has guided all recommendations for preservation, regeneration, and dealings with nature, having emphasized the fact that the ethics of care is the most universal of all; because it can be exercised and experienced at all levels, from the individual to the global.

Care is a loving and non-aggressive relationship with reality. Care is attentive to the vital processes and is concerned with all beings so that they can continue participating in the community of life in such a way that no one is excluded and left alone in his suffering. It is with care, as stated in the Charter, that we can "ensure that communities at all levels guarantee human rights and fundamental freedoms and provide everyone an opportunity to realize his or her full potential" (Subprinciple 3.a).

The Charter in Principle 2 states that we must "care for the community of life with understanding, compassion, and love." Care should be exercised with *understanding*. Understanding is not an abstract process of acquiring the truth about things, but a form of communion with them, i.e., a kind of love. In fact, we only truly know what we love.

Principle 2 also stresses that we should care for the community of life with *compassion*. This word "compassion" is better understood if we take the Buddhist perspective that encompasses two dimensions. The first is to respect each living being and to entirely renounce the desire to possess them (detachment). The second is to care for them, to be together with them in all moments, in happiness and sadness, and, in particular, to not allow them to suffer alone.

Finally, it is necessary to care for the community of life with *love*. Love is the most powerful energy that exists in the human being and in the universe. It is this indomitable and tireless attraction and union force, which looks for a fusion in the sense of a non-duality experience. If, objectively, we are brothers and sisters because of the same genetic code, because of love we, subjectively, want to be brothers and sisters; and we conscientiously propose to ourselves to live this reality. To care with love is to feel united with the most distant star, to the brother bird and to the sister ant, and to be interested in the fate of each person on this planet. To care with love is to be able to declare with emotion: "You are infinitely important to me; you will not suffer unjustly; you will not disappear; you must live."

As we conclude our brief thoughts, we can state: the final effect of this ethics of respect and care is peace on Earth and with Earth. After thousands of years of hostilities between human beings and nature, and the devastation laid to the gifts received from our Great Mother, we must now, if we want to have a future, make an alliance of peace. We must allow the words of the alliance that God made with the survivors of the deluge: "Never more devastation and death; on the contrary, I will make an eternal alliance between myself and all living beings and with all creatures that live on Earth" (Genesis 9:11,16). The rainbow is the symbol of this life alliance. We are all invited to be the rainbow's sons and daughters. ●

# Saving the Landscape of our Childhood and Backdrop for our Dreams

**Homero Aridjis** is one of Latin America's leading writers, many of his thirty-five books of poetry and prose are translated into twelve languages. His work has received important literary prizes in Mexico, Italy, France, the United States, and Serbia. As president of the Group of 100, an environmentalist association of writers, artists, and scientists he founded in 1985, he has been honored with the United Nations Environment Programme Global 500 Award, the Orion Society's John Hay Award, the Presea Generalisimo José María Morelos, *Latin Trade* magazine's "Environmentalist of the Year", the Natural Resources Defense Council's Force for Nature Award, and the Green Cross/Mikhail Gorbachev Millennium Award for International Environmental Leadership. He is a former Mexican Ambassador to Switzerland and The Netherlands, and a visiting professor at Columbia University. He was President of International PEN, the international writers organization, 1997-2003, and currently is President Emeritus. He has been an editorial page columnist since 1994 for the Mexican newspaper *Reforma*.

*"The Monarch Butterfly"*

*You who go through the day*
*like a winged tiger*
*burning as you fly*
*tell me what supernatural life*
*is painted on your wings*
*so that after this life*
*I may see you in my darkness*

The town of Contepec, in eastern Michoácan, is surrounded by hills. The highest is Cerro Altamirano, and every year the monarch butterfly, Danaus *plexippus*, arrives from Canada and the United States to the Plain of the Mules at its summit. Drawn to the microclimate of the oyamel fir pine forests in central Mexico, the monarch is believed to have existed two million years ago. When the sun shines in the clear, bright days of winter, millions of butterflies, layered like tarnished gold on the trunks and branches of the oyamel trees, burst out of their heavy clusters. As the day warms, their flight above and among the trees becomes more frenetic, peaking at noontime when the sky comes alive with a flapping of tigerish wings that rustles like a breeze of dry leaves in the deep silence of the woods. As night falls, the butterflies roost on the trees, disappearing into the perfect camouflage of darkness. As spring nears, a sea of butterflies swoops down the slopes of Altamirano Hill in search of water, turning the streets of Contepec into aerial rivers. Toward the end of March, the colony heads north, only to return, different and yet the same, the following November.

An Indian legend has tried to connect the arrival of the butterflies to the return of the souls of the dead on November 1-2, the Day of the Dead, linking the insect's presence to the ceremonial rites which pay homage to man's ghostly passage on Earth. Coincidentally, the ancient Greeks used the same word, psyche, for butterfly and soul. I think this legend was concocted to answer reporters' questions about the existence of Nahuatl, Mazahua, or Tarascan stories mentioning the monarchs.

I was born in Contepec, and from my house I could see Altamirano Hill, like a bird with outspread wings always about to take flight. We who were used to seeing the million-strong colonies of monarchs each year had no idea the butterflies came from Canada and the northern United States in a migration of several thousand miles, flying at an average speed of nine miles per hour, covering between seventy and ninety miles a day, and that each butterfly was the great-grandchild of a butterfly that had flown away the previous spring. It was only in 1975, following years of research by Canadians Norah and Fred Urquhart, and Americans Lincoln Brower and William Calvert, that Kenneth Brugger happened upon one of the colonies in Mexico and solved the mystery of where the monarchs overwinter.

When I began to write poetry, I would take long walks on Altamirano Hill, home to owls and hummingbirds, coyotes and rattlesnakes, skunks and alicantes, and so the hill became the landscape and the substrate of my memories. At seventeen, I went to Mexico City, and then lived in the United States and Europe until 1980, but every year I returned to Contepec during the win-

Principle 1. Respect Earth and life in all its diversity.

ter months and climbed to the butterfly sanctuary. Peasants told me about logging and fires. Each year more oyamels were felled in the Plain of the Mules, and fewer butterflies came. The natural beauty which had inspired my writings was ravaged and the images which had nourished my childhood were destroyed. The possibility that Contepec could become a wasteland ringed by bare hills, like so many other towns in Mexico, made me desperate; and, the lack of respect for the forest shamed me as a human being. We revere man-made masterpieces in museums, but we blindly destroy the masterpieces of Nature as if they belong to us and we have the right to decide on the survival of a species which has been on Earth since time immemorial.

I understood that for people living in the region it was hard to think about saving butterflies and trees when they had their own urgent needs to satisfy. I also knew that professional loggers were doing more harm than local residents who cut down trees. Once the trees were gone, the people were as poor as ever; but now their surroundings were ruined. The loggers who were breaking the chains of life were committing a social and moral crime by destroying the forest, polluting the water, and eroding the soil – all in the name of economic progress. But what kind of economic progress cripples ecosystems and makes the land barren and unlivable?

I dreamed about Altamirano Hill becoming a national park, although I knew a decree was no guarantee of survival for the butterfly sanctuaries when even the forests on the Popocatepetl and Iztac Cihuatl volcanoes were being destroyed. In April 1986, a year after the Group of 100 first spoke out demanding an end to the environmental degradation of the Valley of Mexico, I convinced the government to give the butterfly overwintering sites official protection. The news was announced on Children's' Day, April 30, as a gift to Mexico's children. Weeks later, I was summoned to a meeting and I learned that only the core – and not the buffer zone – of each sanctuary would be fully protected, and obviously not the entire hill. Worst of all, Altamirano Hill was being left out because a conservationist at the meeting didn't know about the Plain of the Mules. I succeeded in getting my hill included in the presidential decree published on October 9, 1986, designating the areas known as Chincua Hill, Campanario Hill, Huacal Hill, Pelón Hill, and Altamirano Hill protected for the migration, hibernation, and reproduction of the Monarch Butterfly. The core zones were meant to provide the indispensable habitat necessary to ensure "the continuance of the migratory phenomenon...and the gene bank of the various species which live there." A "total and permanent ban on logging and use of the vegetation and wildlife" was decreed. The buffer zones were to "protect the core zone from outside impact, and productive economic activities were allowed, within environmental norms."

However, the felling of trees and the setting of fires continued, even after the official decree. In the winter of 1989, after a fire and unchecked cutting of oyamels on Altamirano Hill, the butter-

flies came but did not stay. They avoid cleared areas, so I felt sure that the delicate balance between climate and habitat had been upset, that the spirit of the place had departed, and that the butterflies would never come back to Contepec. Near the other sanctuaries, the only sound heard at dawn was the buzz of chainsaws, and the only industry which seemed to flourish in the state of Michoacán was lumbering. Smoke-belching trucks piled high with logs hogged the roads.

In the unusually cold winter of 1992, a massive butterfly die-off took place, and up to seventy percent of some colonies perished. We blamed this alarming mortality rate on excessive deforestation. As the eminent monarch butterfly expert, Dr. Lincoln Brower, said, "The oyamel forest, which shields the monarch butterflies from severely inclement weather, had become a blanket full of holes."

At a meeting of scientists and environmentalists in February 1993, we drew up recommendations for conserving the oyamel fir forest, and we predicted the possible collapse of the overwintering phenomenon in Mexico within fifteen years if cutting of trees in the reserve was not stopped. However, five months later, new permits were issued for logging in the sanctuaries protected under the 1986 decree. When I toured the region by helicopter with government officials, my conversations with the ejidatarios, the peasants who earn their livelihood by chopping down the trees, left me with two overwhelming impressions: that they are wretchedly poor, and that they have a prodigious number of children. In the Asoleadero ejido, family size ranged from eight to fifteen children. The head of the Rosario ejido boasted he had fathered forty-five children. When I asked the men how they supported their families, they replied, "By chopping down trees." And when I asked them how their children and grandchildren would survive, they answered, "By chopping down trees." And when I asked them what would happen when there were no more trees, they said, "We'll go to Mexico City or to the United States."

In the aftermath of 1997's severe drought, lack of water forced the butterflies to leave Contepec almost immediately after their arrival. In the 1998-99 season, the monarchs returned to Altamirano Hill. On a visit to the Plain of the Mules with the Mayor of Contepec, among the stumps and wood chips of freshly-cut trees, we saw thousands of crushed butterflies littering the forest floor. Later, I learned that the ejidatario charged with guarding the forest was selling wood to potters in a neighboring town. In 1999-2000, the butterflies came to Altamirano, but did not stay; and the cutting went on, with burros dragging logs to the brick makers at the foot of the hill. Since then, monarchs have been scarce in Contepec, and on the Plain of the Mules the oyamel forest is thinner every year.

During negotiations for the North American Free Trade Agreement in the early 1990s, I suggested the monarch butterfly as the ideal symbol for a partnership between the United States,

Mexico, and Canada, elevating environmental protection to as high a priority as business and trade. Preventing the monarch butterfly migratory phenomenon from disappearing in the coming decades is up to these countries.

In 2000, the government greatly enlarged the size of the Monarch Butterfly Biosphere Reserve to nearly 140,000 acres. In 1996, Brower and I had suggested another possibility for saving the forests: buying or leasing them from their owners, mostly peasant communities, making it more profitable in the short- and long-term to preserve the trees rather than cut them down. The new decree also approved the establishment of a multimillion-dollar trust fund to compensate the owners for not cutting down trees, and payments have been made for several years. However, nineteen years after the first decree, small- and large-scale illegal logging continue; cattle graze in the forests; ecotourism is ravaging the sanctuaries; the human population keeps growing; and the government seems unable or unwilling to enforce protection of the Reserve. What was once an almost continuous forest has become fragmented and degraded. The 2004-2005 winter population of monarchs in Mexico was at its lowest since monitoring began in the late 1970s.

Principle 1 of the Earth Charter addresses the challenge of protecting the monarch butterfly overwintering phenomenon in Mexico while ensuring a livelihood for human beings in the region. If the people living around the sanctuaries could be helped to understand their own interdependence with the forest and the monarchs, and be brought to value the continued existence of the butterflies and the trees, they would be more concerned about preserving the sanctuaries for future generations. Much depends on sincerity and political will on the part of local, state and federal officials, and their ability to foster true participatory democracy among the local communities. Having a genuine and guaranteed stake in preserving their surroundings would encourage residents to realize their full potential and to act in environmentally responsible ways.

In a world where tigers and orangutans may become extinct, where rhinoceri are slaughtered for their horns and elephants for their tusks, where crocodiles are crushed by bulldozers, where thousands of birds and monkeys are captured and sold illegally every year, where nameless organisms disappear en masse, perhaps a hill and a butterfly are not that important. But if we can save the monarch butterfly and Altamirano Hill, the landscape of our childhood and the backdrop for our dreams, from the depredation of our fellow men, perhaps other human beings can save their hill and their butterfly; and all of us together can protect Earth from the biological holocaust which threatens it. Because, after all, is not the long journey of this butterfly through earthly time and space as fragile and fantastic as the journey of the Earth itself through the firmament? ●

Principle 1. Respect Earth and life in all its diversity.

# Our World's Youth: Taking Compassionate Action for a Better Tomorrow

**Jane Goodall**'s landmark study of chimpanzees became the foundation of future primatological research and redefined the relationship between humans and animals. *The Chimpanzees of Gombe: Patterns of Behavior* is the definitive scientific work on chimpanzees and is the culmination of her scientific career. In 1977, Goodall established the Jane Goodall Institute, which establishes innovative, community-centered conservation and development programs in Africa, and the Roots & Shoots education program that has 6,000 groups in more than 87 countries. Dr. Goodall travels an average 300 days per year, speaking about the threats facing chimpanzees, other environmental crises, and her reasons for hope that humankind will solve the problems it has imposed on Earth. Goodall's scores of honors include the Medal of Tanzania, the National Geographic Society's Hubbard Medal, Japan's Kyoto Prize, and the Gandhi/King Award for Nonviolence. In 2004, at a ceremony at Buckingham Palace, Prince Charles invested Dr. Goodall as a Dame of the British Empire, the female equivalent of knighthood.

**Robert Sassor** is an active advocate for social, economic and environmental justice. As a student at Willamette University, Rob began a chapter of Roots & Shoots to introduce service-learning and environmental education programs to the University and local community. He co-founded the Roots & Shoots College Leadership Council and has remained active in the program on the local and national levels. He is the Special Projects Coordinator at the Jane Goodall Institute in Arlington, Virginia. He intends to dedicate his career to bringing forth change in the lives of the world's poorest, and to committing himself to helping realize the vision of a world free from poverty.

I have three grandchildren. When I see how we have damaged this planet since I was their age, I feel deep shame. Our society has become one that makes decisions based on how they will effect the next shareholders' meeting and neglects to address how those decisions will effect the next generation. Whereas, traditionally, many indigenous people made major decisions based on how they would effect their tribes seven generations in the future.

The dangerous consequences of this shortsightedness are only just beginning to play out as our streams, oceans, land, and air become polluted; our food grown with poisonous chemicals; habitats destroyed; species wiped out; and our world's precious resources – trees, land, water, and oil –consumed at reckless rates.

The goal of Roots & Shoots – the Jane Goodall Institute's global program for youth – is to implement positive change through "knowledge, compassion, and action." Roots & Shoots groups, many of whom incorporate the Earth Charter into their activities and classroom curricula, therefore understand the power of the Earth Charter's call to "care for the community of life with understanding, compassion, and love." These words from Principle 2 are compelling – and ones we all must live by if this amazing world of ours is to be saved.

In keeping with the Earth Charter's mission, Roots & Shoots groups are working to improve things for the environment, animals, and their own communities through acts of compassion and understanding. The projects are designed and implemented by the students and reflect the diversity and imagination of our world's youth. In Africa, for example, many groups maintain tree nurseries and distribute seedlings to schools that are otherwise surrounded by sun-baked, packed earth. As the trees grow, it is possible for grasses to survive in the shade below them. School yards are greening, as I write; the soil erosion that once threatened the classrooms is being controlled, and some students grow indigenous fruit trees that help provide much needed fresh food for the pupils.

There are so many projects and so many students who are making them happen. Kids are composting with worms, caring for local parks and highways, and mulching Christmas trees. They are campaigning, always without violence, against the use of synthetic chemicals in food; the feeding of growth hormones and antibiotics, as prophylaxis, to livestock *and the barbaric conditions in which they are typically raised;* the use of pesticides, herbicides, and chemical fertilizers on golf courses, parks, and neighborhood lawns; the use of Styrofoam in school lunch boxes – and everywhere else.

Roots & Shoots students are also promoting the use of renewable resources. A group in Tanzania introduced rice husks as a substitute to precious firewood used in a local brick making business. After less than a year, about seventy percent of the community had switched to rice husks as well, thereby slowing deforestation in the region.

Countless animals and their environments are benefiting from the efforts of children around the world. Students are studying a variety of creatures, from house sparrows to salamanders. They research endangered species and help organizations that are trying to protect them. Students in Salem, Oregon, raise money so that shepherds in the Himalayas can build strong fences around their sheep at night, preventing the endangered Snow Leopards from preying on their livestock and, if caught, getting killed.

Other kids are working to save a variety of insect, such as the Monarch butterfly, threatened along its migratory route by deforestation and the use of pesticides, and the California Cavity Bee, endangered by the introduction of exotic species. There are Roots & Shoots groups that are devoting a great deal of passion to helping to protect sea turtles in India, Israel, America, and Costa Rica; the highly endangered Vancouver Island marmot in Canada, and the Channel Island fox in California. In Beijing, several groups are working to raise awareness about the Yangtse River dolphin. And so many more.

During my travels, I also meet Roots & Shoots students around the world who understand the importance of building bridges between communities. In the Middle East, 350 Roots & Shoots students from Israel and Palestine gathered to hold a parade for peace. In war-torn Kosovo, students flew giant, hand-made doves of peace along the bridge connecting Serbia and Albania. The energy and enthusiasm of these students are my hope for the future. Their efforts are making this a more peaceful world for us all.

The world's youth are embracing the challenges of the Earth Charter. Students are working every day to make this a more peaceful and sustainable world, and recognize the need to supplement their curriculum with service learning programs that reflect the goals that Roots & Shoots and the Earth Charter share. These students see beyond the boundaries of their local community and – through recycling programs, city clean-ups, book drives, and hands-on youth education programs – are playing a critical role in shaping the sustainable practices in their hometowns and beyond.

It is time for us to heed their call. The future of our planet depends not only on the vision of our youth but on the collective actions of all of us to make that vision a reality. Our youth are aware of the challenges that our world is facing and are providing the informed and compassionate leadership it will take to overcome them. Let us follow their lead and do what we can to make this world a better place for all living things. ●

Principle 2. Care for the community of life with understanding, compassion and love.

Wakako Hironaka, Japan. A project descriptive essay which speaks to Principle 3 on using the Earth Charter in the Japanese House of Councillors

# The Aims of the Earth Charter in Japan

**Wakako Hironaka** is a Member of the House of Councillors of the Diet of Japan. She serves as Chair of the Research Committee on Economy, Industry and Employment. Ms. Hironaka is a Member of the Democratic Party of Japan and is now serving her fourth term. In 1993-94, she was State Minister, Director-General of Environment Agency. Ms. Hironaka is also active internationally, as a member, Earth Charter Commission, GLOBE, and Global Environmental Action. She has written several books, essays, translations, and critiques on education, culture, society, and women's issues, including *Between Two Cultures: Woman-Her Work and Family* (1979), and *Politics is Unexpectedly Interesting* (1989).

During the twentieth century, humankind has experienced tremendous economic progress, wealth, and an increase in the average lifespan through advances in science, technology, and medicine. The cost of these developments has been environmental destruction and an increase in the scale of damage caused by war.

Economic growth, for all its benefits, has also given rise to irreparable environmental damage, and social injustices caused by the uneven distribution of wealth. Two world wars, the ensuing cold war, and the regional conflicts that followed have brought about wide-scale loss of life, property, and well-being. War has been the greatest destructive force to the environment. While the twentieth century saw the growth of wealthy countries and prosperous peoples, it also saw growing disparities of wealth among and within nations. People are living longer, but the world's burgeoning population, now reaching over six billion and still growing, puts a heavy burden on Earth's resources.

At present, a mere twenty percent of the nations of the world consume eighty percent of the world's resources. "Global Fairness," the challenge of creating an equitable global society that will break the vicious cycle of conflict and environmental degradation, is the issue of the new century. As members of the human race, we must make the creation of such an equitable society our mission.

Against this backdrop, the Earth Charter was created in an attempt to confront the challenges of building an equitable global society that will break the cycle of conflict and environmental degradation. The Earth Charter sets down principles for preventing further degradation of the environment by amending current patterns of mass production, consumption, and waste disposal; and, by using the earth's limited resources prudently to make society sustainable. The aim is to preserve the entire global environment, while paying consideration to the people, cultures, and ways of life in different regions. Dissemination of the Charter is a peaceful and democratic attempt to create a society that will protect human rights, eradicate poverty, raise literacy levels, and respect women and minorities.

I was fortunate enough to be invited to participate in the creation of the Earth Charter, from the point of its inception, as a member of the Drafting Committee. In this capacity, I was involved in discussions about what should be included in the Charter and what ideas must be emphasized in order to build a sustainable world. Following the launch of the Earth Charter in The Hague in the year 2000, I was challenged to consider what I could do specifically to realize the goals of the Earth Charter, in light of my position as a member of the House of Councillors of the Diet in Japan.

I recognize and place a strong emphasis on the important role of the individual in implementing the Earth Charter. It is not only through businesses and governments, but also, perhaps more importantly, through the widespread action and support of the individual citizen that restoration and preservation of the environment can be achieved. In order to make the Earth Charter more accessible to the public and to increase awareness of its contents, my first project in Japan was to prepare a pamphlet containing a Japanese translation of the Earth Charter. I distributed roughly fifty thousand copies of the translation to my colleagues and constituents and posted it on the internet. With the coordination of the Earth Charter headquarters in Costa

Rica, I petitioned signatures in support of the Earth Charter initiative. Roughly 241,000 signatures were collected at this time.

My next step was to form the Earth Charter Committee of Japan. We invited prominent leaders, in various fields, to the United Nations University in Tokyo to participate in discussions about how to spread the ideas of the Earth Charter throughout Japanese society. After some discussion by the Committee, we decided that a more accessible version of the Earth Charter in Japanese was needed. The Committee jointly produced a booklet that explained the Earth Charter in simple terms. The booklet contains the text of the Charter, both in English and in its Japanese translation, a commentary on its ideas and their significance, and advice on how to implement these ideas.

In addition to producing this booklet, the Committee made the following proposals. First, we would like to see the Earth Charter booklet used as a supplementary reader in schools, with reference to the Charter being made in textbooks across the school syllabus. We aim to spread this trend to universities also, initiating special lectures on the Earth Charter and its implementation. Second, we would like to see the Charter incorporated by businesses in their activities, and thereby introduced to employees. Third, we hope that the Charter will be adopted by prefectural governments, and by city and town administrations, and be reflected in their policy-making processes. Finally, we hope to gain the support of writers and journalists throughout Japan, with a view to seeing the Charter promoted through the media, thus making it better known among the general public.

When creating the above proposals, the Earth Charter Committee of Japan considered the historical path which Japan has traveled. During the post-war period, industrial and economic development was given greatest priority and the environment was almost completely disregarded. This led to severe pollution and environmental degradation, leaving detrimental effects. The government, industrial sector, and civilians on all levels made many efforts to repair this environmental damage, and to a large extent these efforts were successful. In recent years, however, pollution and environmental damage has been caused by the excess consumption and waste of daily life of individuals. Japan is a small country with a large population of 130 million people. Unless care is taken, we could easily become a country once again plagued by pollution and environmental problems.

Looking also at the global situation today, we must remember that no country stands alone in the process of sustainable development. Rapid globalization of both economic and human resources, as well as the global scale of pollution, means every country and individual must consider themselves as but a single member of the greater global society.

Principle 3. Build democratic societies that are just, participatory, sustainable, and peaceful.

When faced with these facts, I, and other members of the Earth Charter Committee of Japan, recognized the benefits and necessity of adopting the principles of the Earth Charter. The powerful and comprehensive message that the Earth Charter contains needs to be internalized by all people and translated into action in their everyday lives.

The aims of the Earth Charter in Japan have also become more important as we have entered the United Nations Decade of Education for Sustainable Development in 2005. In order to ensure that the Charter will feature highly in this Decade, and thus increase its influence throughout Japan and the world, practical implementations of the Earth Charter goals are of utmost importance.

Development of a sustainable world is often misconstrued as meaning simply the protection of the natural environment. As the Earth Charter emphasizes, however, a sustainable environment goes far beyond the preservation of the natural world. It involves ensuring the protection of the rights and freedoms of all humans, as is indicated in Principle 3 of the Charter, namely to allow every person to realize his or her full potential and achieve a livelihood that is secure and meaningful as well as ecologically responsible. Specifically, issues such as the protection of women's rights, the eradication of poverty, and the maintenance of democratic governance must all be addressed in order to build a sustainable world.

The Earth Charter Committee of Japan emphasizes the importance of Japanese Overseas Development Assistance (ODA) in implementing the Earth Charter. No individual country is isolated in the endeavor to work towards a sustainable environment. In addressing the issues mentioned above, such as poverty and women's rights, Japan's role in the provision of ODA is crucial. The Earth Charter Committee of Japan continues to encourage the Japanese government to increase ODA to neighboring countries.

ODA is one area in which Japan has witnessed a change since the collapse of the bubble economy of the eighties. Due to the massive and rapid economic growth during the bubble era, and the consequent strength of the yen, Japan became the world's leading aid donor in 1989. While it retains this position statistically, every year following the collapse of the economy, Japanese ODA has decreased. This may be due, in part, to the fact that many Japanese people believe that in such times of economic recession, the country should put itself first, above the needs of the international community. However, it is my belief that Japan's path to peace will be best achieved by recognizing that we are part of the wider community and by providing support to less fortunate countries. It is towards this end that I, as a parliamentarian as well as part of the Earth Charter Committee of Japan, am urging the government to increase its ODA contributions.

Japan's role in forming a sustainable global community goes beyond these monetary contributions, however. In order to fully realize the aims of the Earth Charter, the Japan Committee is looking to increase awareness of the Charter's values not only within our own country, but also throughout Asia and other parts of the world. In extending the ideas of the Earth Charter to these areas, Japan hopes to help all countries see themselves as part of the whole, and recognize the need to implement strategies that will ensure a sustainable environment on all community levels.

Japan has learned by experience the hard lesson of environmental degradation due to rapid economic and industrial development. Observing a similar process occurring in neighboring Asian countries, we feel impelled to share the lessons we have learned. Environmental protection is often considered a secondary priority in developing nations. This was indeed the case in Japan during the time of her economic development, when serious pollution, health problems, and loss of life were all results of such rapid development. Japan hopes to build on its own experience and encourage developing nations to prioritize sustainable environmental policies on an equal level with economic growth. In these countries, as within Japan, the Earth Charter would be a valuable tool for stimulating public awareness of environmental protection issues, and providing an impetus for the creation of practical methods by which to improve conditions.

Since the creation of the Earth Charter, Japan has experienced an increasing awareness of the Charter's ideals among leaders in various fields and in the general public. We must continue our progress by further translating our awareness into concrete action. I, along with the other members of the Earth Charter Committee of Japan, firmly believe that the Earth Charter presents important and viable principles. We look forward to seeing its continued implementation in Japan, throughout the Asian region, and globally – thus contributing to building a sustainable world. ●

## The Earth Charter in Mexico: Actions to Advance Toward Democratic Societies that are Just, Participatory, Sustainable, and Peaceful

Alberto Cárdenas Jiménez and Mateo A. Castillo Ceja, Mexico. A project descriptive essay on building participation in sustainable development as it relates to Principle 3

**Mateo A. Castillo Ceja** is President of the Ecological State Council of Michoacan and, with many others, has instigated true processes of social participation in the development of environmental public policies for a sustainable Mexico. He is an altruistic person who takes part in the world humanitarian movement. He is considered a national expert in the implementation of local Agenda 21. He has been a representative of civil society in Mexico in many forums and international summits. Castillo is the main developer in Mexico of the Earth Charter and the founder of the National Secretariat. He was awarded the Citizen Merit Prize in 2003, and in 2004 he received honorary mention in the National Prize for Ecological Merit.

**Alberto Cárdenas Jiménez** served as head of the Secretariat of the Environment and Natural Resources from 2003-2005. He has extensive experience as a public servant. In 2001, he worked as the first General Director of the National Forest Commission. From 1995-2001, he was Governor of the State of Jalisco. During his term, he carried out an integral reform of the executive, legislative, judicial branches; and municipal and electoral reform achieving a new state constitution. Also, he initiated the Regionalization Program as a strategy for sustainable, balanced, and just development to confront the problems and challenges of poverty, globalization, and inequality. From 1992-1994, he was Municipal President of Ciudad Guzmán in Jalisco. His political trajectory has taken place within the *Partido Acción Nacional* (Party of National Action) as a member of the National Executive Committee, Secretary of Studies of the Municipal Executive Committee in Ciudad Guzmán, and head of internal and external electoral processes.

To build a democratic society that is just, participatory, sustainable, and peaceful, and is founded on respect for universal human rights, economic and social justice, and the culture of peace, as stated in the third Principle of the Earth Charter, it is absolutely necessary to protect and conserve the environment and natural resources and to acknowledge their vital importance for the security and development of nations. In this twenty-first century, the people of the world cannot ignore that natural resources are essential to sustain life. Not to recognize their social, economic, and political value allows for their destruction and limits the expansion of national and global development.

The natural richness of our planet is our life insurance in a changing world. Humanity's well-being depends on the preservation of all ecological systems. In order to build a world of peace, freedom and dignity for all, we need fertile soil, healthy oceans, and clean water and air.

Mexico acknowledges that the freedom of action of those of us who use and enjoy this richness is conditioned by the needs of tomorrow's societies. Besides owning, administering and using natural resources, the essential duty of sustainability is that we have the responsibility to prevent environmental damage and conserve conditions so that future generations have the possibility to enjoy a healthy environment.

Mexico, in its megadiversity, constitutes a national and world treasure. Thus, towards the end of the year 2000, the President of Mexico, Vicente Fox, declared water and forests as matters of national security. Since then, Mexico's environmental sector has focused on stopping and reversing ecosystems degradation while restoring biodiversity and natural resources, emphasizing that environmental costs should be reflected in the social, environmental and economic value of the services provided by the ecosystems.

Environmental national policies made a qualitative jump forward by prioritizing the sustainable management of water and forests, and converging public policies in order to promote sustainable development. The new environmental policy is based on internal management that applies planning and promotional instruments, supported on a constantly updated legal framework. These axes of the new environmental policy correspond to the principles of the Earth Charter: The inclusion of sustainability criteria in national developmental policies, participation and social shared responsibility, the strengthening of state

Principle 3. Build democratic societies that are just, participatory, sustainable, and peaceful.

environmental management, the fight against environmental impunity, and a scrupulous adherence to the law and accountability.

Different institutions in the federal government responsible for formulating and realizing the economic and social policies in the country have taken on specific commitments in order to progress towards a sustainable development for our country.

This national effort, headed by the Secretariat of the Environment and Natural Resources (SEMARNAT) , has been fruitful. We signed the agreement for the Coastal and Marine Ecological Legislation of the California Gulf, with the participation of the following Secretariats: Tourist, Agriculture, Livestock, Rural Development, Fishing and Food, Marine, Communications and Transport, Environmental and Natural Resources and Administration, as well as the governments of the states of Baja California, Baja California Sur, Sonora, Sinaloa, and Nayarit. This process for Land Ecological Legislation allows for and assures the incorporation of local knowledge and active participation of local communities in the design of the policies for use and usefulness of the land and natural resources.

We have reoriented federal resources towards areas of social and environmental concern, such as Protected Natural Areas where indigenous peoples live, to encourage productive reconversion to sustainable activities that will improve conservation of ecosystems and biodiversity, at the same time that they foster local and regional development. An example of such an effort is the development of ecotourism services by the National Commission of Protected Natural Areas and the Tourist Secretariat. We created a National Program for Energy and the Environment through which the Secretariats for Energy and Environment and Natural Resources designed the basis to foster development of clean energy sources for the country.

© PLAN NEDERLAND / JOHANNES ABELING

Education is a fundamental means to promote sustainable development. That is why Mexico was the first country to sign its commitment to the United Nations initiative which declared 2005-2015 as the Decade for Sustainable Development Education. Since 2001, SEMARNAT has encouraged the establishment of a National Strategy for Environmental Education for Sustainable Development, with the support of Environmental Education State Plans, Training and Educational Communication for Sustainable Development. By mid-2005, we had accomplished twenty-four State Plans plus an environmental education program for the metropolitan area of Mexico City – all products of consensual agreements with organized civil society, reached in workshops with public participation, and emphasizing the Earth Charter as an educational tool in the plans.

In Mexico we have also made important advances in the consolidation of profound transformations towards a development of the political and institutional life of the country. The results are encouraging in terms of society's expression and participation, which offers ever more mature proposals on the priorities of our nation.

In terms of strengthening the institutions of government, changes are also visible. The process of governance recognizes the importance of societal participation in the search for and generation of consensus for adequate public policies in society, the economy, and the environment. We have created and strengthened consultation and participation processes for our society; today we have a Transparency and Governmental and Public Information Law that provides society with opportune and true information.

Knowledge of the Earth Charter motivates social participation and strengthens advancement efforts towards institutional and legal development. In order to advance and the mandates of the Earth Summit and initiate the agreements of Agenda 21, Mexico promotes democratic processes for social participation through a National Consulting Council for Sustainable Development (CCDS) and five regional ones. The main objective of these institutions is to procure ample and informed participation in decision-making and problem-solving related to the environment and development.

The first draft of the Earth Charter

arrived at the CCDS in 1997 as it was looking for consensus in its elaboration. From that time on, the National Council committed itself to the vision of a democratic country – just, sustainable, and peaceful.

The President of the Republic, Vicente Fox, during his intervention at the World Summit on Sustainable Development that took place in Johannesburg, South Africa, in 2002, announced his commitment to support and disseminate the Earth Charter and its principles, and fundamental values for sustainable development. When at this Summit, the Earth Charter Initiative presented the Type II Partnership proposal "Educating for Sustainable Living with the Earth Charter," the Mexican government, through SEMARNAT, underlined the relevance of considering the Earth Charter as an educational tool to develop a better understanding about those critical choices that humanity has to make and the urgent necessity to commit to a sustainable way of life.

Among the results derived during the Summit of Johannesburg, we reached accords between the CCDS and several countries and nongovernmental organizations to implement Type II Partnership. In compliance with these agreements, the CCDS has accepted the task of developing a national strategy to disseminate and consolidate the principles and values contained in the Earth Charter, with the purpose of offering education and training to local communities and authorities on the fundamental principles of sustainable development and its incorporation in the decision making process.

In Mexico, the Earth Charter is integrated in community training and development programs as a guide to introduce sustainable development. One of the main indicators of support of the program is signing the endorsement whereby communities, local authorities, universities and/or companies, ultimately recognize the Earth Charter as an important ethical point of reference for sustainable development, and commit to use it as a guide and ethical framework in decision making, in plans and policy development and as an educational tool for sustainable development. To date, twenty endorsements from municipal presidencies have been attained, fifteen from the main academic institutions in the country, three national nongovernmental organizations and one private organization dedicated to ecosystems management based on ecotourism.

The integration of the National Committee for the Earth Charter complies with one of the commitments made by the CCDS. This committee was formed with representatives of the five Regional Councils for Sustainable Development, the National Council and other institutions directly connected with the project, such as SEMARNAT, through the Center of Education and Training for Sustainable Development, Secretariat for Public Education and various nongovernmental organizations. At the same time, thirty-two states of Mexico continue advancing the national project of the Earth Charter and the Type II Partnership "Educating for Sustainable Living with the Earth Charter."

With efforts in the areas of education, training, communication, information and attention to local communities, the Secretariat has achieved encouraging results by using the Earth Charter as an educational tool and basic guide in the design of workshops directed to raising consciousness of the principles and values of sustainability. . At the same time, the first "Degree on Environmental Education, Communication and Information with the Earth Charter," was implemented, which culminated with the development of a Masters Degree in "Education for Sustainable Development with the Earth Charter" within the Framework of the Decade for Sustainable Development Education.

As part of the effort to make all Mexicans aware of this contribution to sustainability, justice and world peace, to date more than thirty thousand copies of the Earth Charter (adapted for Mexican culture) have been distributed, as well as electronic dissemination via the Internet. In this sense, in a collaborative effort with different educational institutions and nongovernmental organizations, versions have been created for children and youths, as well as translations to the main indigenous languages in the country, such as Purépecha and Maya. A new outreach effort will translate the Earth Charter into Braille so that the visually impaired can also learn of our commitment.

With the conviction that change is possible if we act locally and globally in favor of a more just, sustainable and peaceful world, we recognize that the principles and values expressed in the Earth Charter play a relevant role in the construction of democratic and participatory societies. We recognize that, meaningful social participation entails coordination and compromise of shared responsibility before confronting and resolving environmental problems, actively intervening in the fight against poverty, achieving quality education, gender equality, and respect and recognition of traditional knowledge.

This effort must be congruent with the values of democracy, peace and social justice. We are convinced that humanity can achieve the vital mission of taking care of our planet and can guarantee a shared social existence through solidarity and tolerance. ●

Awraham Soetendorp, The Netherlands. A thematic essay which speaks to Principle 4 on intergenerational responsibility and the Millennium Development Goals

# To Avert the Day of Destruction

**Awraham Soetendorp** is a child survivor of the Second World War. He has been a congregational Rabbi rebuilding Jewish life since 1968 through his Jewish Institute for Human Values. He has been intensely engaged in interfaith and humanitarian and ecological awareness building efforts and as a founding member of Green Cross International. In 1999, he founded the Hope for Children Foundation which fosters the Millennium Development Goal of universal education. He has introduced the Earth Charter into school curricula in the Netherlands. He is a member of the hundred leaders engaged in the dialogue of Islam and the West, initiated by the World Economic Forum. In 2005, he was co-recipient of the Peace Builder Award in Washington, D.C. He is an Earth Charter Commissioner.

Remarkably, the very last words of the biblical Book of Prophets state that the only way the complete destruction of Earth and all its inhabitants can be averted is when harmony is restored between the generations. "Behold, I will send you Elijah, the prophet, before the coming of the great and terrible day of the Eternal, to turn the hearts of parents to their children and the hearts of children to their parents – lest I come, and smite the land with destruction" (Malachi 4:4-6). These words, spoken by an anonymous prophet named Malachi, "my messenger," about the middle of the fifth century B.C.E., resonate with great force in our age.

The Earth Charter is to a great extent a response to this challenge. From the Preamble: "Everyone shares responsibility for the present and future well-being of the human family and the larger living world" (Preamble, paragraph five). From the Principles: "Recognize that the freedom of action of each generation is qualified by the needs of future generations" (Subprinciple 4.a); "Transmit to future generations values, traditions, and institutions that support the long-term flourishing of Earth's human and ecological communities" (Subprinciple 4.b). From the commitments: "Strengthen families and ensure the safety and loving nature of all family members" (Subprinciple 11.c);

"Honor and support the young people of our communities, enabling them to fulfill their essential role in creating sustainable societies" (Subprinciple 12.c); and, "Provide all, especially children and youth, with educational opportunities that empower them to contribute actively to sustainable development" (Subprinciple 14.a). The whole concept of sustainability derives from the notion that the hearts of parents and children have to turn towards each other. In the deep understanding of Native Americans, in all that we do, we should be aware of the effects on the seventh generation.

An ancient Jewish parable addresses these intergenerational responsibilities in simple terms. In the parable, an old man is planting a fruit tree. A young man passes by and remarks, "Foolish old man, you will never be able to reap the fruits of the tree." The old man retorts, "Foolish young man, when I was born I did not come into a desert. My ancestors planted trees for me. And I do not want to leave a forlorn land without trees to your generation." Is this age old truth self-evident at the beginning of the third millennium following a century which experienced indomitable progress and most cruel destruction?

What is desperately needed is the strengthening of compassion and hope. Compassion, in the fine definition of Martha Nussbaum, is to feel the painful emotion occasioned by the awareness of another person's undeserved misfortune. Compassion is not hereditary, it is not transmitted by genes, but it can, and, therefore, must be, taught. Schools must be caring institutions where the capacity of solidarity, of developing what Robert Lifton calls "the species selves" – reaching beyond nationality and race and embracing others – is being taught. To this end, the different spiritual traditions, certainly including the Abrahamic faiths, together with faith traditions from the East, can and must contribute. It is my conviction that the teaching, interpretation, and action based upon the Earth Charter will enhance the capacity for compassion. The holistic approach of integrating respect and care for the community of life, social and economic justice, democracy, non-violence, and peace is indispensable in this effort.

And what about hope? At the end of a workshop devoted to

Principle 4. Secure Earth's bounty and beauty for present and future generations.

58    Part I: Respect and Care for the Community of Life

The Earth Charter in Action

water, in preparation for the large conference of the Parliament of World Religions in Barcelona summer 2004, young people spoke about their experiences and their ambitions in a very moving, sincere way, shaming us the elders who had been much more cautious, blaming others rather than ourselves for not making necessary progress. The last speaker was Michael from California. He felt so privileged having the education, the means, and the time to engage in the protection of water resources, having been born in a place of luxury. However, he was afraid he would not be able to realize his greatest ambition, to become a grandfather, because of the man-made disasters which we would bring upon ourselves – "the day of destruction." It was one of those rare moments when I realized fully why I had to be there. "Michael, when I was born in the Jewish quarter of Amsterdam in war-torn Holland in 1943, my chances of ever becoming a grandfather were zero because of the man-made disaster of those days. But, I am a grandfather today because of the soft forces of compassion that moved my non-Jewish foster parents to give me a home and shelter. I believe that those soft forces will prevail, and that you, God willing, will have grandchildren who will drink living water." This is my basis hope and it gives urgency to the involvement in the struggle for a just and peaceful society. But is it enough?

I recognize Michael's generation's fears and despair. We, the elders, have not planted the healthy fruit trees, at least not enough, and the threat of destruction is real. We can only together retrieve the moral resources needed to rebuild the inclusive world community of decency in which no one is degraded. To this end, the Earth Charter is a moral guide – a compass of conscience. However, it does not stand alone. There exists a necessary, all-empowering connectedness with the goals for the new millennium. How extraordinary! The Earth Charter was inaugurated and presented to Queen Beatrix of The Netherlands in the Peace Palace in June 2000, only months before the representatives of 189 countries signed the declaration of the Millennium Developments Goals. These were the result of powerful parallel processes, which ranged over decades. No one coordinated both these events. Perhaps such a coincidence is but the recognition of the cosmic order which exists but of which we are seldom aware. Taken together the Earth Charter and the Millennium Goals are in continuous conversation with each other, in question and response, beginning with both Preambles.

From the Earth Charter, "We stand at a critical moment in Earth's history, a time when humanity must choose its future....The choice is ours: form a global partnership to care for Earth and one another or risk the destruction of ourselves and the diversity of life" (Preamble, paragraph one and paragraph four).

From the United Nations Millennium Declaration and the Millennium Developments Goals: "We will spare no effort to free our fellow men, women and children from the object dehumanizing conditions of dehumanizing poverty, to which more than a billion of them are currently subjected....We are committed to making the right to development a reality for everyone and to freeing the entire human race from want..." (III.,11.).

The Millennium Development Goals call for the formation of a global partnership, and the political leadership of the world community responded with an unprecedented alliance of concern. The moral appeal to conscience and responsibility, expressed in unambiguous, interconnected principles and commitments, was translated by the governments of almost all nations in a detailed and realistic roadmap of action:

- to reduce the proportion of people living on less $1 US a day from twenty-eight percent to fourteen percent;
- to ensure universal education;
- to eliminate gender disparity in schools;
- to reduce the rate of mortality of those under five years old by two-thirds;
- to reduce the maternal mortality ratio by three-quarters;
- to halt and begin to reverse the spread of HIV/AIDS and the incidence of malaria and other infections diseases;
- to integrate the principle of sustainable development into country policies and reverse the loss of environmental resources;
- to provide safe drinking water to a billion people, who have not access to date, and basic sanitation to 1.5 billion people;
- to improve the lives of at least 100 million slum dwellers;
- to strive for open rule-based governance, more generous aid for reducing poverty and debt relief for developing countries.

Political leadership astounded the world community by agreeing, not only to these detailed, concrete steps to alleviate poverty; but, by attaching to these efforts a fixed timetable, they dared to choose a truly prophetic time path leading to 2015.

During the 1992 United Nations Conference on Environment and Development in Rio de Janeiro, politicians repeatedly told the spiritual leaders who had also assembled, "Please keep pressing us to take measures that may contravene national self-interest but are necessary to safeguard the planet." During the UN Millennium Summit, they at least made a start in putting the interest of the most impoverished citizens of the world community before the direct self-interests of the various governments.

The Earth Charter community of concerned citizens tries to assure that the audacious steps taken by the governments will be sustainable. The channeled energy to fortunately alleviate this desperate generation from what Don Helder Camera called "misery beyond poverty" should not endanger the survival of future generations. And, we can only achieve this intergenerational aim by changing attitudes, values, and patterns of consumption. The question is not whether I can afford a second car, but whether the world community can afford me having a second car. How essential the cooperation is between the value-orientated Earth Charter and the moral activism of the Millennium Development Goals is shown throughout, but, in particular, in the statement in the Preamble of the Earth Charter that states, "We must realize that when basic needs have been met, human development is primarily about being more, not having more" (paragraph four). The ethical imperative is to redouble our efforts as one global community to meet the basic needs within the next decade, and at the same time to prepare ourselves for new ways of responsible living with each other in reverence for the diversity of life. As the Preamble says, a change of heart and mind is required.

Another conclusion of the Earth Charter that is of paramount importance in trying to realize the Millennium Development Goals is that "our cultural diversity is a precious heritage and different cultures will find their own distinctive ways to realize the vision…" (The Way Forward, paragraph two). Cultural diversity is not a threat to the cohesion in our societies. On the contrary, it is a blessing. Different cultures and spiritual traditions enrich and inspire the common effort towards justice and peace. Study of the Earth Charter itself would contribute greatly towards mutual understanding of the various worldviews and enhance cooperation. I suggest that the various spiritual traditions undertake the writing of a commentary from their belief systems and ways of life which will then be shared and studied. In this respect, the notion emanating from Buddhist tradition that we have to deal with the threat posed by inner pollution could be incorporated into the Earth Charter. The challenge is to take away the stumbling blocks of ignorance and mistrust and thus to allow the unimpeded flow of wisdom and experience emanating from the different cultural and religious traditions. Thank God, there are many ways leading to the truth.

And, there is more than a glimmer of hope. The experience of Israelis and Palestinians discussing the challenges posed by the Earth Carter together in workshops over the last few years shows how beneficial this intercultural, interreligious exchange is for the fostering of mutual trust.

Furthermore, the Earth Charter points out that an innovative and strengthened and strong partnership of government, civil society, and business is essential for effective governance. Amongst the many ways to forge this partnership, I suggest the following: the extra contribution of a millennium share of 0.1% of one's income by every individual citizen in the countries of relative wealth during each year of this coming decade. Not only would such a voluntary taxation provide an estimated $50 billion US annually, but the concentrated expression of willingness to support the Millennium Developments Goals would help to convince the political leadership in the various states to raise the level of GNP towards the agreed 0.7%. Yes, every individual, family, and organization has a vital role to play. In the The Netherlands, we came very close to realizing this proposal in 1999. Trade unions and employers' organizations, both partners in the Millennium Labour Council (http://www.mlc.org.za/origins2.asp), agreed in principle to having 0.1% set aside during wage negotiations for financing increasing efforts towards universal education as a millennium gift to the world. Unfortunately, at the last minute they did not

dare to go beyond a recommendation. But, this occurred before the Millennium Declaration. I firmly believe it is doable. Trade unions and employers' organizations will work together towards this goal, when the urgency is felt, even more determinedly.

Jeffrey Sachs, Special Adviser to the United Nations Secretary General on the Millennium Development Goals, is right when he calls upon us, now that we have committed ourselves to halving poverty by 2015, to end extreme poverty by 2025. Those dates may make us feel uncomfortable, but they are the benchmarks of a decent behavior, urging us to fulfill our minimal requirement. In the words of another prophet, Micha: "to do what is just, loving mercy."

The Earth Charter helps us to be continuously aware that there are not "them" and "us", that while we are working day and night to finally eradicate poverty for others, we are doing it also for ourselves, to be whole. "To move forward we must recognize that in the midst of a magnificent diversity of cultures and life forms we are one human family and one Earth community with a common destiny" (Preamble, paragraph one). We truly form one body; when one part of the body aches, the whole body feels the pain. We can only restore the health of the planet community when we have cured all the inhabitants. The prophet Malachi realized that this state of universal health can only be achieved when the healthy relationship between the generations is being restored. It is the custom of Native Americans to hand the elders a feather and ask them to relate to the young generation what particular lesson they want them to hold to, all through their lives. In my own experience, I have come to realize how important it is also for the elders to hear and learn the ambitions and hopes of the young. Sharing experiences and ambitions helps to interlink, even stronger, to learn to be always inclusive, and to practice sustainable living. The Earth Charter and the Millennium Development Goals together interlink the lessons and the hopes of succeeding generations and help to internalize them.

At the start of this decade of responsibility, I share my own lesson, the experience of a baby seeking refuge. The man of the resistance, holding me in a suitcase with holes in it, knocked on the door. Ria and Bertus van der Kemp opened the door. In a split second, they had the choice to take care of this Jewish baby, with all the risks entailed, or to close the door. By opening the door widely they gave me life. More and more, I see myself, I see ourselves, holding the doorknob in our hands. The door is ajar. Do we open or close the door? Millions upon millions of children in desperate need are staring at us with frightened eyes. Do we close the door, or open it widely? ●

Principle 4. Secure Earth's bounty and beauty for present and future generations.

60    Part I: Respect and Care for the Community of Life

The Earth Charter in Action

Laura Westra, Canada. A thematic essay which speaks to Principle 4 on legislation regarding harm to nature

# Securing Earth's Bounty for Present and Future Generations

**Laura Westra** has held offices in the International Society for Environmental Ethics, Science for Peace Group, Occupational Ethics Group, and Society for the History and Philosophy for Science and Technology. She is on the editorial boards of many philosophical and scientific journals, including *Environmental Ethics*. She has been a member of many boards and committees, including the IUCN Commission for Environmental Strategy and Planning, and the Planning and Implementation Group for the Earth Charter. She has been a consultant for the World Health Organization, the University of Peace, and the Ontario Government. Most of Westra's work is on environmental ethics, policy and law, with special emphasis on human rights and global justice. Westra has published more than seventy five articles and fifteen books, including *Just Integrity* (2002); *Ecoviolence and the Law: Supranational, Normative Foundation of Ecocrime* (2004). She has also received a second Ph.D. in International Law.

At a recent meeting of the World Health Organization (WHO), Budapest, Hungry, June 23-25, 2004, on the "Rights of the Child to Health and the Environment," David Stanner of Denmark stated that "children are today's canaries," referring to the proverbial "canary in the mine" used to alert miners to the fact that the mine's conditions were unhealthy, possibly even lethal. I found this concept extremely disturbing, as it acknowledged an aspect of the status quo that further emphasized the widespread ecoviolence to which we are all exposed in various degrees. Children are exposed to violent attacks on their physical integrity and normal function long before they are born. In addition, children are far more vulnerable than adults to most environmental assaults and exposures, or ecoviolence, because of their different physiology and their specific health needs. Finally, children are the most vulnerable among us, because they can neither move and change their location or living conditions, nor protest what is being done to them.

In this essay, I will explore, as a legal scholar, the state of law as it relates to the right of future generations. Children should be considered the "first generation" when future generations rights are named, as they are in many international and domestic instruments, and are explicitly cited as worthy of protection, as we shall see below, although the preborn should also be considered part of the first generation. Thus the environmental justice for which I have argued from both a legal and a moral point of view, does not encompass only North/South issues in its present synchronic aspect, as justice among peoples or intragenerational justice, but it has even stronger implications from the diachronic standpoint, as the human race as such appears to be at stake.

There is one major case in law in which children and future generation rights are explicitly linked – that is the case of Minors Oposa v. Secretary of the Department of Environment and Rural Resources, 33 I.L.M. 173 (1994):

> 1. The Rights of The First Generation and The Future
> This case, however, has a special and novel element. Petitioners minors assert that they represent their generation as well as generations yet unborn. We find no difficulty in ruling that they can, for themselves, for others of their generation, and for succeeding generations, file a class suit. Their personality to sue on behalf of the succeeding generations can only be based on the concept of intergenerational responsibility insofar as the right to a balanced and healthful ecology is concerned.

This appears to be the only judgment that appeals specifically to intergenerational equity in international law. Barresi goes on to point to the significance of the case: "... it was decided by a national court on principles of intergenerational equity for future generations of nationals of that national state". This, I believe, is only partially correct: appeals to future generations for ecological purposes and to preserve "environmental rights," a "nebulous concept" according to J. Davide, have far wider implication that the protection of the area's citizens, present and future, as they affect a much larger proportion of the Earth, than appears, *prima facie*, to be the case.

From our point of view, what is particularly important is the

Principle 4. Secure Earth's bounty and beauty for present and future generations.

appeal to *parens patriae* doctrine, as the minors request explicitly, "protection by the State in its capacity as *parens patriae*." I have argued in the discussion of the rights to health and the environment of children and the preborn, and found the *parens patriae* doctrine to be the best approach to governmental and institutional responsibility for the rights of the first generation. That doctrine progressed from being used, initially, purely for economic and inheritance problems, to juridical use in cases that are exclusively medical and protective. Now we note that the same doctrine is used for the protection of life and health of children and future generations, by means of the preservation of naturally "supportive" ecology. This case, therefore, explicitly links the two major areas of concern of this work: children's life and health and the environment.

Nevertheless, despite its explicit support of intergenerational equity and the novel use of *parens patriae*, subsequent cases did not follow in the footsteps of *Minors Oposa*. In 1997, the Courts in Bangladesh took an opposite position in fact.

At any rate, the major work on intergenerational justice and the law is that of Edith Brown-Weiss. Hence it might be best to approach the topic with a review of the "Sustainable Development Symposium" where she revisits her 1990/1992 argument and responds to the critiques brought against it:

> 2. Obligations to Future Generations in the Law: The Proposal of Edith Brown-Weiss
> What is new is that now we have the power to change our global environment irreversibly, with profoundly damaging effects on the robustness and integrity of the planet and the heritage that we pass on to future generations.

What are the main characteristics of Brown-Weiss' position? The first thing to note is that her proposal comprises both rights and duties, and that these include both "intragenerational" and "intergenerational" aspects. Intergenerational duties include the obligation to pass on the Earth to the next generation in as good a condition as it was when that generation first received it and a duty to repair any damage caused by any failure of previous generations to do the same. Thus, every generation has the right "to inherit the Earth in a condition comparable to that enjoyed by previous generations". In addition, each generation has four duties. First, to conserve the diversity of the Earth's natural and cultural resource base; second, to conserve environmental quality so that the Earth may be passed on to the next generation in as good a condition as it was when it was received by the present generation; third, to provide all members with equitable access to the resource base inherited from past generations; and fourth, to conserve this equitable access for future generations.

These duties impose non-derogable obligations, especially on affluent Western developed countries who are clearly in a position of power, as most of the degradation, disintegrity, elimination of biotic capital, and other serious ecological ills proceed directly from the practices of the powerful West, to the vulnerable South. I have argued that these obligations should be viewed as *erga omnes* (or universal obligations), and they should also be considered as founded on jus cogens (or non-derogable) norms as the proliferation of harmful chemicals, the exploitation of natural areas, the many activities exacerbating global climate change, represent a form of institutionalized ecological violence, or ecoviolence, on vulnerable populations. As gross breaches of human rights, they should be thus considered to be ecocrimes (that is, crimes perpetrated through the environment), and treated accordingly.

In contrast, some have argued that both limitations on economic expansion and commercial activities on one hand, and the demand for increased respect for the preservation of endangered areas and species on the other, only represent a Western, imperialistic conceit – one that flies in the face of the South's needs and cultural practices. Guha, and others, contrast the Western concern with the environment as a source of leisure-time amenities, rather than understanding its role as foundational to survival, as has been demonstrated by many, including the WHO.

But this misrepresents the role of ecological integrity in human survival. The Earth Charter correctly links the two by listing Ecological Integrity as its second Part, right after the one we cited above. Principle 5 calls for us to "Protect and restore the integrity of Earth's ecological systems, with special concern for biological diversity and the natural processes that sustain life." Essentially, Klaus Bosselmann has noted that there is a dissonance between most environmental ethics theories, which do not really address social justice issues, and theories of social justice, that do not fully appreciate the impacts of ecological problems. His analysis of the problem starts by noting that "a theory of either environmental justice or eco-justice is lacking". He cites a definition of environmental justice that views it as "equal justice and equal protection under the law without discrimination....", but he also points out that such a view ignores the intergenerational aspect of the concept. He adds, "But like the 'rights' issue, the liberal approach of justice tends to foster the very problems we are trying to overcome...." Bosselmann wants to link intra- and intergenerational justice, citing Brown-Weiss's own proposal and extending the meaning of "future generations" to non-human animals. I have proposed going even beyond that, by including all life under the same protective umbrella, thus including the unborn, as an integral part of the first generation as well. By starting with the consideration of health and normal function, thus relying not only on ecology, but also on epidemiology and the work of the World Health Organization, the form of ecojustice here proposed is indeed radical. But, by connecting existing regulatory regimes not only to their *explicit* environmental, even if non-anthropocentric thrust, but also to their *implicit* interface with all human health, I believe this proposal for ecojustice might be the most extensive one, best suited to inform supranational and international law regimes. ●

Principle 4. Secure Earth's bounty and beauty for present and future generations.

# Part II. Ecological Integrity

# Principles

5. Protect and restore the integrity of Earth's ecological systems, with special concern for biological diversity and the natural processes that sustain life.
   a. Adopt at all levels sustainable development plans and regulations that make environmental conservation and rehabilitation integral to all development initiatives.
   b. Establish and safeguard viable nature and biosphere reserves, including wild lands and marine areas, to protect Earth's life support systems, maintain biodiversity, and preserve our natural heritage.
   c. Promote the recovery of endangered species and ecosystems.
   d. Control and eradicate non-native or genetically modified organisms harmful to native species and the environment, and prevent introduction of such harmful organisms.
   e. Manage the use of renewable resources such as water, soil, forest products, and marine life in ways that do not exceed rates of regeneration and that protect the health of ecosystems.
   f. Manage the extraction and use of non-renewable resources such as minerals and fossil fuels in ways that minimize depletion and cause no serious environmental damage.

6. Prevent harm as the best method of environmental protection and, when knowledge is limited, apply a precautionary approach.
   a. Take action to avoid the possibility of serious or irreversible environmental harm even when scientific knowledge is incomplete or inconclusive.
   b. Place the burden of proof on those who argue that a proposed activity will not cause significant harm, and make the responsible parties liable for environmental harm.
   c. Ensure that decision making addresses the cumulative, long-term, indirect, long distance, and global consequences of human activities.
   d. Prevent pollution of any part of the environment and allow no build-up of radioactive, toxic, or other hazardous substances.
   e. Avoid military activities damaging to the environment.

7. Adopt patterns of production, consumption, and reproduction that safeguard Earth's regenerative capacities, human rights, and community well-being.
   a. Reduce, reuse, and recycle the materials used in production and consumption systems, and ensure that residual waste can be assimilated by ecological systems.
   b. Act with restraint and efficiency when using energy, and rely increasingly on renewable energy sources such as solar and wind.
   c. Promote the development, adoption, and equitable transfer of environmentally sound technologies.
   d. Internalize the full environmental and social costs of goods and services in the selling price, and enable consumers to identify products that meet the highest social and environmental standards.
   e. Ensure universal access to health care that fosters reproductive health and responsible reproduction.
   f. Adopt lifestyles that emphasize the quality of life and material sufficiency in a finite world.

8. Advance the study of ecological sustainability and promote the open exchange and wide application of the knowledge acquired.
   a. Support international scientific and technical cooperation on sustainability, with special attention to the needs of developing nations.
   b. Recognize and preserve the traditional knowledge and spiritual wisdom in all cultures that contribute to environmental protection and human well-being.
   c. Ensure that information of vital importance to human health and environmental protection, including genetic information, remains available in the public domain.

*The text of the Earth Charter continues with Part III on page 82.*

# Ecological Integrity – A Commitment to Life on Earth

**Brendan Mackey** is a Reader in Environmental Science at The Australian National University where he undertakes research and teaching in the fields of environmental biogeography, conservation science, and cross-disciplinary studies in sustainability. Dr. Mackey co-chairs the Ethics Specialist Group within the IUCN Commission on Environmental Law. He also serves as Chair of the International Education Advisory Committee to the Earth Charter Initiative. He has worked to promote the Earth Charter at a national level within Australia. Earlier, he served as a member of the core team who assisted in the drafting of the Earth Charter during the global consultation process.

The essential contribution of the Earth Charter is in promoting a global moral community based on shared values and principles for a more just, sustainable, and peaceful world. Because it is grounded so strongly in the ecological integrity concept, the Earth Charter ethic requires an unprecedented planetary scale of moral reflection. Integrity implies a wholeness that is nurturing and necessary for human well-being. The ecological integrity pillar of the Earth Charter ethic ties the current and future well-being of humans, and the greater community of life, to the ongoing care and protection of Earth as our home. In this essay, I provide a scientific perspective on ecological integrity, examine how the concept is articulated within the Earth Charter[1], and consider case studies of how the Earth Charter's principles, inclusive of ecological integrity, have found expression in real world action.

Who can hear the word "tsunami" and not recall the devastation wrought upon Indonesia, Sri Lanka, and other countries on 26 December 2004. History is replete with stories of the destructive powers of wild nature with fire, flood, drought, earthquakes, and plagues having brought misery to human societies in all ages. It is understandable then that most people fear wild nature and measure progress by the extent to which we are removed and protected from the associated forces. Such reali-

ties resonate with the observation in the Earth Charter that, "the forces of nature make existence a demanding and uncertain adventure…." (Preamble, paragraph two).

In the face of experiences like the Indian Ocean tsunami of 2004, the concept of ecological integrity can seem puzzling. But, only recognising the destructive dimension to wild nature yields an incomplete understanding, as there are also constructive natural forces at play. It is actually the interplay between the processes of synthesis and decay that has made Earth inhabitable for human and non-human life. This interplay is evident in the co-evolution of life and Earth's environment. While the actual genesis of life on Earth remains a mystery to science, the geological record shows that life first emerged on Earth around 3.5 billion years ago. However, the evolutionary journey has not been a matter of life simply responding to changing environmental conditions. Rather, life has continually interacted with the surrounding environment, thereby creating the very conditions necessary for life on Earth[2].

At a global scale, the most powerful example is the relationship between living organisms and Earth's climate. The amount of solar energy stored within Earth's atmosphere is regulated by the atmosphere's chemical composition (in particular, through the albedo and greenhouse affects). This energy in turn drives Earth's climate. All living organisms, including humans, continually exchange gases with the surrounding environment (e.g., through plant photosynthesis and animal respiration). The affect of this exchange between living organisms and their environment over the course of billions of years has been to transform the chemical composition of the atmosphere, Earth's energy balance, and hence Earth's climate.

At a local scale, ecosystems also work to modify the local environment. The cover of plants and soil regulates the flow and quality of water from a catchment. The fungi and microorganisms in the soil help recycle mineral nutrients enabling plants to continue photosynthesising and producing new biomass. Local ecosystems on land and in the oceans provide humans with food, other useful chemical substances, freshwater, and fibre for clothes and shelter. Particularly in developing nations, local communities are directly dependent on the renewable natural resources provided by the surrounding ecosystems, unmediated by technology.

The continued functioning of ecosystems does not require human intervention, as they are self-generating and self-sustaining. By definition they are dynamic systems whose internal components (including the communities of plant, animal, bacterial, and fungal species) change through time and in response to external conditions. The wild processes that sustain the ecological integrity of ecosystems include the evolution of new species and the dispersal of existing plant and animal species and their propagules. Ecosystems are effectively "managed" by natural selection that ensures the best-adapted species persist in the system given prevailing conditions.

From this perspective, ecological integrity refers to the continued healthy or proper functioning of these global- and local-scaled ecosystems and their ongoing provision of renewable resources and environmental services. Humans can intervene in these systems in ways that undermine their self-sustaining capacities. For example, humans can harvest substances from ecosystems at rates exceeding the system's capacity to regenerate. Thus, we can log wood from forests at a rate faster than the trees can regrow, and harvest fish from the ocean faster than the fish populations can be replenished. At the extreme end of human intervention, we clear the land of the evolved ecosystem and replace the landscape with a land cover that is maintained by continual inputs of human capital, technology and labour. At larger scales the impact of human actions accumulates to degrade the global ecosystem. The degradation of the ozone layer and the ongoing and now chronic influence of greenhouse gas emissions from burning fossil fuel on Earth's climate are powerful examples of humanity's capacity to collectively degrade ecological integrity at a planetary level[3].

The concept of ecological integrity is unpacked in Principles 5 through 8 of the Earth Charter. However, the concept is reflected throughout the document. The Preamble makes clear the overarching dependence of human well-being on Earth's ecological integrity, "...Earth has provided the conditions essential to life's evolution. The resilience of the community of life and the well-being of humanity depend upon preserving a healthy biosphere with all its ecological systems..." (Preamble, paragraph two) and, "The choice is ours: form a global partnership to care for Earth and one another or risk the destruction of ourselves and the diversity of life." (Preamble, paragraph four).

Most of the principles in Part II, Ecological Integrity, are of a different kind to the principles in Parts I, III, and IV. The first four principles in Part I, Respect and Care for the Community of Life, state a basic set of aspirational values defining the kind of world we seek to create and leave as our legacy. The ecological integrity principles are largely "directive" as they suggest actions that can or should be taken to avoid or minimise our ecological footprint. Many of the principles reflect scientific-based understanding of practical steps needed to protect wild nature, for example, Subprinciple 5.b, "Establish and safeguard viable nature and biosphere reserves, including wild lands and marine areas, to protect Earth's life support systems, maintain biodiversity, and preserve our natural heritage." Another example is Subprinciple 5.e, "Manage the use of renewable resources such as water, soil, forest products, and marine life in ways that do not exceed rates of regeneration and that protect the health of ecosystems."

Principle 6 and supporting subprinciples present a strong reinterpretation of the precautionary principle that builds upon that articulated in the Rio Declaration and the UN Framework Convention on Climate Change. Subprinciple 6.b is particularly challenging as it asks us to "Place the burden of proof on those who argue that a proposed activity will not cause significant harm, and make the responsible parties liable for environmental harm."
If this idea were to be implemented, it would dramatically alter how major developments proceed. For example, environmental impact assessments would be not only obligatory for all major projects, but would need to be conducted in a highly rigorous and comprehensive manner with greater concern for long-term and accumulated impacts, as proposed in Subprinciple 6.c. Of course, being a Peoples' Charter, the Earth Charter is not a legally binding treaty. Therefore, endorsing the Earth Charter does not impose any legally enforceable obligations. Principles such as 6.c, at this point in the history of international law, simply point to how planning and decision-making need to evolve if we are to ensure human activities do not cause serious harm to Earth's ecological integrity.

Principles within the Ecological Integrity theme also make a bold attempt to integrate the two main drivers of global change, namely, the rapidly increasing human population and the seemingly ever-increasing rates of material consumption. The former is seen as the prime cause of environmental degradation by many in the global north (e.g. USA), and the latter by people in the global south (e.g. India). In reality, both factors combine to increase the environment load on Earth's ecosystems. Thus, the wording of Principle 7 is both novel and important, "Adopt patterns of production, consumption, and reproduction that safeguard Earth's regenerative capacities, human rights, and community well-being."

Principle 7 suggests our concern for ecological integrity stems from far more than just a sense of enlightened self-interest based on the environmental services provided by global and local ecosystems. This is especially so if we interpret "community" in the sense of Principle 2's reference to the "community of life," and remain mindful of our responsibilities to future generations in Principle 4. From an Earth Charter perspective, ecological integrity is necessary for all life, human and non-human, including future generations – even species yet to exist – thereby ensuring we give consideration to the full evolutionary potential of life on Earth. Finally, Principle 8 stresses the importance of education and the transfer of the knowledge necessary to protect ecological integrity. Scientific investigations are necessary to understand how Earth's ecosystems work and the current and potential impacts of human activities. We are also increasingly appreciating the contributions of traditional ecological knowledge to sustainability.

The starting point for the Earth Charter was a review of values and principles already embedded within existing international declarations and treaties. This draft Earth Charter was then modified and added to many times through an extensive global consultation process. It is no surprise, therefore, to find that the values and principles of the Earth Charter find expression in communities, organisations, and enterprises throughout the world. The unique contribution of the Earth Charter is to integrate environmental and social justice concerns within a common ethic. This ethic is exemplified where we find people choosing to find ways in which social justice can be advanced through protecting and restoring ecological integrity.

In collaboration with other non governmental organisations (NGOs), including the Wildlife Conservation Society and agencies such as the Ugandan Wildlife Authority, the Jane Goodall Institute has established in Uganda an integrated chimpanzee conservation programme[4]. A model has been developed called Community Centred Conservation that maintains the local community as its nucleus and guide. This approach empowers local communities with the tools and resources needed to manage their natural resources for long-term economic gain and environmental prosperity.

Elements of the conservation programme include *in situ* conservation activities in remnant forests, management of other issues threatening populations such as poaching, together with ecotourism enterprises. A major Earth Education Programme has commenced that aims to train and supply primary and secondary teachers and community members with environmental knowledge, skills, and curricula. Ngamba Island Chimpanzee Sanctuary was established in October 1998 to care for orphaned chimpanzees that have been rescued by the Uganda Wildlife Authority from poachers and/or traders, with no chance of survival back in the wild.

The Jane Goodall Institute has endorsed the Earth Charter; and its programmes in Uganda, and elsewhere, demonstrate how economic development for local communities and the conservation of wild nature can work together. The Institute's work is an exemplar of the Earth Charter's ethic that brings together social justice, environmental, and animal welfare concerns in a way that reflects an integrated, ethical framework. Real world solutions are only sustainable when all three dimensions are present; development is sustainable when justice is served to the poor; the ecological integrity of Earth's ecosystems is promoted, not degraded; and the intrinsic value of all life is respected.

Earth Charter Principle 7 calls for more sustainable patterns of production and consumption. Towards this end, Subprinciple 7.d recommends we "Internalize the full environmental and social costs of goods and services in the selling price, and enable consumers to identify products that meet the highest social and environmental standards."

These market-based innovations would help ensure that the economic system better reflects important, yet ignored, environmental and social values. Currently, many of the negative impacts on ecological integrity from market-based transactions are not factored into the cost of production, and consumers remain ignorant of the environmental consequences of their investment and consumption decisions. Various systems are being developed around the world in response to this challenge, such as the Dow Jones Sustainability Index (DJSI) and the FTSE4Good Index Series. RepuTex is the registered brand of a small, fully independent, rating agency based in Melbourne, Australia.[5] The company is dedicated to the delivery of the RepuTex Social Responsibility Ratings (SRR). A RepuTex SRR is an assessment of the extent to which an organisation is performing in a socially responsible manner and managing its social risk exposures in terms of criteria in four domains, namely, Corporate Governance, Workplace Practices, Social Impact, and Environmental Impact.

The Earth Charter is used by RepuTex in a number of innovative ways. First, as a key reference in the formulation of RepuTex evaluation criteria, such that Earth Charter principles, concepts, and language are reflected throughout the RepuTex system. As RepuTex extends its system to the global market, the Earth Charter is providing a set of shared values and principles that helps the criteria remain relevant throughout the regions of the world.

The Earth Charter has assisted The Wilderness Society Australia, an environmental non government organisation, to integrate concerns for wild nature with sustainability for local communities and justice for indigenous communities. This new thinking has found expression in a number of forms. First, the WildCountry project was born as the key visionary conservation theme for the organisation. WildCountry has a long-term vision to ensure the conservation of Australia's extraordinary natural heritage and biodiversity. The purpose is to protect, promote, and restore wilderness and natural processes across Australia for the survival and ongoing evolution of life on Earth. In this way, WildCountry is helping to realize Principle 5 of the Earth Charter that urges us to "Protect and restore the integrity of Earth's ecological systems, with special concern for biological diversity and the natural processes that sustain life," and Subprinciple 5.b, "Establish and safeguard viable nature and biosphere reserves, including wild land and marine areas, to promote Earth's life support systems, maintain biodiversity, and preserve our natural heritage."

To give effect to such vision demands a collaborative approach based on forging partnerships and alliances with the capacity to conserve biodiversity across land tenures. In this way, Wild-Country reflects the sentiments of The Way Forward, the concluding section of the Earth Charter, where it states, "The arts, sciences, religions, educational institutions, media, businesses, nongovernmental organizations, and governments are all called to offer creative leadership. The partnership of government, civil society, and business is essential for effective governance" (paragraph three).

The other area where this new thinking has found expression is in the Wilderness Society's endeavours to integrate indigenous concerns into their core mission. Again, the Earth Charter proved to be a valuable reference point on this crucial issue with respect to Principle 12. Subprinciple 12.b states the need to "Affirm the right of indigenous peoples to their spirituality, knowledge, lands and resources and to their related practice of sustainable livelihoods."

Aside from desert biomes, the most extensive areas of the world's remaining wild lands occur in the tropical savannah of Northern Australia, parts of Kalimantan and Borneo, Indonesian New Guinea and Papua New Guinea, the Russian boreal, the Canadian boreal, parts of the Congo Basin, and the tropical forests of the Amazon basin. In all these cases, indigenous communities have inhabited the landscapes for thousands of years, and in the case of Northern Australia around 50,000 years – the oldest continuous human culture on Earth. Unfortunately, new conservation areas and policies aimed at protecting these remaining wild lands can serve to further alienate already displaced indigenous peoples and may ignore their need to undertake sustainable economic developments. Many non-government environmental organisations have ignored the values, aspirations, and rights of indigenous peoples in wild lands. Such a perspective only serves to reinforce existing injustices and can be counter-productive to conservation aims. Traditional ways of living in these regions have found accommodation with wild natural processes – both destructive and constructive – and in many cases traditional ecological knowledge holds the key to understanding sustainable paths of development in the future.

Following a process of dialogue with indigenous peoples, The Wilderness Society Australia developed an Indigenous Rights policy which recognizes, among other things, that "indigenous peoples are the traditional custodians who have managed the environments of Australia since time immemorial." The organisation also helped launch the *Malimup Communique* that was developed at a meeting of indigenous representatives, staff of government land management agencies and representatives of non-government environmental groups at Malimup Spring, Western Australia. The communique is concerned with indigenous people and the management of areas reserved or zoned as "wilderness." The Wilderness Society Australia has endorsed and now integrated the Earth Charter into their organisation's new guiding principles. Thus, the Earth Charter remains a guiding ethical framework for the unfolding vision of WildCountry and the emerging partnerships with indigenous peoples and other communities throughout Australia.

Currently, the human endeavour is rushing towards a future where the integrity of ecosystems is degraded beyond repair, and we risk the Earth system flipping into a different state which is not supportive of human well-being, nor that of the greater community of life. The Millennium Ecosystem Assessment meticulously details the scientific basis of these concerns.[6] In such circumstances, our well being becomes increasingly dependent on technology and engineered solutions to provide the necessary life support systems.

We may well survive in a world where Earth's ecological integrity is destroyed and our well-being is totally dependent on machines, but there may be little wild nature, and poverty may still engulf communities around the world. There will be, no doubt, a future for humanity one way or another; but, will this be a future worth having? The Earth Charter asks us to make a choice about the kind of world we want our children to inherit. A commitment to the Earth Charter ethic rejects cataclysmic futures in favour of continuing efforts to secure a just, sustainable, and peaceful life on Earth for all. With our knowledge, technology, and wealth, we have the means to find a balanced future without poverty, and where ecological integrity is ensured – a future where people live with, not against, wild nature. Herein lies humanity's choice and fate in the coming century. ●

### Notes

1 Also, see discussion in Mackey, B. (2004). The Earth Charter and ecological integrity – some policy implications. *Worldviews: Environment, culture, religion* 8(1): 76-92.

2 This concept was first raised in the 1920's by Vadimir Verdansky in his book The Biosphere, and subsequently developed by James Lovelock's Gaia hypothesis (Lovelock, J. (1979). Gaia – a new look at life on Earth. Oxford: Oxford University Press), and more recently by Victor Gorshkoves biotic regulation theory (see Gorshkov, V., Gorshkov, V.V. & Makarieva, A.M. (2000). *Biotic regulation of the environment: Key issues for global change.* Springer Praxis Books.)

3 See the reports of the Intergovernmental Panel on Climate Change. Available from: http://www.ipcc.ch/ [accessed 1 February 2005].

4 Material from this section was based on personal communications with Debbie Cox and the IGS web site. Available from: http://www.janegoodall.org/africa-programs/programs/ [accessed 1 February 2005].

5 Further details can be found at the company's web site. Available from: http://www.reputex.com.au/ [accessed 1 February 2005]. The author is a volunteer advisor to RepuTex.

6 The Millennium Ecosystem Assessment. The MA was launched by U.N. Secretary-General Kofi Annan in June 2001 and was completed in March 2005. The MA was governed by a Board comprised of representatives of international conventions, UN agencies, scientific organizations, and leaders from the private sector, civil society, and indigenous organizations. A 15-member Assessment Panel and a Review Board, composed of leading social and natural scientists, oversaw the technical work of the assessment supported by a secretariat with offices in Europe, North America, Asia, and Africa, and coordinated by the United Nations Environment Programme. Its reports are available from www.MAweb.org.

# Using the Earth Charter in Local Campaigns against Genetically Modified Organisms

Khyn P. Yap, The Philippines. A project descriptive essay as it relates to Principle 5 on preventing introduction of harmful organisms

**Khyn Yap** is President of Eco Trekkers Society, Inc. (ETSI) a non-profit youth NGO. While coordinating for ETSI, he was employed as community organizer working on micro-finance to help the poor. He is now studying nursing at Riverside College in the Province of Negros Occidental. Mr. Yap involved with the Earth Charter Youth Initiative after visiting the website of ECYI. From then he has used the Earth Charter as a guiding principles in activities and introducing it to other youth organizations in The Philippines. Later in life, he looks forward to mentoring the youths who will follow in his path.

The Philippine government has shown a positive attitude towards bioengineering and the introduction of genetically modified organisms by granting permits to corporations despite various protests from local people and concerned citizens who are affected by the field trials. The first officially-granted permit to commercially propagate Yeildgard, a genetically engineered corn variety popularly known as "Bt Corn," was issued in December 2002, whereas field trials had already started back in 1999. The planting of Bt Corn has been approved on my island of Negros Occidental, one of the five provinces that compose Western Visayas. Negros Occidental can be found near the center of the Philippine archipelago of 7,107 islands.

When news reached us about hunger strikes and other forms of protest by different activist groups in Manila calling for a moratorium on the commercialization of Bt Corn in 2003, my youth organization, Eco Trekkers, joined the local campaign against genetically modified organisms that was started by Greenpeace activists. Eco Trekkers was founded in 1999, by a group of amateur outdoor enthusiasts, as a campus club at the Technological University of the Philippines – Visayas. It was created solely as an adventure club with members' interests focusing on mountaineering and outdoor activities. Most of our activities at that time were mountain climbing and nature tours. Negros Island has only three forest areas left after logging firms have almost completely ravaged the natural forests leaving us with only three percent forest cover left. Passing by forest areas affected by timber poaching and illegal forest activities triggered us to widen our club's objectives to focus on environmental awareness and education. In 2002, we decided to formally register our club as a non-governmental youth organization. From the name Eco Trekkers Club, it was changed to Eco Trekkers Society, Inc. or ETSI.

The goal of ETSI is to advance the role of the youth and actively involve them in the protection and promotion of sustainable development. The percentage of youth involvement on sustainable development and other youth related issues is very low. Many of the Filipino youth don't even know that their problem of unemployment is inter-related with the environmental issues of the country. Most of them have not even participated in any volunteer work nor are they involved in any youth organization. Against this background, our main focus is on organizing the youth from the grassroots where poverty and lack of education hinders them from actively participating in finding solutions to issues that affect them.

Parallel with our vision of creating a sustainable world, we decided to endorse the Earth Charter as our guiding principles and ethical framework. The Earth Charter calls on young people to act locally and collectively towards the common goal of fostering sustainable development. The Earth Charter Youth Initiative gave us the opportunity to link up with other groups and individuals around the world and exchange successful projects and activities that can be replicated by others. That is why we joined the program of Earth Charter Youth Groups in July 2003. By using the ECYG-label we seek to demonstrate our connectedness to other youth around the world who promote the vision of the Earth Charter in their local communities. In addition, it strengthens our efforts of disseminating the Earth Charter in our community and our networks. Among the institutions we will encourage to give their endorsement is the national Youth for Sustainable Development Assembly, which consists of nine Filipino youth-serving organizations. The Youth for Sustainable Development

Principle 5. Protect and restore the integrity of Earth's ecological systems, with special concern for biological diversity and the natural processes that sustain life.

Assembly network eventually included a workshop on the Earth Charter in the Kamp Kalikasan (Nature Camp) 2004 as one of its program highlights.

Our campaign against the introduction of genetically modified organisms is based on Earth Charter Principle 5.d.: "Control and eradicate non-native or genetically modified organisms harmful to native species and the environment, and prevent introduction of such harmful organisms."

Most people in our community are unaware of the dangers that go along with the introduction of genetically modified organisms such as the contamination of other non-genetically modified corn plants as a result of cross-pollination. Scientists have warned that genetically modified organisms pose serious risks to the environment as the crops are depending on herbicides and beneficial insects are killed by the usage of these herbicides. We have seen, from one of the field visits organized by PEACE.Net on Bt corn plantations in Cauayan, that snails have mutated and changed their shapes. We are not yet concluding that it is the effect of the Bt toxins present in the soil, yet as the Earth Charter wisely suggests, a precautionary approach should be applied when scientific knowledge is inconclusive.

While other activist groups lobby for the government's rejection of genetically modified organisms, Eco Trekkers Society, Inc. is focusing on local awareness-raising and education. Our goal is to let the people know that genetically modified organisms are a threat to our health and environment. They must know their rights and power as consumers. Therefore, we have organized small, group discussions in our school, distributed flyers and brochures in our community, and put up exhibits which warn about the risks of introducing the engineered crops and educate the visitors about their rights as consumers to be informed about whether the food they eat is genetically

modified or not. In our forums, which are held once a month during the semester and are attended by around eighteen to twenty-five students respectively, we provide information on the issue of genetically modified organisms, such as lists of these types of food sold in markets, and then we engage the participants in discussions. Earth Charter Principle 5.d. has been discussed thoroughly, and short debates and controversies about its consequences have made discussions more lively and interesting.

Another issue that we have been discussing intensely is the negative impacts of the introduction of genetically modified organisms on our national economy. Farmers who will plant Bt crops will not be allowed to save, exchange, or improve the seeds that they are using, which makes them rely on the multinational corporations who own patents on these modified crops. So, in the years to come farmers will be depending on the herbicides and seeds of these corporations, and, thus, will be even less autonomous and self-reliant.

The only alternative we see and strongly propagate in our campaign is the intro-

duction of sustainable agriculture and the usage of technologies that are appropriate to our environment. We also strongly endorse the mandatory labeling of the genetically modified food sold in the markets. It is so ironic that while most first world countries banned genetically modified crops to enter their food supplies, we in the third world countries seem to accept them with open arms. Against this background, the Earth Charter provides a prudent and holistic strategy of addressing these interrelated challenges of global economic injustice, threats to the integrity of Earth's ecological systems, and poverty.

Our involvement in the Earth Charter Youth Initiative made us realize that we are not alone in striving to make our world a better place, but that there are individuals like us who persistently pursue peace and sustainable development. We became aware that small local actions, like cleaning up garbage in our cities' shoreline or our campaigns against harmful genetically modified organisms, make a big impact nationally and internationally. And if we all acted together, who says that we cannot build a sustainable and peaceful world? ●

Principle 5. Protect and restore the integrity of Earth's ecological systems, with special concern for biological diversity and the natural processes that sustain life.

Ruud Lubbers, The Netherlands. A thematic essay on the precautionary approach and globalization as they relate to Principle 6

# The Shift from Economy to Ecology

**Ruud Lubbers** played a leadershiprol in the Earth Charter. He is an active Steering Committee member. Ruud Lubbers is an economist and former Minister for Economic Affairs (1973-1977) in The Netherlands, and from 1982 to 1994, he served three terms as Prime Minister. Since then, he was Professor of Globalization at the Catholic University of Brabant and visiting Professor at the Kennedy School for Government at Harvard University, USA. He was president of World Wildlife Fund. Most recently, Ruud Lubbers was the United Nations High Commissioner for Refugees (2001-2005).

In the 1960s I lived, as I do now, near the river Maas in my hometown of Rotterdam. Its port became one of the biggest in the world supplying and exporting products to and from the European heartland to the world. Around it the chemical industry was developing quickly. The Netherlands was prospering, but I came to realize that this had its costs. The neighborhood was rapidly changing. In my own youth, I saw foxes in the meadows; now there were not even fish in the river any more. I would play in the garden with my young children where we could smell the chemicals and draw with our fingers in black dust on the table. The river was so polluted that one could develop photos in it!

This is where I started to worry, as a young father and as a businessman. The city did economically well and was expanding with the growth of international trade, but something had to change in its environmental impact. My reading in 1971 of the Club of Rome's *Limits to Growth* strengthened my ideas. The report focused on global trends and saw economy and ecology in a greater, overarching perspective. It was an extrapolation of worrisome trends – worrisome for nature and, therefore, for humankind. Here, in retrospect, were already the seeds for my intellectual development towards the 1990s, my transformation from "economy" to "ecology," from the short-term to the long-term.

If the Earth Charter is about the paradigm-shift from economy to ecology, the introduction and application of the precautionary principle is an important tool and proof of that transition. If one is wondering about the pros and cons of substantially increasing the application of an existing technology, or of applying a new technology, one normally makes an assessment of the environmental impact and the risks in relation to nature. Doing so, one has to work with a calculation of risks. Sometimes it is very clear that certain environmental impacts are not acceptable at all; sometimes it is clear that those impacts are no problem at all.

But in many other cases, it is more complicated. There is a risk and one starts to quantify the risk. The economist tends to make a plea for a calculation to see if the benefit merits the risk. In doing so the economist "discounts" benefits and risks, taking into account the time factor. A risk after hundreds of thousands of years is for an economist almost zero. For an ecologist it is different. He does not "discount" risks. Almost on the contrary, the future – our responsibility vis à vis generations to come – is at least as important as the actual. And the actual negative impact on environment and nature has to be balanced against the capacity of new technologies to increase consumption.

As an economist, your work is to produce something because you have scarce capital, so you work it into an efficiency of capital. In ecology, it is the other way around: you don't look for the short term, you look for the long-term. So to simplify, ecology is long-term, economy is short- term. Here again, economists tend to prioritize the increase of the economy and ecologists tend to prioritize the protection of environment and nature.

To strengthen the ecological dimension in calculating such risks, one can introduce the precautionary principle. It advises us to "Prevent harm as the best method of environmental protection and, when knowledge is limited, apply a precautionary approach" (Principle 6). Further, it calls upon us to "Ensure that decision-making addresses the cumulative, long-term, indirect, long distance, and global consequences of human activities" (Subprinciple 6.c).

Principle 6. Prevent harm as the best method of environmental protection and, when knowledge is limited, apply a precautionary approach.

If there is uncertainty in relation to the ecological impact of certain projects, the precautionary principle calls upon one to err on the safe side, to abstain from actions or projects, from new technologies if one is not sure. We have a proverb in the Dutch language, "In geval van twijfel steek [de straat] niet over" that says, "In case you are not sure, do not cross a street."

When I became Economy Minister in the Netherlands in 1973 and developed a policy of "selective economic growth," I tried to solve the great intrinsic dilemma of economic growth: how can it be made compatible with the environment?

Much later, the outcome of the Rio Summit became the agenda for the twenty-first century. It laid the foundations for the Earth Charter. And for me, it was the start of a new phase in my thinking, already sown in the decades before – an intellectual transformation from economy to ecology, from the short-term to the long-term, from the confrontation inherent to globalization and its rebounds, to the harmony of seeing the planet as a whole. This reflection process deepened a few years later, after I left my political office in 1994.

I started to think about an important new trend that came up those days – globalization. With its many faces and interpretations, globalization became to be known as such only after the demise of the Soviet Union, in 1989. In the same period, it came to a series of global summits: on women (Beijing), on population and reproductive health (Cairo), on social development (Copenhagen) and, of course, the first one, the Earth Summit in 1992 in Rio de Janeiro. All these summits exemplified the global interest for global issues and were themselves the very expression of globalization – not only governments gathered there, but, even more,the non governmental organizations (NGOs). And indeed, all these summits produced global commitments as if we were becoming more "one."

The first five years of the new millennium showed again a diverse picture from the global point of view. On the one hand, we saw the Millennium Declaration, a powerful commitment of the United Nations to the Millennium Development Goals, and a successful Monterrey Summit; on the other hand, the attack on September 11, 2001 in New York and a very visible Al Qaeda. The world, and, in particular, its lead country, the USA, became obsessed by "security" concerns. By choosing a classic, ideological strategy – a preventive strike against a rogue nation because of the risk of weapons of mass destruction in the hands of the axis of evil – the Bush administration disqualified the United Nations as the global guardian of security. At the same time, the struggle of Islam with modernity, in particular in the homelands of the Moslems, coincided unfortunately with two "globalizing" dimensions. First, there is the perception that globalization and Americanization threatens Islam and the Islamic way of life. And second, there is the perception that America protects corruptive leadership in the Islamic world. In addition to this, there is the on-going degradation of the United

Nations as a producer and protagonist of justice by the humiliating lack of capacity to perform in the conflict between Israel and Palestine, between Jews and Palestinians. The United Nations High Commissioner for Refugees' mandate for the Palestinian victims of violence and persecution has existed for fifty-five years; and there is no doubt in the hearts and minds of Moslems that this is the proof of ongoing injustice and double standards.

In these senses, globalization, and anti-globalization or anti-Americanism, are the opposite of everything the Earth Charter stands for – the interconnectedness of people and peoples, a common future, with sustainable development, with harmony. Instead, globalization, in its success and its rebound, seems to inflict the contrary – it divides peoples.

In the meantime, the need for a global answer is more urgent than ever. This answer is not only on the level of summits or concrete measures and negotiations. It goes deeper. To illustrate this, I go back to the beginning of the 1990s. I had, after twelve years being prime minister in the Netherlands, more time to reflect. The concept of inclusivity – to include people, to include dimensions of life – grew more important to me. I started to understand the call for a paradigm shift, which was put forward by NGO's at the Rio Summit.

An important influence in this transformation was my acquaintance with the way indigenous people look at life. Indigenous people succeeded in Rio to introduce two fundamentals that go beyond good environmental policies reducing and controlling emissions. The notion of preventing harm, of thinking of future generations, is one fundamental. The second fundamental that found ground in Rio was the positioning of the "indigenous" way of relating to nature – a relationship of "awe." While the Enlightenment resulted in more and more exploitation and plundering of Earth, the indigenous – economically at the lowest level – had totally different concepts. They celebrate nature. They have a different concept of time. They think about harmony, about Mother Earth, respect, and equity.

These fundamentals are, with many other insights, integrated in the Earth Charter. To handle the great challenges and responsibilities we have towards Earth and to counter the negative globalization trends, we can make full use of the Earth Charter. The civil society of the globalizing world, "we the people" need a constitution – a document describing the values to be respected and to be pursued. The Earth Charter gives us a holistic, comprehensive, inclusive constitution. ●

Hazel Henderson, USA. A thematic essay which speaks to Principle 7 on regenerative economies and the economics of sustainability

# Beyond Economism: Toward Earth Ethics

**Hazel Henderson** is an independent futurist, worldwide syndicated columnist, and consultant on sustainable development. Editor of *Futures* (UK) and *WorldPaper*, she also serves on many boards, including Worldwatch Institute and the Calvert Social Investment Fund, with whom she co-created the Calvert-Henderson Quality-of-Life Indicators. Dr. Henderson has been an ardent supporter of the Earth Charter since its inception. Her book *Paradigms in Progress: Life Beyond Economics* (1991) included references to the Earth Charter's early Principles. Since then, she has tirelessly promoted the Earth Charter in her books, speeches, and editorials, including a chapter in her new book with Daisaku Ikeda, President of Soka Gakkai International, *Planetary Citizenship* (2004).

The Earth Charter is the single most important people's declaration of the shared common values that lie beyond economics and money-measured indicators of "success," "wealth," and "progress." The twentieth century saw the zenith of economics as the arbiter of human progress and its gradual takeover of private and public decision-making. By the 1980s and the rise of Margaret Thatcher in Britain and Ronald Reagan in the USA, economists were fast becoming elevated to the role of philosopher kings in both industrial and developing countries. This takeover by economics of public policies, mass media, political discourse and the narratives of business, entrepreneurship, human motivation and social organization has been termed "economism."

The economics profession gradually became pre-eminent in government agencies across the board – from education to health, welfare, environment, even the arts and recreation. Policy analysis in all these sectors of societies began to be subsumed by economists and their methodologies, particularly those of cost-benefit, risk-assessment, and valuations of everything from the monetary worth of family and social cohesion and human life itself, to ecological sustainability. The myopic focus of economics on money-based transactions and measures of "value" began to seriously distort public and private decision-making.

Indeed, even today, most economic textbooks still teach an obsolete model of "human nature" based on the primitive stage of early human experience, coded in our reptilian brains. For economists, rational behavior is the maximizing of individual self-interest in competition with others – implying that humans' equal capacities for cooperation and sharing are "irrational." These errors in economics are compounded by the discounting or ignoring of human and social "capital" and ecological assets. The often heavy costs of economic exploitation of such human and environmental resources are a result of economic theories of "discounting" their value and "externalizing" such social and environmental costs to society, future generations and the environment.

The Earth Charter is a major bulwark reasserting the widely-shared values associated with the totality of human existence and preservation of options for our survival and common future on this planet. Thus, the Earth Charter has become a powerful reassertion of these broader values that lie beyond the narrow calculus of monetary profit and loss. I believe that this is why the Earth Charter has found such worldwide acceptance and endorsement in so many countries and cultures. Institutions at all levels and in all sectors of society have endorsed the Earth Charter, from municipalities, civic, academic and professional groups to companies such as the USA-based Calvert Group of socially-responsible mutual funds on whose Advisory Council I serve. Furthermore, the Earth Charter has become a reference point for many efforts to articulate other declarations of global ethics, such as the Prague Declaration of Forum 2000 and those of the Parliament of the World Religions.

There is hope in the unfolding public debates of this twenty-first century, for example, between the business-as-usual views of most participants in World Economic Forum meetings in snowy Davos, Switzerland and those of global civil society at the World Social Forum in sunny Porto Alegre, Brasil. The world's mainstream media have so far failed to adequately understand or reframe these worldwide debates between proponents of economic and technological globalization, which threaten the

*Principle 7. Adopt patterns of production, consumption, and reproduction that safeguard Earth's regenerative capacities, human rights, and community well-being.*

broader social and environmental values held primarily by the vast grass-roots majority of human beings.

An example of such debates involves education and how it is treated in the national accounts of most countries, i.e., their Gross National Product (GNP) and its narrower Gross Domestic Product (GDP) indexes. Education, which is arguably the most important investment any country makes in its future, is treated as a "cost." Yet, in this twenty-first century Information Age, politicians and leaders worldwide stress the key role of education as the bedrock of human development and social progress. Many economists have now widened their horizons accordingly and acknowledge that the wealth of nations lies in educated, productive citizens, increasingly described as "human capital."

The World Bank began acknowledging such new forms of capital in its Wealth Report in 1995 when it conceded that its previous narrow focus on financial and built capital (money and factories) was misplaced. The Wealth Report explained that sixty percent of its measure consisted of human capital, twenty percent environmental capital (nature's resources), and that finance and factories only constituted twenty percent of the real wealth of nations. Since then, the Bank has focused on education – particularly of girls – as one of the most productive investments that governments, businesses, and individuals can make. Of course, parents knew this all along!

Yet, most economic textbooks, models and national accounts – GNP and GDP – still categorize these investments in education as "consumption," or "expenses," as if these funds were just money down the rat hole! Such persistent errors force these crucial investments in our most precious resource, our children, to compete in annual budgets of local, state, and national governments with roads, police, sewage treatment, sports stadiums, and even weapons.

The growing breed of statisticians of quality of life and sustainable development (see for example, the Calvert-Henderson Quality of Life Indicators, www.calvert-henderson.com), have called for correcting such errors in national accounts for decades. In 1992 at the UN Earth Summit in Rio de Janeiro, 170 governments pledged, in Agenda 21, to implement these corrections by including human resources, unpaid work, ecological assets, and subtracting pollution and resource-depletion. The Earth Charter grounds all these new indicators in its sixteen principles.

It is vital for Earth Charter supporters, educators, and all those concerned with our children's future, to insist that economists at the International Monetary Fund, the World Bank, and in national governments, re-designate investments in education as just that: investments. Once this is accomplished, these education investments should also be added to the new asset accounts recommended by statisticians of quality of life. Education is a key part of the infrastructure of all societies that pays

dividends over at least twenty years and produces our precious "human capital." When all these taxpayer-supported infrastructure investments are properly accounted as assets in GNP, they balance out and reduce the public debt accordingly. This lowers interest rates countries must pay. Doing this would open the door to more long-term planning, motivate positive investment, and ensure a brighter future for society and our children. Earth Charter values are slowly entering the thinking of many corporate executives of the 2000 companies that are signatories of the Global Compact principles launched by Kofi Annan, Secretary-General of the United Nations.

We can all hold economists to account to see that the errors in their models no longer compromise our children's future. Remember, economics is not a science, just a profession, with less quality control than most others. Never again should educators, parents, and concerned citizens have to fight annual budget battles over education. With correct accounting, these investments, and those in vital public infrastructure, would be safely protected as the long-term assets they truly are.

Earth Charter supporters can challenge economism and claim the full legitimacy in public and private decision-making for all the Charter's life-affirming values and principles. Economists need not be embarrassed by this unmasking as a profession rather than a science. Many honorable professions are content with this term: those who practice law, medicine, engineering, architecture, and other such applications of knowledge. Lawyers in particular are happy to be known as advocates. Similarly, we now know, economists have always been advocates of various government policies, regulations or deregulation, and of the interests of their clients who are most often bankers, financial firms, and corporations in general.

There is no quarrel with these advocates, whether lawyers, economists, or lobbyists, or their roles in policy-making. All that is necessary is clarity on the part of these professionals and all advocates so that the public is fully informed, and the issues are argued honestly. Economists can no longer falsely claim scientific status for their arguments nor confuse the public by pretending to be scientists. Why not embrace the truth and call the profession "economic advocacy"? After all, the Information Age has already morphed into the Age of Truth.

Today, advocates of the Earth Charter stand on even firmer ground as we advocate progress toward the Millennium Development Goals, addressing needs for clean water, health, education, and providing global public goods and infrastructure. Rebalancing human notions of "progress" and "development" beyond the false ideologies of economism is necessary for human survival on this endangered planet. The Earth Charter represents humanity's best roadmap to diverse regenerative economies and peaceful, just societies for a brighter future for all. ●

# The Earth Charter on its Way through Germany

Principle 7. Adopt patterns of production, consumption, and reproduction that safeguard Earth's regenerative capacities, human rights, and community well-being.

**Hermann Garritzmann** has served as an expert on adult education in the Archbishopric Paderborn and an advisor for a project of quality development and quality assurance for institutions of vocational education. He was Coordinaor of Agenda 21 processes in the district of Höxter. Since June 2001, he has been the German Earth Charter Coordinator at the Ecumenical One World Initiaive. For over twenty-five years Garritzmann has been active as freelance in the educational work of the Bishopric Development Organization, MISEREOR. Currently he is a member of the steering committee of a pilot project for vocational education: "Complete Living in the One World – Global Learning in the Third Lifeage" – a project to connect sustainable development and adult education for senior citizens.

*Our planet is the only home we have.*
*Where should we go, if we destroy it?*

This simple but provocative question was once raised by the Dalai Lama. The German Earth Charter Team gladly used this line as heading for an advertisement with which we raised awareness for the Earth Charter in more than fifty trains of the German Railway Company. We were given the chance to put our message on the cover of the itinerary-bulletins which were placed on each seat. For four weeks in early 2004, these trains cruised back and forth through Germany and transported the message that the Earth Charter seeks to inspire a new sense of global responsibility based on respect and care for the community of life. Our announcement concluded with the invitation: "Together, we can imaginatively develop the vision of a sustainable way of life and live in a different and better way." Yet for many passengers the question remains: a sustainable way of life – what is it and how does it work?

In a wealthy country like Germany, people listen very closely and critically when in Earth Charter Principle 7 it is said: "Adopt patterns of production, consumption, and reproduction that safeguard Earth's regenerative capacities, human rights, and community well-being." This especially holds true when Sub-principle 7.f expresses this point even more explicitly: "Adopt lifestyles that emphasize the quality of life and material sufficiency in a finite world."

The task of adopting economic patterns that help to protect and restore the ecological and social systems of Earth poses a special challenge for the developed countries. The "ecological footstep" each citizen of the industrialized countries leaves on this planet gives clear evidence of this challenge: if every person on the planet would live like an average German citizen and consume and waste as much resources as we do, we would need four planets Earth to serve that need. Therefore, sustainable patterns of production and consumption are essential for safeguarding the well-being of our ecosystems. In the meantime, a sustainable use of resources is also a matter of fairness and justice towards the people in the global South who cannot afford a lifestyle compared to ours.

The Ecumenical One World Initiative (ÖIEW), which has served as the German focal point of the international Earth Charter Initiative since spring 2001, was created to assist in achieving exactly this goal. It was established in the mid-seventies when the first wave of awareness for ecology and global interdependence arose. Its aim is to encourage the adoption of a new way of life – a way of life which is dialogical, solidaric, simple, and ecologically sound.

The membership of the ÖIEW is constituted by individuals who perceive themselves as part of the One World with its rich diversity of plant and animal life. And, we perceive ourselves as part of the One Humanity which embraces all peoples, cultures, and religions. Both of these aspects are addressed by the Greek word "ecumene".

As members of the ÖIEW, we meet on the common ground of a certain set of personal commitments, which we consider as guidelines for our lives and which we hope to implement in our communities. These are:

- to contribute to justice, peace, and the conservation of nature through conscious life decisions;
- to take small steps towards peace, justice, and sustainability in our everyday life;
- to develop conscious patterns of consumption and to assist in making the power of the consumers become politically relevant;
- to harmonize personal behaviour and political claims in a trustworthy way;
- to financially support initiatives that focus on ecology, peace, one world issues, and human rights through a freely-chosen self-taxation;
- to engage in non governmental organisations and campaigns that promote a sustainable way of living;
- to strive for making an ethic and practice of sustainability a dominant motive for the personal behaviour of the people, as well as for the economic and political structures.

A workshop held on the perspectives of the Initiative showed that in the future the members of the ÖIEW want to give special emphasis to the following programmatic lines: the endeavour to adopt sustainable ways of living; the dialogue about an ethic of sustainability; and the vivid exchange of ideas about a spirituality of global responsibility.

We have found all these issues in the Earth Charter. The Charter calls on us to *be* the change we want to see in the world; it is an ethical prerequisite to start the global transformation with changing one's own conduct. From early on, our members have translated the first drafts of the Earth Charter into German and discussed its meaning. Serving as the official German Earth Charter focal point since 2001, we are intensely trying to make the Earth Charter known in Germany and our German-speaking neighbouring countries and to also make it become relevant within the structures of local and national decision making.

Together with Friends of the Earth Germany, we publish a German Earth Charter brochure that has reached its fourth edition, which means that by now we have distributed around 35,000 copies in schools, faith organisations, Local Agenda 21 groups, and other institutions of civil society. In the meanwhile, the Earth Charter has been reprinted in numerous other publications such as the German edition of Mikhail Gorbachev's book, *My Manifesto for the Earth*, and it can also be found on various websites on the internet. Additionally, we publish a quarterly news bulletin about the Earth Charter Initiative entitled "Erd-Charta Themen" – "Earth Charter Topics" and have started to train some "Ambassadors for the Earth Charter" to use their unique skills and experiences to bring the Earth Charter into discussion in their personal environments. In this way, we try to enhance the dissemination of the values of sustainable development from the bottom up, starting with the individuals, reaching out to grassroots organisations, and, thus, building the ground for involving more and more people and influencing the conduct of our local municipalities and national governments.

In this regard, a first success was achieved when we were given the chance to introduce the Earth Charter to our National Council for Sustainable Development, which has been established by Chancellor Gerhard Schröder to prepare the German Strategy for Sustainable Development. The Council acknowledged the Earth Charter as an important international people's treaty and dedicated its annual meeting in 2004 to the issue of "values for sustainable development" where the Earth Charter has been discussed.

More governmental support was reached through our participation at two round table discussions organized by the Ministry of the Environment to evaluate the role of faith communities in the public endeavour of protecting the environment. These discussions helped us strengthen our links to various faith communities in Germany which now spread the values of the Earth Charter among its members.

However, lobbying the government does not hold our main priority. The shift towards sustainable development requires the assistance of all members of society. At its core, this shift requires alternative approaches to defining the quality of life, which lies in being more, not in having more, as the Preamble of the Earth Charter holds. Fortunately, various academies and other educational institutions, major religious events like the recently held "Kirchentag" of the Lutheran Protestant Church that brought around 300,000 Christians together, and even the International Horticultural Show in Rostock in 2003, have given us the chance to present the Charter and foster dialogues about the universal responsibility each one of us has as a citizen in the One World. We prepared several workshops for the first National Social Forum in Germany that was held in July 2005.

One highlight of our work in this field, surely, was the seminar on the topic "Does the World have a Conscience? Earth Charter and Global Ethic" held in February 2005 in cooperation with the Protestant Academy Berlin and the Global Ethic Foundation. This workshop helped us to identify the common ground of the Earth Charter Initiative and the renowned Global Ethic Foundation, which seeks to foster understanding between the world religions by distinguishing four broad ethical principles which all the various religions have in common.

Another important partner in these activities is the Club of Budapest International which included the Earth Charter into their campaign "You can change the world." Our joint press release in celebration of the World Ethic Day, which is commemorated on September 22, helped us to attract major public attention.

Another main priority of our work is educating for sustainable living. In 2002, the influential German Catholic Bishops' Organisation for Development Cooperation dedicated a whole edition of their teachers' periodical to the Earth Charter. This cooperation helped us to make the Earth Charter known and used in

Principle 7. Adopt patterns of production, consumption, and reproduction that safeguard Earth's regenerative capacities, human rights, and community well-being.

schools throughout Germany. Due to unfortunate financial constraints, we had to postpone a project of major importance: With the appropriate resources, we would love to translate the Earth Charter into a language that is relevant for youth and to also invite young people to develop ideas and activities to bring the vision of sustainability to life in their specific contexts.

We are gaining some more support for our educational efforts through participating in the national round table for the United Nations Decade for Education for Sustainable Development where we stress the importance of personal commitments for achieving a sustainable way of life. The Decade can be seen as one example of several positive developments. Other heartening trends are the Ten-Year Action Plan for Sustainable Patterns of Production and Consumption, adopted by the United Nations at the World Summit on Sustainable Development, as well as many inspiring examples where bioregional means of production have been reinforced throughout Germany and other parts of the world. These developments show that the question of sustainable ways of living becomes more and more relevant again, whereas sufficiency approaches to sustainable development were formerly belittled as petty forms of abstinence and asceticism. While the ÖIEW has been working on these topics for so many years against all odds, it is heartening to see how the issue of personal responsibility is gaining new impetus.

In 2006, the ÖIEW will celebrate its thirtieth anniversary. We are still sorting out the most appropriate form for this celebration, yet we hope to bring together women and men who helped to create the Initiative thirty years ago with women and men who were born in 1976 and who then will be thirty years old. It would be hopeful if the quest for a holistic and global ethic, a sustainable way of life, and a spirituality of universal responsibility could thus be passed on through the generations. ●

Hans van Ginkel, Japan. A project descriptive essay on the Ubuntu Declaration as it relates to Principle 8 on advancing sustainability education and knowledge

# The Ubuntu Alliance: Mobilizing Knowledge for Sustainable Development

**Hans van Ginkel** started his career as a teacher in secondary school, became a teacher trainer, curriculum developer and formulator of national examination programmes. He became the longest serving university rector in the history of The Netherlands at Utrecht University, 1986-97. Now he is the Rector of the United Nations University, Tokyo. Dr. van Ginkel is also vice-chair of the Board of Trustees of the Asian Institute of Technology, Bangkok. He was the treasurer of the Netherlands Foundation for International Cooperation in Higher Education, board member and vice-president, of the European Association of Universities and board member, vice-president, and president of the International Association of Universities. He was one of the initiators of CRE-Copernicus, IAU's Kyoto Declaration, and the Ubuntu Alliance. He has received many distinctions and awards, including Knight in the Order of the Netherlands' Lion, which he received from Queen Beatrix in 1994.

Education for Sustainable Development means what it says: it is not just environmental education or even sustainable development education, but education for sustainable development. It is not a topic that can be taught in a few weeks just at a certain age, but should rather be given attention in all sectors of education, and at all levels in relation to relevant, already existing subjects in an integrated manner. In this way Education for Sustainable Development gives orientation and meaning to education for all. Education for All and Education for Sustainable Development are two sides of the same coin. To develop the curricula and courseware needed – and regularly update these – and to inform teacher training and re-training in effective ways is a primary goal of a consortia of eleven of the foremost educational and scientific organizations – the Ubuntu Alliance[1].

The Alliance members signed the Ubuntu Declaration at the World Summit on Sustainable Development (WSSD) in Johannesburg in 2002. The Declaration strives to ensure that educators and learners from primary to the highest levels of education, taking part in both formal and non-formal education, are aware of the imperatives of sustainable development. The Alliance aims at an inclusive and flexible process, mobilizing all who have something to contribute in primary, secondary, and tertiary (including higher) education. Specific attention will be given to online learning and the contributions of the media. The Johannesburg Plan of Implementation will give guidance with regard to the issues to focus on, in particular, such as water, energy, health, agriculture, and biodiversity (WEHAB) and, of course, the Millennium Development Goals (MDGs).

The Earth Charter gives important perspectives and concepts to build upon while constructing curricula and training teachers. The Ubuntu Alliance is also working hard to tailor existing knowledge in science and technology to the very different conditions and needs of the different parts of our mega-diverse planet, as well as to develop knowledge on new themes like access and benefit-sharing and bio-diplomacy. Indeed, the Ubuntu Alliance has endorsed the Earth Charter and put it at the heart of our vision.

The United Nations has designated 2005 as the Year and 2005-2014 as the Decade of Education for Sustainable Development (DESD). The process of the year and decade must be inclusive and flexible, the framework challenging and enabling, not limiting and harnessing. The challenge that might mobilize many and serve to give focus to their contributions might be to create jointly a Global Learning Space for Sustainable Development (GLSSD), based on Regional Centres of Expertise (RCEs). Regions are seen here – as in common language – as parts of countries like Bretagne, France; Tohoku, Japan; or Catalunya, Spain. The regional centres should include institutions of primary, secondary, and tertiary education; research institutions; science museums; non-formal education; zoos/parks; and others. As it is important to mobilize many, initially, prizes could be awarded for innovative, joint projects of two or more institutions from different sectors. The RCEs might be identified in a comparable way to the monuments on the world cultural heritage list. This would have the

Principle 8. Advance the study of ecological sustainability and promote the open exchange and wide application of the knowledge acquired.

advantage that local/regional conditions can be fully taken into account. The DESD would in this way have as a visible output a global network of such regional centres of expertise. In the process, it would be possible to mobilize many, learn from their creative ideas, build on diversity, and promote international cooperation in education for sustainable development. The regional centres of expertise together, and their mutual relations, would form the Global Learning Space for Sustainable Development.

Education serves as a powerful tool for moving nations, communities, and households towards a more sustainable future. For over fifteen years now, institutions of higher education have been rethinking their roles, among others, to find new ways to respond to the challenges of sustainability and prepare future generations to deal with sustainability issues in their careers and lives. Higher education institutions play a vital role, not only in shaping the future by educating the professionals of tomorrow, but also by creating a research base for sustainability efforts, and by providing outreach and service to communities and nations. They are extremely well-placed to help achieve Principle 8 of the Earth Charter. At the same time, the Earth Charter is well-designed in order to inspire the people working and studying in higher education institutions to contribute to sustainable development. The commitment of individual academics to the Earth Charter will be crucial for moving the education for sustainable development (ESD) initiative forward.

Education for sustainable development builds the capacity of nations to create, broaden, and implement sustainability plans. ESD improves sustainable economic development by improving the quality and skills of the workforce while addressing the overarching need for true democracy, environmental integrity, and social justice. ESD also creates an informed public that can support enlightened environmental,

social, and economic policy and legislation, and raises the quality of life for all members of society. ESD has four major goals: improve access to quality basic education; reorient existing education to address sustainable development; develop public understanding and awareness; and provide training programs for all sectors of private and civil society.

The RCEs, proposed by United Nations University and promoted by the Ubuntu Alliance, will assist with the vertical alignment of curriculum from primary through university and with linking formal and non-formal sectors of the education community. This alignment and linkage is essential to the success of a holistic ESD programme for all citizens in the region. Institutions of higher education are central to the development of such an integrated regional approach in bringing the best of knowledge from the natural sciences, social sciences, and humanities together and integrating this knowledge with the best of educational practice of their community and regional partners, and in doing so, to promote the principles of the Earth Charter. The RCEs will be crucial in promoting informed international cooperation in ESD. This sharing and cooperation will be made possible, and efficient, through the use of integrated computer technologies and facilitated by the RCE-Global Service Centre. This service centre will, among others, house the Global Higher Education for Sustainability Partnership Resource Project.

At the United Nations University-UNESCO conference on "Globalization and Education for Sustainable Development" held in Nagoya, 28-29 June 2005, the programme to promote the development of RCEs and GLSSD was launched. Five initiatives were presented, based in Toronto, Canada; Heerlen, Netherlands; Sendai, Japan; Suva, Fiji; and Kumasi, Ghana. The aim is to have twenty strong RCE initiatives by the end of 2006. At the end of the United Nations Decade of Education for

Sustainable Development in 2014, a partnership for ESD, created through the RCE effort, will flourish around the globe. Indeed, the Regional Centres of Expertise and Global Learning Space for Sustainable Development will likely be the most tangible and stimulating outcome of the Decade, providing an excellent base to achieve Principle 8 of the Earth Charter. ●

**Note**

1   For the full Ubuntu Declaration and list of signatories see www.unesco.org/iau/tfsd_ubuntu.html

# Part III. Social and Economic Justice

## Principles

9. Eradicate poverty as an ethical, social, and environmental imperative.
   a. Guarantee the right to potable water, clean air, food security, uncontaminated soil, shelter, and safe sanitation, allocating the national and international resources required.
   b. Empower every human being with the education and resources to secure a sustainable livelihood, and provide social security and safety nets for those who are unable to support themselves.
   c. Recognize the ignored, protect the vulnerable, serve those who suffer, and enable them to develop their capacities and to pursue their aspirations.

10. Ensure that economic activities and institutions at all levels promote human development in an equitable and sustainable manner.
    a. Promote the equitable distribution of wealth within nations and among nations.
    b. Enhance the intellectual, financial, technical, and social resources of developing nations, and relieve them of onerous international debt.
    c. Ensure that all trade supports sustainable resource use, environmental protection, and progressive labor standards.
    d. Require multinational corporations and international financial organizations to act transparently in the public good, and hold them accountable for the consequences of their activities.

11. Affirm gender equality and equity as prerequisites to sustainable development and ensure universal access to education, health care, and economic opportunity.
    a. Secure the human rights of women and girls and end all violence against them.
    b. Promote the active participation of women in all aspects of economic, political, civil, social, and cultural life
       as full and equal partners, decision makers, leaders, and beneficiaries.
    c. Strengthen families and ensure the safety and loving nurture of all family members.

12. Uphold the right of all, without discrimination, to a natural and social environment supportive of human dignity, bodily health, and spiritual well-being, with special attention to the rights of indigenous peoples and minorities.
    a. Eliminate discrimination in all its forms, such as that based on race, color, sex, sexual orientation, religion, language, and national, ethnic or social origin.
    b. Affirm the right of indigenous peoples to their spirituality, knowledge, lands and resources and to their related practice of sustainable livelihoods.
    c. Honor and support the young people of our communities, enabling them to fulfill their essential role in creating sustainable societies.
    d. Protect and restore outstanding places of cultural and spiritual significance.

*The text of the Earth Charter continues with Part IV on page 116.*

# Using Earth Charter Principles to Assess Social and Economic Justice in Latin America

**Yolanda Kakabadse** has worked for more than twenty-five years towards the national, regional and global environmental agendas. She has served as Minister of Environment in Ecuador, Executive President of the Fundación Futuro Latinoamericano and President of the World Conservation Union (IUCN). She has developed programs and processes to strengthen sustainable development through the integration of multi-sectorial efforts. Dr. Kakabadse coordinated the participation of civil society at the Earth Summit, Rio de Janeiro 1992. She has also been Counselor to the Vice President for Environment and Sustainable Development of the World Bank and Senior Advisor to the Global Environment Facility. She has been a member of the boards of directors of the Worldwide Fund for Nature International, the World Commission on Forests and Sustainable Development, and the World Resources Institutes Global Council. She is an Earth Charter Commissioner.

Part III of the Earth Charter, Principles 9, 10, 11 and 12 related to justice in the social and economic realms, was born of the fundamental concern that today's society is characterized by inequity. Social expressions such as racial, cultural, generational, or gender discrimination, as well as the marked differences among the economic classes, are present in all continents and nations. In this essay, I will use the experience of Latin America as a lens through which to view the key concepts in Part III of the Earth Charter.

Have we made progress towards the elimination of these behaviors in Latin America? Are we now in a better situation than ten years ago? In some aspects, we have and we are. In fact, in some issues related to equity, we have gone from commitments on paper to specific experiences which, although not to the full extent, are still part of the agendas of national and international politics within the framework of sustainable development. On the other hand, it is evident that people and societies have difficulty internalizing the true meaning of justice and understanding it as something different from a sense of compassion.

In order to illustrate this apparent progress in the fulfillment of the challenges proposed by the Earth Charter, we can look at some specific processes which, although they illustrate progress, point at the large contradictions that the Latin American continent witnesses.

While Principle 9 suggests working towards the "eradication of poverty as an ethical, social, and environmental imperative," the reality is that the number of poor people and the level of poverty in the world have risen and become more serious. What are the causes? Primarily, a myopic and short-term vision of development.

The processes of wealth creation in all societies of the world have been based on the use of natural resources. It is difficult to think of a development process without water, sources of energy, without land or any vegetal or animal species. From food to medicines, from textiles to cosmetics, all have their origin in a renewable or nonrenewable source. However, on many continents, as is the case of Latin America, the exploitation of natural resources has resulted in riches for few and poverty for many.

Even today, at the beginning of the twenty-first century, the common citizen in Latin America is influenced by a culture based on extraction and the irrational use of natural resources that is benefiting only a few. The abundance of natural resources in our region does not help a change of attitude. We have not learned to save and be austere. On the contrary, we have placed our resources in the category of the non-extinguishable and unimportant. In fact, they are part of the national accounts only when they have been totally exploited. The forests of the region, the rivers, the biological diversity, and other resources only now are being considered for their economic value as potential resources for ecotourism.

The positive aspect is that from Mexico to Patagonia important tourist industry, based on the acknowledgement of natural and cultural resources, has been developed. This has fostered new alliances between sectors – the owners of the resources who are generally local communities, and the tourist sector with business acumen – which traditionally, were separated due to social, economic, or cultural differences. The results are already visible.

There has not only been an improvement in the economy of both parties, but an explicit acknowledgement of the value of nature. From the Andes to the mangroves, from tropical forests to marine resources, all have gained a new meaning in the life of the region – their protection has economic value.

However, new contradictions appear in national agendas. The reaction of indigenous and peasant communities of the Andean counties to attempts to privatize water illustrate this situation; it is a rebellion against inequity. It goes beyond the need to define rules to control its use. The fight is not about the resource – it is about the principles and the values related to the ownership of the resource and its use. Traditionally, restriction and distribution systems originated in the communities themselves and have been based on principles of justice and equity. Their protest is born from the attempt to benefit only the wealthy and exclude the poor.

Through their participation in national and international debates about issues such as access and distribution of benefits generated by the use of biodiversity, indigenous peoples are now participating in establishing criteria related to benefits that should derive from the use of indigenous species or from traditional knowledge.

A brief analysis of the conflict in Latin America leads us to estimate that approximately seventy percent of the conflicts in the region are related to natural resources. Land ownership and water distribution, forest exploitation, and air pollution are only a few of the recurrent issues that are connected by the common thread of action or intention to use the natural resource indiscriminately or for personal benefit. The search for equity requires changes in individual behaviors as well as in institutional structures. Principle 10 establishes that we need to "ensure that economic activities and institutions at all levels promote human development in an equitable and sustainable manner."

The governmental programs designed to improve the economic conditions of the poorest people are based on a policy of assistance, but the majority of them are inconsistent with other capacity-building programs. There are, however, some notable accomplishments, especially when they are the result of intersectorial alliances. As a result of the decentralization of development programs, local governments have recharged their capacity to generate and implement participatory processes. These programs do not always achieve direct economic benefits, but they do open spaces that permit different parties to have access to information, to soft-money loans, and to technologies and other capacities that enable the development of non-traditional economic activities. The interesting factor about these processes is that, in many cases, they are born from associations between various sectors – the local government with non governmental organizations and with the productive sector interested in new markets for non-traditional products.

We cannot talk in Latin America about a large productive sector that is visionary and aware of its social and environmental responsibility. However, in each country, there is a formal or informal association of leaders of the productive sector that have formulated, and practice, new values based on equity and solidarity. These processes are characterized by relationships that emphasize human values and reject traditional patterns that perpetuate differences.

In the productive sector, the circle of individuals who are convinced of the need to promote philanthropy is becoming more significant. In the Latin American context, philanthropy is not only about economic contributions, but also about the direct and active participation in the process of generating social and economic change.

In several cities and countries in the region, business councils for sustainable development have clarified their roles and have strengthened their strategies to contribute to socially responsible development. These are slow steps and the impact is not always visible, but it builds towards a vision of long-term development.

In Latin America the numbers are clear. In the last two decades the growth of poverty has been alarming and little has been done for those who are most vulnerable. The growth of urban centers as a result of migration from the countryside is proof of the lack of attention to development policies, to the importance of food production, to the need to assure land ownership for the most needy, and to the imperative need to reinforce the economy of the farmer and small entrepreneur.

In the last years, Central America and the Andean regions have witnessed intense negotiations to establish free trade treaties with the United States of America. Central America has concluded its process of negotiation as a block while Colombia, Ecuador, and Peru are in the final phases of the debate.

The competitive nature of human beings and of nations establishes commercial codes that do not meet the standard set by Principle 10. The search for the well-being of others is not a characteristic of our modern society. On the contrary, we search for immediate benefits without concerning ourselves with the welfare of others. We sense that the tenets of the Free Trade Agreement are not very clear as to what the real benefits are for those in most need. The ones who most benefit will be, once again, a small minority. The risks for the poorest and the least protected are not measured or accounted for in equal terms. On the other hand, the formula of debt forgiveness for poor countries, though appearing to promote solidarity, actually reaffirms relationships of inequality between rich and poor countries. Most of the debt reductions are a new way of control, and, in real terms, they do not affect the economy of the donor country, thus maintaining the inequality.

One of the areas that has made most progress relates to Principle 11: "Affirm gender equality and equity as prerequisites to sustainable development and ensure universal access to education, health care, and economic opportunity." In political spaces, the obligation to preserve gender equality has been legislated in electoral processes. Beyond the law, the participation of women in the political sphere is more and more noticeable; in the private sector, there has been a growth in the leadership of women who are prominent by their professional qualities. In the academic field, the balance in gender is unquestionable. However, this phenomenon is more common in higher economic classes than among the poor and the marginalized. Access to education for girls and women of meager economic means is still limited.

Finally, let us look at Principle 12: "Uphold the right of all, without discrimination, to a natural and social environment supportive of human dignity, bodily health, and spiritual well-being, with special attention to the rights of indigenous peoples and minorities." Equity among people and nations is one of the most difficult social principles to attain, especially in societies where the concept of charity has been viewed as the way to share. If we critically look at the process of the construction of the agenda and the results of the World Summit on Sustainable Development in Johannesburg in 2002, we find two situations that clearly show the difficulty of putting equity processes into practice. First, the industrialized nations did not honor their commitment to donate 0.7% of their Gross National Product for the support of the development of poor countries. Its implementation would have made a significant difference in enabling several nations to address conditions that perpetuate poverty. Second, generating more visibility was the decision to contribute to the fight against poverty in Africa through actions that targeted the symptoms of the problems, and not the causes. In conclusion, charity—which does not take great effort—has not improved the situation of the poorest continent of the planet, and justice has not entered the discussion.

In terms of the environment, the rights of indigenous peoples have been rooted in defending their environment and their ecosystem against threats generated by processes of exploitation of natural resources which attack their stability, their security, and their right to live in an integral and secure environment. Oil exploitation, for instance, is progressively more responsible in its use of technologies that reduce the impact on the environment. Consequently, there are fewer attacks against local communities and nature itself. Additionally, there are more spaces for dialogue between the interested groups attempting to define priorities by working together. In the Amazonian countries, the plans for petroleum exploration used to be defined and executed with the exclusive participation of governmental authorities and investors. Today, the law and, for the most part, practice involve those who may be affected by the implementation, to discuss measures for the reduction of social and environmental impact.

If our departing point is the analysis of the advancement of the Principles of Part III of the Earth Charter, it is evident that, even though some processes are taking place in Latin America, much is still needed. The most important aspect is that debate has been generated among development policy-makers and society has become aware of the challenges in recognizing the rights and the obligations of the state and its citizens.

Thus, in Latin America, contradictions are commonplace; the discourse is starting to change, but the political culture moves slowly. We live amidst an array of contradictions that arise from the abyss that exists between what is and what might be. We live in a continent that is characterized by its richness and cultural and natural diversity. However, the very essence of inequity and poverty has not changed in the majority of the continent's countries. Its rivers and water sources, forests and mountains, marine and coastal resources, and, in general, its great biodiversity should allow the continent to ensure that no inhabitant would endure hunger, insecurity, or ignorance. We have the necessary conditions for its peoples and nations to attain sustainability in development.

In order to achieve change, we must respond to several challenges:

First, the construction of a sense of belonging within a nation or continent, maintaining the cultural values on which our current societies are built.

Second, the challenge in the short run is not to combat poverty, but to administer wealth. There remains, however, the question of whether, in order to manage wealth, must we assign a monetary value to all resources? Can religious, spiritual or cultural values, or even beauty, be valued in terms that are not monetary? The most important step towards the recognition of the values of our environment, and thus the generation of new behaviors to combat inequity, could be to internalize the sense of belonging with our own history and environment.

Third, the weak social investment in education, health, and other needs in almost all the countries of our continent and the perception of this as an expense, not an investment, needs to be the first objective of change.

I feel that the new generations have better conditions to meet these challenges. On the one hand, their rebellion against the patterns of discriminatory and abusive behavior of past generations, and against the way of designing and putting into practice the so-called developmental policies which respond to the interests of the few, is evident. Additionally, this generation has a clear vision for the future and its role in bringing about change. Thus, we have the obligation to invest in the construction of spaces in which to take action. ●

Erna Witoelar, Indonesia. A thematic essay which speaks to Principle 9 on using the Earth Charter to eradicate poverty

# The Earth Charter and the United Nations Millennium Development Goals

**Erna Witoelar** is the United Nations Special Ambassador for Millennium Development Goals (MDG) for the Asia Pacific Region. She is the former Indonesian Minister of Human Settlements and Regional Development, and founder of the Partnership for Governance Reform in Indonesia. Before joining the government, she pursued a long career in civil society where she was President of the Indonesian Consumer Foundation, founder and first Executive Director of the Indonesian Forum for the Environment, and President of Consumers International. She is currently an Earth Charter Commissioner, Chairperson of the Indonesia Biodiversity Foundation, and a board member of the Asia Pacific Philanthropy Consortium.

Only a few months after the Earth Charter was launched, world leaders from 189 United Nations (UN) Member States unanimously adopted the Millennium Declaration in September 2000. It called for a fully-inclusive, people-centered and rights-based approach to development. They thereby reaffirmed the commitment of their nations and the international community to the achievements of the Millennium Development Goals (MDGs), an ambitious agenda for reducing poverty and improving lives. As UN Secretary General Kofi Annan said, "We will spare no efforts to free our fellow men, women, and children from the abject and dehumanizing conditions of extreme poverty, to which more than one billion of them are currently subjected."

The Millennium Development Goals are eradicating extreme poverty and hunger; achieving universal primary education; promoting gender equality and empowering women; reducing child mortality; reducing maternal mortality; combating HIV/AIDS, malaria and other diseases; ensuring environmental sustainability; and forming a global partnership for development.

Seven of the eight goals have been translated into quantitative and time-bound targets, thereby allowing measurement and reporting of progress through objectively verifiable and interna-tionally comparable indicators. The targets are quite specific, unlike in the past when the same goals were set only in rhetorical terms.

The MDGs are not just national governments' commitments to the UN or the international communities; they are these governments' commitments to their own people. The Goals are global in their scope, but targets and indicators can be tailor-made to shorter time scales, higher targets, and local circumstances. The Goals are inter-related. The synergy among goals is a unique characteristic of the MDGs. Conversely, lack of progress in one goal is a barrier for achieving progress in another. Since a single intervention will achieve advances in multiple goals, working across sectors is much more effective than working in a single sector.

But the MDGs are not just about targets and statistics – they're also about values, stated clearly in the Millennium Declaration. The Values stated in the Millennium Declaration are:

Freedom: men and women have the right to a life of dignity, free from hunger, violence, oppression, and injustice.

Equality: no individual or nation must be denied the opportunity to benefit from development. Men and women must have equal rights.

Solidarity: costs and burdens of global challenges must be distributed fairly in accordance with equity and social justice.

Tolerance: human beings must respect one another in all their diversity. Diversity is a precious asset of humanity.

Respect for Nature: current unsustainable patterns of production and consumption must change in accordance with the precepts of sustainable development.

Shared Responsibility: global challenges must be addressed multilaterally. The UN must play the central role.

Principle 9. Eradicate poverty as an ethical, social, and environmental imperative.

86    Part III: Social and Economic Justice

The Earth Charter in Action

Reading all these values, one cannot deny that they resemble very much the values shared by the Earth Charter in building a just, sustainable, and peaceful global society.

"Freedom" and "Equality" bear a resemblance to the Earth Charter principles of Part III: Social and Economic Justice. They are the base for achieving the goals of poverty and hunger eradication; of equal access to basic health, education, shelter, water and sanitation services, and of gender equality and empowerment of women. While the MDGs focus on the achievement of economic and social human rights for all, the Charter further elaborates on justice and ethics.

"Tolerance" and "Respect for Nature" have similarities with the Earth Charter principles of Part I, Respect and Care for the Community of Life, and Part II, Ecological Integrity. Diversity of nature and humanity is very important in all attempts to ensure environmental sustainability. This goal is further targeting to integrate principles of sustainable development into country policies and programs; reverse the loss of environmental resources; and significantly increase access to safe drinking water, basic sanitation, and secure tenure for slum dwellers.

"Solidarity" and "Shared Responsibility" are a common force throughout the Earth Charter as well. Both the Declaration and Earth Charter are advocating for the importance of these values at global, national, and local levels. Both instruments seek to inspire in all the people a new sense of global interdependence and shared responsibility for the well-being of the human family, among countries as well as within each country. The Earth Charter widens it to all forms of life in the larger living world, while the MDGs focus more on how to implement this global solidarity. It is stated in Goal 8 that the aims are more and better aid, more open and just trade systems, debt cancellation, access to technology, and more job opportunities for youth. As a whole, both in the long-term vision as well as the underlying principles and values, the Millennium Declaration, including its goals, is very much in line with the vision and principles of the Earth Charter.

The momentum of renewed global solidarity, pledged formally by governments and all international and regional agencies through processes towards and during the MDG + 5 Summit in September 2005, can and should also be used to renew people's commitments to the Earth Charter. By now, most UN member countries realize that successful achievement of the MDGs requires addressing their links with other issues identified in the Millennium Declaration, such as human rights, good governance, peace, and security. These are all concerns strongly declared at the Earth Charter, but received retaliations from many government delegates during the tireless efforts by the Earth Charter Secretariat and Commissioners to seek endorsement of the Earth Charter by the UN.

Even though MDGs do not expressly refer to civic participation in decision-making or the role of civil and political freedoms,

which are strongly stated in the Earth Charter, these are important elements of the Millennium Declaration. Civil society campaigns on MDGs mostly advocate a rights-based approach, with inclusive decision-making involving women, the poor, and the marginalized. The path to achieve the Goals has to be paved by access to information; access to participation in planning, monitoring and evaluating; and access to means of making governments accountable.

The relationship between realization of MDGs with conflict resolution and peace building are also more and more recognized, not only in countries where conflicts exist, but also in many regional and international forums discussing regional and global challenges for achievement of the Goals. Missing the MDG targets and conflict can be cyclical: hardships, especially when accompanied by sharp inequalities, can breed violence; while poverty and unequal distribution of scarce natural resources is a potential cause of conflict. Hence, conflict directly and indirectly weakens achievement of other MDGs. It undermines economies, destabilizes governments, provokes mass movements of people, and destroys infrastructure. Working to achieve the MDGs should align efforts with the Earth Charter campaigners towards peaceful conflict resolution.

What is keeping the world from achieving the Goals is not the lack of finances or technical capability – it is the political obstacles or the lack of political will. This is not news. What is news is that there is now an explicit recognition of this fact in the UN system at the highest levels, and this is symbolized in the conception of the Millennium Campaign. The explicit object of the Campaign is to encourage and facilitate "we, the people," at a national and international level, to hold their governments and other key actors accountable for their promises in the Millennium Declaration and the Millennium Goals.

The Earth Charter can be used as a tool to advance the MDGs as it promotes environmental sustainability and responsibility for a way of life that can inspire commitment, cooperation, and change. Environmental sustainability, including sustaining the biodiversity of all the world's ecosystems and sustainable provision of water for life, is ensured by the maintenance and protection of the ecological integrity and rehabilitation of degraded ecosystems. Further, sustainable access to safe drinking water and basic sanitation for the urban poor can be integrated into all urban slum-upgrading programs – which can also ensure secure tenure for slum dwellers.

One-fifth of the world's population live in extreme poverty while 800 million people are chronically hungry, which is the primary concern of the Millennium Development Goal 1 on Poverty. Again, women disproportionately suffer the burden of poverty. Sufficient clean drinking water and adequate water for other household, agriculture, and economic activities can be instrumental in eradicating poverty and hunger. Urban and rural poor are buying more expensive water than the affluent people.

Provision and pricing of water, therefore, need to give greater weight to increasing access instead of fiscal gain. Water is a basic human right, not a commercial commodity.

The mere fact that poverty, health, education, gender, and environment became the millennium goals is due to a lack of political and resource commitments to achieve them as a whole. In many countries, the policy framework is not yet aligned with the MDGs and the fundamental objective of reducing human poverty. Poverty reduction is still seen as an automatic by-product of economic growth and macroeconomic stability. The Earth Charter can balance this by providing a values framework to translate the concept of "pro-poor policies" into specific and practical policy measures.

Even though the Earth Charter has not been fully endorsed by the United Nations in its totality, it has directly or indirectly influenced UN processes and products in quite significant ways. Unlike the Millennium Declaration, which is a more government-led process, the Earth Charter came about through a very participatory process involving thousands of individuals and hundreds of organizations. There is much to learn from this process to campaign for the MDGs.

The Millennium Declaration, including the MDGs, and the Earth Charter are really complementary to each other. There are cross-cutting issues and overlapping concerns, but each declaration also has its own niche in the segments of society. Even as the MDGs are more acceptable to governments at national, regional, and global levels; so the Earth Charter is more easily adopted by the civil society, media, parliamentarian, local governments, private sector, academicians, religious groups, and so on. These are target groups on which the Millennium Campaign is focusing. Hence, is it then still relevant to seek endorsement of the Earth Charter by the United Nations?

Today's world has the resources, technology, and knowledge to eradicate poverty with a people-centered and rights-based approach to development, and to integrate principles of sustainable development into national policies and programs. This campaign is about everybody's participation, and if the Millennium Development Goals advocates and Earth Charter supporters can build synergy and campaign together, then we will be the first generation that can really see poverty eradicated. We have no excuses. ●

A.T. Ariyaratne, Sri Lanka. A thematic essay which speaks to Principle 9 on recognizing the ignored, protecting the vulnerable, and serving those who suffer

# Awakening and the Earth Charter in Sri Lanka

**A.T. Ariyaratne** is the founder and President of the Sarvodaya Movement of Sri Lanka. For half a century the Movement he founded has been advocating a Ten Basic Needs Satisfaction approach to sustainable development—Development from Below. The concept and practice of community self-governance and has been in the forefront of the environmental movement in his country. Dr. Ariyaratne has won many international awards including the Ramon Magsaysay Award, the King Boudouin Award for International Development, and the Gandhi Peace Prize. He is an Earth Charter Commissioner.

E ach of us is called to utilize our brief passage on Earth wisely, with awareness of the footprints we leave behind in our journey through life, as well as of the interdependence of causes and effects. Beginning as a teacher and now with the perspective of fifty years with the Sarvodaya Movement, I have come to understand the principles of the Earth Charter, not as beliefs, but as multifaceted gems of wisdom.

Like any lesson, these principles must be shared in practice for them to have the impact for which they were intended. Indeed it is that word *sharing* that has served as the core of the value system which has animated the Sarvodaya Movement. It is the motivating force in thousands of villages – the interconnecting web of understanding that shapes what village people have known for generations.

Today, Sarvodaya is Sri Lanka's largest and most broadly embedded people's organization, with a network covering fifteen thousand villages, thirty four district offices, and over one hundred thousand youth. The aim of the movement is to use shared work, voluntary giving, and sharing of resources to achieve the personal and social awakening of everyone – from the individual, to the village, and continuing up to the international level. "Awakening" means developing human potential, and is a comprehensive process taking place on the spiritual, moral, cultural, social, economic, and political levels. Sarvodaya

strives for a model of society in which there is neither poverty nor excessive affluence. The movement's holistic approach is based on the Buddhist principles of goodness, sympathy, and tranquility; and on the Gandhian values of truthfulness, nonviolence, and self-sacrifice.

Particularly now that the Indian Ocean tsunami of December 26, 2004, has brought worldwide attention to this part of the globe, the application of Earth Charter principles has become urgently imperative. Nature has given us notice, and we can ignore her call to awaken only at our own peril. The humanitarian, political, and economic response has been heartening. But, it also calls for circumspection. Not all the projects generously offered take into account the long-term interests of the affected people and of the living environment. This cautionary note is sounded on the basis of Sarvodaya's experience with sustainable development. Let me give some examples to illustrate how principles of the Earth Charter have been actualised by Sarvodaya, and let me also highlight some of the challenges that face us in the future.

Sarvodaya has long been involved in financing the use of solar power. Our micro-credit scheme and village banking systems undertaken by the Sarvodaya Economic Enterprise Services (SEEDS) are now being called upon more than ever before to construct thousands of homes and set up small businesses. These projects and enterprises could take the conventional course and build unsustainable communities on behalf of tsunami survivors. But, together with its organisational partners, Sarvodaya has consciously opted to follow a different path. Permaculture instructors from the Global Ecovillage Network have assisted us to develop model approaches to housing. As of this writing, more than a thousand homes will utilize solar power and their numbers will increase.

Sarvodaya's Living and Learning Centre in Thanamalwila in the south of Sri Lanka has attracted students from throughout South Asia and the world to its courses on sustainability. After five years, the Sarvodaya Saliyapura Organic Demonstration Farm near Anuradhapura in the North Central Province and our bio-diversity conservation programmes reach out to farmers,

Principle 9. Eradicate poverty as an ethical, social, and environmental imperative.

Principle 9. Eradicate poverty as an ethical, social, and environmental imperative.

gardeners, agro-foresters, and students who attend training in village and district centres. Sarvodaya produces and distributes effective microorganisms to reduce reliance on pesticides. We have supported the generation of dendro power and other forms of biomass utilisation, composting and recycling, and youth environmentalist programmes to clean up our lakes and waterways.

If one spends more than one hour in any urban centre of our beautiful country, the negative effects of urbanisation and commercialisation become strikingly evident. Air pollution and reliance on non-renewable energy restrict our very ability to breathe. The transportation infrastructure required to move vast quantities of unnecessary and artificial consumer goods from port to village is woefully inadequate. From outer space one can see this island, once covered by rain forests and teeming with wildlife, as a crowded patchwork of roadways choked by a gridlock of people leaving home and family to manufacture clothing and goods for consumption at retail prices far in excess of what those workers themselves can afford. The "Made in Sri Lanka" label on your garments may carry with it a short-term benefit but a long-term curse.

Though one can be paralysed by despair at such trends, Sarvodaya and the Earth Charter are rooted in a distinctly different way of thinking and acting. Instead of giving in to the intense violence of civil war, Sarvodaya has seen that mass meditation involving more than two million ordinary people has, at critical moments, established an overwhelming ambience and psychosocial disposition for peace. Visitors to Sri Lanka's most notorious prisons are now finding that meditation programmes sponsored by Sarvodaya have loosened the shackles of retribution. Jailed hardcore criminals have become remarkably less violent. Sarvodaya programmes in gender relations and children's and women's rights focus on "the spirit of the law" as well as the questionable workings of a legal system that, in general, provides little succour to the poor.

Discussing details of projects, however, does not adequately communicate the fundamental principles of the Earth Charter to masses of Sri Lankans and their counterparts across the globe who endure unspeakable suffering. Just as economic poverty or isolation rob villagers of even a modicum of happiness in their struggle to stay alive from one day to another, a comparable spiritual poverty and sense of alienation render hollow the material comforts of post-industrial societies. That is why the awakening of all which Sarvodaya and the Earth Charter envision is of a more fundamental nature.

Even the best initiatives of governments, and of partisan politics, will not produce desired results if the individual citizen does not understand them or willingly participate in them. We will all benefit if we can help ordinary people to experience the joy and accomplishment of self-governance through participation. Nations can gather deliberate and make declarations. We can sign ceasefire agreements and stop killing each other in one pocket of violence. The separateness of such efforts will not allow us to nurture the very wholeness that we seem to have neglected.

If we are wise and dedicated, we can turn good intentions to noble acts whose cumulative momentum may well allow all of us a longer and more joyous sojourn on this Earth. We can actualize the hope that all beings be well and happy, even in the briefest moments of that journey. ●

Michèle Sato, Luiz Augusto Passos, and Carlos Maldonado, Brazil. A project descriptive essay on the many inspirations and applications of the Earth Charter in Mato Grosso, Brazil

# Mato Grosso Writes Its Earth Charter

**Michele Sato** holds a doctorate in science and is a full member of the Commission of the Earth Charter of the State of Mato Grosso, Brazil. She is the leader of the Research Group in Environmental Education at the Federal University of Mato Grosso.

**Luiz Augusto Passos** holds a doctorate in philosophy and is a full member of the Commission of the Earth Charter of the State of Mato Grosso, Brazil. He is a philosopher and educator, with a practice in homeopathy.

**Carlos Maldonado** is national coordinator of the Earth Charter in Brazil and full member of the Commission of the Earth Charter of the State of Mato Grosso. He holds a degree in law and is currently doing his doctoral research on formal systems of education.

*Sometimes we neglect our internal values in exchange for material aid. But without political foresight, dollars and international help are useless. For instance, we need to prove the viability of Extractive Reserves as an alternative to Amazonian development. In the meantime, these reserves become remote islands in a sea of misery and injustices, if the political under-standing is not clear. We need to strengthen the alliance with the environmentalists without losing our own characteristics as workers who want a ecologically responsi-ble society, where we can live with dignity, social justice, and also enjoy what wisdom, science, and technology have to offer us.*
Chico Mendes

Conceived in the utopia of civil society, the Earth Charter remained a draft for a long period, so that regional interests could re-write it and place it in the unique context of each beating heart of this immeasurable ecosphere. Thus, in the Brazilian Central West Region, Mato Grosso claimed a politico-educational reality of the Earth Charter because, being aware of the conflicting sides among subjects, it bet on the pedagogy of transformation. As it paid attention to plurality, many times silent, we recognize that, as with all propositions, our Earth Charter was somewhat fragile, as well as embedded with virtues which forced us to place the Charter next to conceptual, methodological, and axiological endeavors dedicated to environmental education.

Our first steps did not begin at the International Conference of the Earth Charter (1998), but with the dialogues of its preparatory process, with the collective organization among various institutions and players who enable it to be a project for all. Thus, our efforts attempted to dialogue on the religious, ethical, political, artistic, conceptual or tactical differences, and on our willingness to build propositions that could express our desires to change life – reinventing passion. This task has not been easy; and perhaps our greatest difficulty resides in overcoming the dichotomy society-nature, which carries a strong illuminist influence which, to this day, continues to exist. It impacts different concepts and attitudes among the players who work with environmental education, and their desires to reaffirm the Earth Charter as one of the political platforms of great complexity. Another challenge was to insert ourselves in the international context recognizing that humankind is a stage for conflicts and tensions, and that there was never the intent to eliminate differences, since we are aware that the biggest challenge we face is the difficult task of mutual co-existence (Passos and Sato, 2002).

To overcome the divorce between nature and culture, between environment and people, between state and nation, there is an on-going dynamic in the heart of Latin America, and in the center of Brazil We understand that the clarity of the

Principle 9. Eradicate poverty as an ethical, social, and environmental imperative.

Earth Charter is not isolated from society, that it reflects its ideology-producing trends, many times reaffirming merely economic development models. The movement is slow and does not bring any explosive revolution. But certainly, the Earth Charter's impact is long-lasting because we are fighting with fervor against isolation, dialectically transforming and being transformed, and, in particular, looking for altering the terrible "integrating-disintegrating" process, which in the majority of the cases only brings pain to the dramatic wish to change life toward social inclusion and environmental justice.

The Mato Grosso Earth Charter does not represent a hope that humankind becomes sensitive of its impact on nature, but rather that it has multi-referential political bases, which insistently believe that the ecological movement cannot continue to be at the margin's edge of economic and social issues (Botkin, 1992). The emphasis in the "Sustainable Development" discourse may represent a strong financial bias of nations, bringing the "myth of the victory of good against evil, of the strong and able against the weak and mediocre, and above all reinforcing a manichaest and positivist approach to reality" (Rummert, 1998, p. 10), increasing a hegemonic world behind the globalization discourse, and above all obfuscating the Earth Charter's importance.

Thus, in Mato Grosso, the Earth Charter movement is allied with that of environmental education in a political manner to stimulate the collective, without promoting competition which leads to social atomization, and in a critical ability to accept conflicts in a field of uncertainties, and having solidarity as a commitment of its participating members. We recognize the existence of a vast field of multiple types of knowledge, which are not confined to academia. We also promote social inclusion, which has been wasted principally by private sectors. We give preference to uniting efforts with all players interested in the movement. The "new" discourse, which in the name of reform hides an exclusionary agenda, brings intolerance with popular values and local culture survival, and obviously promotes the increase of consumerism, particularly in the "techno-globalization" era and the standardization of the human civilization.

We live in a time of separation from the State, exactly in a moment when we need to redefine the State. Discontinuity of individual and collective projects, based on competitiveness and on exclusion of solidarity, affects the construction of sustainable societies and not of sustainable development. Thus, we reject competition and the retreat of democracy, looking instead for the political support of the relationship between society and nature, and, above all, we are immersed in the project of communion with the sixteen principles contained in the Earth Charter.

However, a great question remains in the tense and dialogical-reality which is at the core of the world's and universe's movement. Is this question sufficiently addressed in the Earth Charter's text? Sometimes it does not appear so. At times, the Earth Charter still reveals a predominantly lyrical, wishful point of view, missing the understanding of the contradictions and the ruptures inherent to life, to the movement's status, to the energy of development and change.

Existing trends in the core of the Earth Charter's movement represent a very complex whole. Any claim to characterize them, as we try to do now, is arbitrary because we are inclined to do it in a uniform manner. There are, however, trends that show up frequently. One of them is the opinionated outcry for peace without taking into account that humankind is a stage for conflicts and disagreements. Another is the reproduction of the hegemonic discourse on "sustainable development." Other contradictions may exist, but these two are enough as they regrettably reflect the reactionary approach to cultural matters, the adoption of an incomprehensible static attitude on matters of dynamic movements, particularly pertaining to the disrespect of the various manifestations of human society. This preoccupation may be responsible for the presence of false poets, mere pamphleteers, handlers defending life, or artists who lack any understanding of the meaning of the cycles of life and death.

Our approach, in this sense, does not imply realization and perfection. We believe that a continuous review of concepts and approaches is necessary, using epistemological honesty and a firm, political purpose in opposition to those who preach pre-established concepts. The dominant players want to push for an ideal psychological type based on life's universal values – all this with the purpose of making the Earth Charter just another experience, showing trends and solutions and controlling the esthetical content. We emphasize that there are very beautiful things in its principles, but if one does not see the criticism, personalities may mask the greatness of the movement which, like everything else, has progress and limitations.

Wouldn't this also be the value of the traditional education? Is school apt to face uncertainties, to risk facing surprises or accepting diversity? The liberating educator must be a revolutionary by education (Freire, 2000), gifted with an almost magic power to tear down all acceptable trends and seek freedom. A dream education must invade art, philosophy, science, and technique. It must overcome the resistance of the times, their current disciplines with closed ranks, and strangling logic. It must overcome the hegemonic standardization which has prevented the development of educational diversity (Passos and Sato, 2002).

It is not possible to build an ecological conscience divorced from the dramatic interaction of opposites and of metamorphosis, which dizzily circulates in the entire universe (Santos, 2001). The living and dynamic dialogue depends on a productive, creative, and transforming esthetics which will implement, divulge, and make the Earth Charter's policies adherent and welcoming.

The Earth Charter, when we understand that the great synthesis of its principles is based upon respect without borders with all forms of life, will demand, as a trade-off, the banishment of all unnecessary and prolonged cruelty and suffering, espousing an esthetic sensibility that is positive and dynamic.

The Earth Charter, when proposing sentiments of compassion and understanding with the community of life and geared toward tolerance, rights, and freedom, seeks to cement among co-responsible people a culture of peace. In this endeavor, it supposes a continuous and daily war against premature, pointless, unnecessary death and the demolition of totalitarian and condescending paradigms. It needs to destroy all presumption of perfection and to open itself to all types of difference, seeking knowledge in wisdom and courage to immerse itself in life's events (Passos and Sato, 2002). It is necessary to create a "conviviality" (Morin, 2000) of a new esthetics which will be conducted from the point of view of recreating "feelings" and types of joy and pleasure, personal and collective, which nowadays are misinterpreted daily by the cultural industry. Joy trails all values, without co-responsibility for its consequences. The implementation of the Earth Charter's principles also assumes a personal and collective re-education, favoring non-conformity with the guidelines of collusion.

Having addressed these points of view, we believe that the Earth Charter must be at the technical corners of each segment of society, and in particular at schools. It should also be in the difficult aspects of collective works, in the expressions of students and the entire school community. The relevant Earth

Charter esthetics must defend the joy that comes from gestures, symbols, and feelings which realize and reaffirm the ethical-praxiological decision of remembering, expressing, and living in tension together and in solidarity with all.

To be in the world is inevitably to witness its barbarism, as a volcano that erupts in the gulf, following the tyranny of a discourse that does not allow dissensions but imposes only one way. To look at the world in this manner is not only to understand it externally but also to care and protect its core. This is the view that emerged from the Earth Charter, stimulating our capacity to defend life in the waves of rebellious movements against the political castration of a development-driven economy. We may not have undertaken an explosive revolution but the influence of our praxis pulsates slowly and beautifully on the engagement of the ones who not only want to follow destiny but also want to guide changes.

As we conclude, we do not pretend to be definitive on or to represent a replicable paradigm of the universal method of the Earth Charter. These are thoughts lived in the interior of Mato Grosso life, whose texture thus discloses that our thinking, and our remarks and our poetry care for the words and essences of the existence of beings. To re-experience and recreate the senses is a continuous task for those who reveal a pattern by pulling the loose threads of the yarn, and by including others who are not used to embroidering old clothes made by others' hands. The continuous act of separating threads and of weaving represents the inexorable movement of the past, present, and future. For us to sustain does not mean to freeze ideas – on the contrary, it means to transform them in a surrealist metamorphosis. An international network for the Earth Charter may be a dimension of the complexity, which is weaved and understood through a pattern of multiple nuances coloring environmental education, subject to equilibrium and pauses. The rhythm is the constructed

time, often escaping through our hands, but built on the eternal courage for taking chances to write a charter of ecological and cultural utopias – an Earth Charter. ●

## References

Bachelard, G. (1990). *Air and dreams: Essays on the imagination of movement.* Sao Paulo: Martins Fontes.

Bornheim, J. (1996). The "Bon Sauvage" as a philosopher and invention of the perceptible world. In Novaes, A. (Ed.). *Libertines, libertarians.* Sao Paulo: Companhia das Letras.

Botkin, D. (2002). What ecology for the XXI century? In Barrere, M. (Ed..). *Earth, common heritage: science to the service of the environment and development* (p.15-26). Sao Paulo: Nobel.

Freire, P. (2000). *Pedagogy of indignation.* Sao Paulo: UNESP.

Mendes, C. *Amazonia.* Retrieved August 8, 2002, from http://www.amanakaa.org/rodrig.htm

Mondolfo, R. (1967). *Figures and ideas of the renaissance philosophy.* Sao Paulo: Mestre Jou.

Morin, E. (1997). *My demons.* Rio de Janeiro: Bertrand Brasil.

Passos, L.A. and Sato, M. (2002). Esthetics of the Earth Charter: for the joy (in tension) of living with diversity! In Ruscheinsky, A. (Ed..). *Environmental education – Multiple approaches* (p.15-36). Porto Alegre: Artmed.

Rummert, S.M. (1998). Identification projects: in dispute, dreams and worker's identity. In *Living Democracy* (IBASE), 4, 7-17.

Principle 9. Eradicate poverty as an ethical, social, and environmental imperative.

Dumisani Nyoni, Zimbabwe and Ismail Serageldin, Egypt. A project descriptive essay on equitable employment for the future as it relates to Principle 10

# Youth Employment: A Global Priority for Sustainability, Peace, and Prosperity

**Dumisani Nyoni** is driven by a passion for poverty eradication and the realization that the causes of poverty are multi-dimensional. He believes the Earth Charter offers a framework which helps to heal the wounds that current systems and patterns of human life are creating. In 2000, Dumisani launched the Earth Charter Youth Initiative from the Secretariat of the Earth Charter Initiative in San Jose, Costa Rica. Through hosting workshops and giving speeches, presentations, seminars, and writing, Dumisani has incorporated the Earth Charter as a tool used in connecting and inspiring youth around the world. Following the September 11, 2001 attacks on the United States, Dumisani and friends coordinated a youth dialogue in Boston using the Earth Charter as a reflection piece to bridge divides and create constructive responses to the shocks of these events. He helped to incorporate the Earth Charter in the Youth Employment Summit Campaign during his tenure as its Youth Coordinator.

**Ismail Serageldin** is Director of the Library of Alexandria and chairs the Board of Directors for each of its affiliated research institutes and museums. He is also Distinguished Professor at Wageningen University in The Netherlands. He serves as Chair and Member of a number of advisory committees for academic, research, scientific and international institutions and civil society efforts which includes the Intitut d'Egypte (Egyptian Academy of Science), TWAS (Third World Academy of Sciences), the Indian National Academy of Agricultural Sciences, and the European Academy of Sciences and Arts. Dr. Serageldin has also served in a number of capacities at the World Bank, including as Vice President for Environmentally and Socially Sustainable Development (1992-1998), and for Special Programs (1998-2000). He has published over fifty books and monographs and over two hundred papers on a variety of topics including biotechnology, rural development, sustainability, and the value of science to society.

A young man in the crowded neighborhood of Cairo, Egypt, or in the seemingly empty streets of Bulawayo in Zimbabwe asks the same question every day, "Where can I find a job, or any means that will enable me to make a living, gain some respect, and contribute to the well-being of my family?" The inability to afford electricity for domestic use, the proper medical attention, or decent meals on a regular basis stirs up an intense frustration within him. That frustration turns to an anger that somehow must be expressed and released. Where does he direct it? What does this mean for those around him in his community? What does this mean for a planet where billions of other youth in thousands of cities and settlements share that reality?

According to UN statistics, there are presently over three billion people on the planet living on less than $2 USD per day, and poverty continues to escalate. In many countries, especially in the developing world, half of those people are under the age of twenty-four. In almost all countries, improvements in living standards have been minimal and reflect no substantial change in the lives of the vast majority. In at least twenty countries, conditions are worsening considerably. The number of young people globally is the largest that the planet has ever had.

At present, more than fifty percent of the population is under the age of twenty-five, or just over three billion individuals are youth or children. Young people alone, between the ages of fifteen and twenty-four, exceed 1.3 billion! This means that approximately one person in five is between the age of fifteen and twenty-four years, or seventeen percent of the world's population can be considered to be "youth." The implications for instability represented by this overall scenario are alarming and likely to continue.

The on-going challenge is that of meeting the needs of people around the world, ensuring economic development and rights to livelihoods, and at the same time, safe-guarding the planet from over consumption and the sheer depletion of its resources. A fundamental question that must be answered asks, "How we can eradicate poverty and its associated ills and at the same time protect the ability of future generations to have productive and sustainable livelihoods?"

A shift is required in the way in which livelihoods are generated—and a change in economic organizations is needed. In the vision of the Earth Charter, humanity is challenged to "ensure that economic activities and institutions at all levels promote human development in an equitable and sustainable manner" (Principle 10). As stewards of our Earth's natural resources, and as a community that recognizes the interdependence of living organisms and believes in the equality of people everywhere, we have a responsibility to design institutions that will realize such equality and sustainability.

Unrestrained economic growth alone will not solve the deep and complex problems caused by poverty and unemployment. Our whole approach to the challenge of sustainable development and wealth creation must change. People need to be at the center of the strategies, policies, and initiatives that are developed. Opportunities need to be created for people to generate healthy incomes and to build safe communities. Furthermore, the definition of resources used in this struggle must be expanded. Youth must be recognized as key players in this effort—their numbers alone justify this, as does their productive potential. When more that fifty percent of the world's brainpower, energy, and labor force is left untapped to solve the problems we are faced with, is that not the greatest loss we can ever suffer?

The Earth Charter calls for all peoples to "honor and support the young people of our communities, enabling them to fulfill their essential role in creating sustainable societies" (Principle 12.c). Young people have a greater stake in seeing the establishment of a more sustainable path to the future. As a generation, youth will be around longer and will have to deal with the consequences of today's actions and decisions for a long, long time to come. It is in their interests as a collective to address these complex issues, to reverse the impacts of poverty, and to build a more

sustainable society. Therefore, creating employment opportunities for youth through job creation programs, or the promotion of entrepreneurship models, is essential and urgent in giving young people the direct capacity to make a meaningful contribution to the state of the world.

We know that it is possible to create livelihood opportunities that do not harm the environment or rely on the perpetuation of the current unequal relationship that humanity has with the planet. Opportunities abound to use natural resources to build sustainable enterprises, meeting the livelihood needs of millions and addressing key development challenges such as providing safe, renewable energy, ensuring clean water, and combating hunger.

In September 2000, the Earth Charter Initiative connected with the Youth Employment Summit Campaign, a project of the Boston-based Education Development Center. Together, a project was developed with the support of the Global Environment Facility and the World Bank focusing on the "promotion of youth-led enterprises in off-grid renewable energy." The collaboration was inspired by Principles 10 and 12.c of the Earth Charter. Through collaboration with the Earth Charter Initiative, and in launching the multi-year project focusing on creating sustainable livelihoods, the YES Campaign shifted the emphasis of employment creation for youth to include environmental sustainability as a core piece of the framework through which the vision of the global campaign can be executed.

An online database of effective practices in renewable energy has been launched (www.yesweb.org/gkr/), with several publications and newsletters highlighting the importance and offering practical advice and research on generating jobs and promoting entrepreneurial opportunities that also take care of the planet we live on. Most excitingly, five entrepreneurs from Ghana, Malawi,

India, Peru, and Georgia were supported in launching renewable energy enterprises of their own, demonstrating that young people can indeed succeed in addressing economic needs and building sustainable communities.

The Earth Charter is a tool that helps to define important conversations around the globe—challenging the planet now. It enables creative, practical solutions to emerge while at the same time keeping a focus on the essence of sustainable development. The experience of the linkages between the Earth Charter and the YES Campaign tells an important story of the power of connecting the core issues of sustainable community development and economic empowerment, coupled with the energy and passion of the younger generation.

At the center of the spirit of the Earth Charter is the need to establish a global ethic that promotes respect and care for the community of life, ecological integrity, social and economic justice, democracy, non-violence, and peace. A world plagued by poverty, and where over half of its citizens are without opportunities to meet their needs, cannot ever see these principles become common practice. There is a direct linkage between the overall vision of the Earth Charter and the ability for people to make a living. Otherwise, why should anyone bother to willfully protect, defend, or contribute to any system which does not offer them a chance at a healthy life?

We cannot disconnect the security and prosperity of nations across the globe from the crushing challenges that are born out of the depths of poverty and failure to meet the most basic of needs. The future of the planet and of humankind rests on our ability to overcome these daunting challenges. If the future is now, and youth are the future, then now is the time to make youth employment a global priority. ●

Rene Ledesma and Josephine Espaillat, The Dominican Republic. A project descriptive essay on equitable and sustainable human development as it relates to Principle 10

# The Earth Charter: A Beginning of Sustainable Development in the Dominican Republic

**René Ledesma** was Undersecretary of Environmental Management from 2000-2004 and represented the Dominican Republic at the Conference on Sustainable Development in Johannesburg in 2003. At this conference, he was a key figure in motivating the member states of the United Nations to endorse the Earth Charter. As Director of the Fund For Nature (Pronatura) he provided institutional support for the diffusion of the first and second drafts of the Earth Charter. He belonged to the National Committee of the Earth Charter and participated in various consultations and revisions of materials at national and international levels. Today, from the private sector, he is dedicated to the inclusion of an environmental dimension in development projects.

**Josefina Espaillat Acevedo** is an educator and agricultural engineer at the Universidad Autonoma of Santo Domingo. She is pursuing a doctoral degree in Social Intervention and Cooperation at the University of Oviedo, Spain. She joined the "family of the Earth Charter" in 1997 at Río +5. In 1998, she became the coordinator of the National Committee for the Earth Charter and is responsible for fostering the first and second consultation on the drafts of the Earth Charter in the Dominican Republic. She participated in the meeting that took place in the city of Cuiba, Mato Grosso, Brazil, giving a presentation of the report on the Earth Charter Consultation. In 2001, she received the Duarte, Sánchez and Mella Medal for Merit at the level of *Caballero* for her work in this initiative and her constant fight for the incorporation of ethical values in the field.

*hay un país en el mundo,*
*colocado en el mismo trayecto del sol,*
*oriundo de la noche*

*There is a country in the world,*
*placed in the same route of the sun,*
*that comes from the night*

Pedro Mir

Since the Rio+5 Forum in 1997, the Dominican Republic enthusiastically became part of the Earth Charter project. This article is a recollection of the challenges and rewards that this project has left us with. The most important aspects are the impressions on our thinking, feelings, and daily practices as professionals and citizens of a country with many great possibilities, but also with many great social, economic and environmental problems. We learned that we are unique beings in the universe, but at the same time, we are an imperceptible speck in this universe. We learned that uniqueness-dignity, liberty-independence are binomials that constitute our most profound reality and they remind us that we are part of one single community of life.

The Dominican Republic, like many developing countries, faces grave problems of social exclusion and inequality, corruption scandals in public administration, lack of transparency, as well as a progressive deterioration of our natural and environmental resources. We perceived many of these situations as external; we felt impotent and lacked hope for the future. In this context, the ethical proposal of the Earth Charter was a light that illuminated a new path, a new call to hope and shared responsibility. It provided a reminder that "together we can"; we can take the reins and assume that we can always do something rather than simply be witnesses to the problems. That is the reason we warmly welcomed this Project and we took it as a challenge to society. There was a great integration of diverse sectors of the Dominican people and with great enthusiasm students, educators, mass media, and community groups joined in.

In early 1998, the National Committee of the Earth Charter was formed with ample participation of institutions and people from civil society, the government, the private sector and agencies of cooperation, journalists, artists, educators, students, and others. The working tool was the draft of the Earth Charter. We developed a broad awareness and socialization campaign for this document through different actions: press conferences; interviews and articles in the major newspapers of the country; consultations with various professional groups; meetings in major

Principle 10. Ensure that economic activities and institutions at all levels promote human development in an equitable and sustainable manner.

regions of the country; and drawing, singing, and poetry contests in educational centers; and publication of the local Earth Charter Bulletin. All these activities were realized with our own funds managed by local members. The Committee meetings, which were held twice a month to supervise the program, kept the press informed and contributed to the success of the awareness and the consultation process.

In this process, questions such as the following filled our hearts and minds: "Is it possible to maintain the logic of accumulation, unlimited and lineal growth and, at the same time, avoid the breakdown of ecological systems? Is our paradigm of existential hegemony not antithetical to the conservation of the cosmic earth community? Would it not be irresponsible, and thus unethical, to continue in the same direction?"

We answered our own questions by affirming that we need profound changes in our values, institutions, and ways and styles of life. We are not all, neither are we the only ones. This means that besides us, there must be space left for others who also have rights and autonomy. We assert that we ourselves need an awareness and a sense of mutual belonging that will tie us to an Earth that is our first and last homeland. This process strengthened our commitment to make our country, the Dominican Republic, a country more respectful of its natural and cultural resources, a country more inclusive and democratic, a country more compassionately and humanely habitable.

If it is a fact that the divide between rich and poor has deepened in the country because neo-liberal economic policies are still predominant, it is not less true

that, today, we are less naïve, more sensitive, and critical towards the reality of exclusion and impoverishment. We are more conscious of the interdependence between development, economy, environment, and natural resources. We recognize that the globalization that we are witnessing, which is dominated by inequitable economic relationships, is exacerbating deterioration of the lives of human beings and of nature. In response, we take a critical and proactive stance of repudiation.

Since August 2000, we have a General Law of Environmental and Natural Resources and a State Secretariat of Environmental and Natural Resources. Measures to evaluate the environmental impact of new projects, and the compliance of the ones already in place, have been established. In this context, one of the most significant actions was the social movement "Save the Protected Areas," which was generated to avoid the approval of a sectoral law for the Protected Areas System that would significantly hurt the ecosystems and extension of several National Parks.

The principles and values of the Earth Charter have contributed in forwarding the process of civil society engagement and public action. Today, environmental problems, as well as poverty and matters of social exclusion, occupy an important place in the mass media, mobilizing public opinion to address these issues. In the most remote communities in the country, groups of people organize to present proposals for action connected to their resources and local problems and also to reclaim their right to a dignified life.

The principles and values have also provided a vision of ongoing commitments and challenges. For example, real incorporation of environmental education as a cross-cutting theme in the Dominican educational system is required to address issues such as the public sphere, the rural-urban relationship, production models, and planetary interdependence. Collaborative research efforts between universities and local environmental groups need to be facilitated to strengthen the integration of local and academic knowledge. The citizenry requires access to more appropriate and timely information from the mass media and through the establishment of a National System of Environmental Information and Natural Resources, in order to make better informed decisions about environmental and natural resource issues. The Society-State-Civil Society relationship on environmental issues requires strengthening through the formation of organizations such as the National Council for the Environment and Natural Resources and through consultation with the citizenry for the implementation of mega-projects. Finally, the challenge remains to further the participation of groups such as ecological societies, non governmental

organizations, educational centers, and municipalities in the process of elaboration and implementation of policies for management, such as co-management of protected areas, identification of economic incentives, and economic valuation of environmental services.

These challenges will be more rapidly addressed if we ensure that the activities and economic institutions at all levels "promote human development in an equitable and sustainable manner," as expressed in Principle 10 of the Earth Charter. Society in its totality will have to reorganize the economy using market decisions that clearly manifest actions related to environmental sustainability and to ensure the establishment of mechanisms of social equity.

In order to "promote human development in an equitable and sustainable manner" (Principle 10), the market economy will have to appropriately evaluate the goods and services that Mother Earth conveniently provides us and should respect the limitations that nature demands in order to reach sustainable production. We should at least strive to reach what the economist Jeffrey Sachs accurately expresses: "The tragic irony of this moment is that the rich countries are so rich and the poor so poor that a few added tenths of one percent of GNP from the rich ones ramped up over the coming decades could do what was never before possible in human history: ensure *that the basic needs of health and education are met for all impoverished children in this world*"[1] (author's emphasis).

The challenge according to Lester Brown, founder of Worldwatch Institute, is not only to alleviate poverty but also, when doing so, to create an economy that is compatible with the planet's natural systems; an economy that can sustain progress.[2] This implies a reengineering of the food economy and the energy economy, moving away from the use of fossil fuels to the use of renewable energy and the efficient and

sustainable use of the limited water resources that we still have available.

Finally, we believe that we can build an economy that "promote[s] human development in an equitable and sustainable manner" (Principle 10), if we manage to foster an economic growth that does not destroy our ecosystems and, in that way, we will be able to achieve *one single community of life* where the basic necessities of all people on the planet are provided for and a world of which we can feel worthy. ●

### Notes

1  Sachs, J. (2001, November 21). One tenth of 1 percent to make the world safer. *The Washington Post*, p. A23.
2  Brown, L.R. (2003). Plan B: Rescuing a planet under stress and a civilization in trouble. New York: W.W. Norton & Company.

# The Earth Charter and the World of Business and Economics

**Oscar Motomura** is the founder and Chief Executive Officer of the Amana-Key Group, a center for excellence in management, a network of associates with global reach, based in São Paulo, Brazil. The purpose is to serve as a world reference for radical innovation in management that is capable of generating genuine development of people, organizations, communities, and the greater whole. The Amana-Key Group has adopted the Earth Charter as a global reference for its education programs and innovation retreats. Thousands of leaders from corporations and the government take Amana-Key programs every year, where their awareness of global issues affecting all of humanity is expanded along with their understanding the importance of contributing to our collective evolution, through ethical and conscious management practices.

In the process of making things happen that will be the focus of the next phase of the Earth Charter process, we cannot underestimate the strength of the culture of searching for increasing economic results that prevails in the global society today. Competing for economic growth and profits has become a worldwide obsession.

Rigorous application of the Earth Charter principles necessarily presupposes a reinvention of the way we try to generate economic development. Inherent in the vision expressed by the Earth Charter is a reinvention of the whole system, including inoculating it with safeguard mechanisms to make it impossible to distort the reinvented system through manipulation, corruption, and other unethical practices.

Such a complete reinvention will also require a radical change in the culture underlying the prevailing system, including the re-education of leaders, many of whom have been trained to be effective at competing, neutralizing competitors, creating strategies for growth and profits, and lobbying for laws that are favorable to their businesses. They believe that they are doing good and that they are the productive members of society. But to the degree that they ignore the negative by-products of their actions, they live in a state of illusion. They must be awakened and re-educated along the lines of a broad, new benchmark document like the Earth Charter.

Will this process of awakening people from their illusions and their distorted mental models be an easy task? Of course not. It is entirely possible for many people to go through a well-designed education program and come to a new understanding from a logical point of view, but their core beliefs about life not will change that easily. The real change that is needed entails a fundamental change in consciousness. It is *not* from the mental dimension that principles like those in the Earth Charter will be fully implemented. What is required is a degree of commitment that comes only from spirit.

While those who are successful in the prevailing system may be willing to start playing a new game, with new rules, they have enormous resistance to "letting go" of what they have achieved so far. To truly adopt the principles of the Earth Charter will require a full exercise of the value of detachment.

A new political, economic, business system capable of restoring balance worldwide will be possible if everyone works both for his or her own sake and for the sake of the common good. But the prevailing system is still driven by obsolete theories and beliefs, such as the idea that greed is good, that are still taught, paradoxically, in our schools and reinforced in the daily media.

The Earth Charter was created through an outstanding process involving thousands of people from all nations of the planet. If the next phase of the Earth Charter process is to focus on the reinvention of the larger system, it will require an even better process, now involving billions of people. But involving billions of people in what? What specific "equations" will they have to solve in order to make the necessary reinvention happen? The word "equation" is being used here in the sense of a difficult problem that can only be understood if all its elements are taken into account.[1] The formulation of the "right" equations will be key to this process. Otherwise, the energy and creativity of those billions of people will be wasted in solving "peripheral" issues or in working on symptoms and not on the essential ori-

Principle 10. Ensure that economic activities and institutions at all levels promote human development in an equitable and sustainable manner.

gins of the problem. Following are some examples of equations that are strategic in nature and consistent with the idea of reinvention rather than incremental change.

Equation 1: How can the peoples of the planet join forces to ensure the total reinvention of the political-economic-business system, both locally and globally, so that everything is geared toward the common good, toward global well-being?

Equation 2: How can the press and the media help to reveal the flaws in the prevailing system and promote the reinvention of systems from scratch, using the vision embedded in the Earth Charter as the essential platform?

Equation 3: How can the leading educational institutions of the world be involved with the Earth Charter principles and be stimulated to create innovative programs capable of catalyzing effective transformation of senior leaders, not just through the mental dimension, but also through emotion, deep contact with the realities in contrast with reported realities, of the world, and the elevation of consciousness?

Equation 4: How can the peoples of the world join forces for the sake of replacing the prevailing assumption that "greed is good" with a new premise that everyone on the planet should work for his or her own well-being while working at the same time for the well-being of the whole? How can the peoples of the world join forces to make sure that those who have, help the have-nots to ensure one hundred percent inclusion, thus making the concept of the common good tangible with the velocity that is necessary?

Equation 5: How can the intelligentsia of all nations be mobilized to prove to senior leaders in all sectors that such a "utopia" will make business flourish at unprecedented levels, making the "market" tens of times larger and sustainably healthier?

Equation 6: How can the press and the media, together with scientists and the intelligentsia of the world, endorse the importance of a healthy transition – even at a short-term loss – to a new level of global well-being? How can we make this short-term sacrifice an "in" movement, worthy of wide appreciation from all sectors of society?

These are equations specifically formulated for reinventing the system. We need more than mere change. We need a complete turnaround. A radical transformation. We must acknowledge that, globally, we are operating with obsolete structures, systems, and institutions, and that we have learned to live with them, to get by with the distortions. Through that process, we have gradually become more and more distant from the ideal, from perfection. It all happened step by step. With our consent. A concession here. Another there.

One day, a document like the Earth Charter is produced. Not by corporations. Not by governments. Not by institutions of the political system, the economic system, the financial system, the business system. Not by abstractions that came to life, but by a charter created by the peoples of the planet.

The Earth Charter reveals a vision to all of us. A vision of the ideal, of perfection. Some of us realize how far we have strayed from that ideal. But many of us, trapped in a state of illusion, do not see the problems our political, economic, and business systems have generated. We are blind and insensitive to the reality around us. We live fragmented, virtual lives, conditioned by the system.

For the few who can still see, the responsibility is enormous. They all must go further with visions like the Earth Charter. It is time for action. It is time to make things happen. It is time to do what we need to do – even when what we need to do seems to be an impossible task, like completely reinventing the systems around us. And, on top of that, we do not have much time. Speed is key. And we must act on a worldwide scale.

That's why we need help. We need billions of people involved in the new phase of the Earth Charter. People from all over the world. From different professions. Not orchestrated through a mechanical, hierarchical process full of rules and controls, but all organized biologically, based on a few universal principles.

The Earth Charter honors the complexity of the planet's overall situation. The issues that deserve our attention are many if we are to resolve that mega-equation in a systemic way. But, in the next phase of the Earth Charter process, we will have to select a few "acupuncture points" to leverage the process. Chief among those points are the political, economic, and business systems.

Maybe the Earth Charter's next phase should focus exclusively on that key reinvention. Why? Because as long as individual ambition worldwide is geared toward personal gain, a "little god" is actually driving the process of life – generating the deterioration and the illness of the planet as a whole. As we realize, on the other hand, that our purpose must be the well-being of the whole, the pursuit of the common good without any kind of exclusion, we – as humanity – return to the path of wisdom from which we should not have deviated in the first place. In that sense, the Earth Charter seems to be a tool that the Creator has placed in our hands. Another one. Again. To help all of us. Shall we use this extraordinary opportunity effectively this time? ●

**Note**

1 Formulating equations is the gist of systems change. Equations are the clearest and most encompassing possible statements of all the vital aspects to be addressed in order to make a system advance toward a desirable end state or vision. This kind of definition allows the breaking of the path to a desired state into all of its attributes, components, and general features. Hence the formulation of equations prevents us to leaving out any crucial aspect on the path to a desired end state.

Sixto K. Roxas, The Philippines. A project descriptive essay on humane sustainable development in national economic policy

# Giving the Earth Charter a Local Habitation and a Name in The Philippines

**Sixto K. Roxas**, a noted Philippine economist, has served as the country's chief economic planner and member of Cabinet as Foreign Affairs Undersecretary for International Economic Relations. He serves as Chair, Maximo T. Kalaw Institute for Sustainable Development. He is also Chair of the Foundation for Community Organization and Management Technology and President of SKR Managers & Advisors, Inc. in Manila. Roxas serves as Chair of the Green Forum, Vice Chair of the Philippine Rural Reconstruction Movement, and Vice Chair of the Foundation for Philippine Environment. He has received numerous awards for his leadership in management, economics, and environmental protection. He has been President of the Asian Institute of Management, Chief Executive Officer of the Bancom Group, and Vice Chairman of American Express International. He is considered as a pioneer in investment banking in the Philippines. He retired from banking in 1982 and has been engaged since then in developing a system of local community management.

In March 1987, the World Commission on Environment and Development drew the world's attention to the "trends that the planet and its people cannot long bear: the failures of development and the failures of environmental management." Out of the two failures emerged the apocalyptic twins that threaten the very survival of the planet:

persistent poverty and environmental destruction. The Philippines stands out as a dramatic victim of these deadly twins. The country's present plight might be the planet's future. At the same time, in the Filipino people's deep and continuing involvement in the composing of the Earth Charter and in the carrying out in practice of its principles, the world may also view the model for the intellectual revolution, the moral transformation, and the institutional changes that mark the path to recovery.

The Philippines is a microcosm of all the major issues of the planet: poverty, environmental crisis and, social conflict. The root cause of these problems – the disastrous impact of an inappropriate theory and strategy for development – is nowhere more starkly viewed than in a country of fragile islands. The delicate balances of nature – the genesis of the Philippine cosmos and the Filipino's habitat, its internal balance, the evolution of man, and the human community in this country – are a cameo of the planetary process.

The Laws of Nature and the processes of her settlements are sharply depicted in this archipelago, as are the pathologies to which she is subject. A territory of seven thousand islands, formed over one hundred fifty million years of geological, volcanic, and biophysical processes on which originally a few hundred tribes dwelt in a lifestyle of harmony with their habitats, was brought into the Western historical

stream by a Spanish invasion and colonization in the sixteenth century. Four hundred years of Spanish civilization transformed these tribes into the Filipino nation of mainly Christian and Muslim faiths. Nearly a half-century of American colonization brought individualism and its modern enterprise culture.

An archipelago in the tropics has vulnerabilities peculiar to it. Made up not only of thousands of islands but also of thousands of micro-ecological niches which, over a period of several million years, by a process of selection, the Filipino archipelago species of flora and fauna have adjusted. Because of the multiplicity of those niches, there is a tendency to have a multiplicity of species and subspecies of both flora and fauna, but with relatively few individuals in each one. The worst possible force to release on the Filipino's island habitat were the waves of development interventions driven by single-purpose, sector-specialized entrepreneurs pursuing dreams of amassing personal wealth from the exploitation of nature. These interventions drew their scientific and ethical justification from the intellectual and ideological baggage of the eighteenth and nineteenth century revolutions in Europe and America.

Modern technology put tremendous physical power in the hands of man before it raised his awareness and his ethic to a level where he would use the power wisely. The self-seeking, profit-maximizing, achievement-driven class of

Principle 10. Ensure that economic activities and institutions at all levels promote human development in an equitable and sustainable manner.

so-called entrepreneurs, who raped the environment, marginalized, and alienated great masses of the people, was glorified as the heroes of present day society. Their virtues were proclaimed. Over four generations, theirs were the values the youth were taught to glorify. A fragile ecosystem – what nature took one hundred fifty million years to build – took only a single generation of Filipinos to destroy.

Communities in nature are formed in families, villages, and towns which find their natural balance with their environments. "Livelihood systems" integrate with social, religious, and political systems. When powerful business and government forces take a sectoral view, they, in fact, disintegrate these natural forms and attempt to regroup them into sectoral-oriented and specialized institutions – into sugar towns, logging settlements, mining villages, industrial and commercial centers, and export processing zones. This process never succeeds in completely reintegrating the natural communities that are first disintegrated. Entire segments of the original population in a natural habitat become "marginal" to the new communities. The so-called "progress" itself recruits the prime talent of every community to the ranks of business and management with this style. The natural communities lose all of their leadership to this process, either through business or government

The approach to the Philippine problem requires a fresh ideology. A way must be found – and found quickly – to bring on a convergence among the activities that make people rich, those that give communities sustainable and adequate livelihood and those that restore and preserve the natural resources. This will require a new view of nature as having laws of its own that dictate the poise and balance of self-sustenance, and which man must respect if his use of nature for his own needs is to be sustainable as well. It will also require a new view of economic, social, and political organization that recognizes the natural human community as the modality nature

designed which best molds man's operational institutions to the imperatives of his habitat.

Further, the new ideology will require the translation of that view into the ethical norms, values, laws, institutions, and project modalities that govern man's day-to-day transactions in society. In short, humanity needs a code of sustainable behavior. It needs an Earth Charter.

Crises breed the leadership that responds to the needs and the social movements that transform anguish into the outrage that mounts forces for change. It was inevitable, then, that early on leaders emerged who pioneered action in civil society to awaken consciousness and combat the forces of destruction in an attempt to reverse the tide.

Maximo Kalaw, Jr.'s personal history eminently suited him to become the leader of the movement in the Philippines, organizing the Philippine Institute for Alternative Futures, transforming Haribon into an activist environmental foundation, forming a coalition of over 800 foundations, peoples, and organizations into the Green Forum. This Forum conducted nationwide participatory consultative sessions in eight regions of the country in order to draw from the people their own notions of what sustainable development means for them and their local communities.

On February 21, 1986, the bloodless "People-Power" revolution toppled the Marcos regime and Corazon Aquino assumed the Presidency of a revolutionary government. In 1987, a new Constitution restored a democratic republic. In the same year, the Brundtland Commission report on Environment and Development highlighted the twin problems of failed development and failed environmental management – failures that created the catastrophic twins of poverty and environmental destruction. Shortly thereafter, the sustainable development

movement began in the Philippines. In February 1988, a Conference on Spirituality and Development entitled "Kabuuan," the Filipino words for wholeness, brought together government, academe, non governmental organizations (NGOs), students, farmers, fisherfolk, laborers, religious organizations and spiritual movements of all faiths, indigenous peoples, women's groups, artists, business groups – consumers who produced the Kabuuan Declaration of Principles for Spirituality in Philippine Development. This was considered the precursor of the Philippine Contribution to the Earth Charter of 1991.

A draft Filipino Earth Charter was ratified on September 7, 1991. Prior to the United Nations Conference on Environment and Development (UNCED) in June 1992, the Philippines expected that a Global Earth Charter would embody the covenants of the nations of the world as a basis for a sustainable development path. A People's Earth Charter, which embodied the Southeast Asian Contribution, was drafted at the Paris NGO Summit in La Villete, France, in December 1991. In June 1992, UNCED in Rio de Janeiro adopted Agenda 21 but, unfortunately, not an Earth Charter. Nevertheless, the Philippine Earth Charter process continued.

It is important to note that the Philippines was the first country to have had an official Earth Charter, recognized by their government in June 1995. This was not the text of the Earth Charter that we have now; it was a text drafted in the Philippines through a process of consultation with communities and government. It was a follow-up to the Earth Charter 92 process and a contribution to the drafting of the international Earth Charter. President Fidel Ramos signed this Filipino Earth Charter, known as The Filipino Contribution to the People's Earth Charter, in 1995.

On June 17, 1995, representatives of the Philippine government and civil society adopted the Philippine Contribution to the People's Earth Charter (PCPEC) at a gathering about Human and Ecological Security, a Conference on Population, Environment, and Peace. Signatories to the PCPEC were members of the Philippine Council for Sustainable Development and local government officials. This Charter embodied principles from the original Filipino Contribution to the Rio Earth Charter but was enriched by the experience of state and civil society collaboration to advance a virtues-driven agenda for Philippine development.

During this same time, there were efforts to link the process of articulating a Filipino covenant for pursuing a development modality that preserves Mother Earth to the older Filipino struggle for freedom from the shackles of colonialism, and to ground this struggle in the sacred and esoteric roots of the national independence movements and the ideals of our national revolutionary heroes. By linking Earth Charter dedication rituals to sites and dates dedicated to memories of the Philippine Revolution against Spanish colonialism, the Charter principles became associated with the memories and emotions related to events defining our people's struggle for freedom. For example, the signing of the June 1995 Filipino Contribution to the People's Earth Charter marked the centennial of the signing in the Pamitinan Cave in Rizal Province of the Covenant that launched the Philippine Revolutionary Movement in April 1895.

The principles of sustainable development were first articulated in grassroots discussions all over the Philippines, embodied in formal declarations at different levels, enshrined in a final document called the Philippine Contribution to the Earth Charter Process, and solemnized in religious rituals and State ceremonies. This merged the movement with the spirit of the Philippine revolution of 1896 and made the Earth Charter process an integral part of the sacred historical traditions of the Filipino nation. The Philippine Contribution thus rose from the depths of peoples'

concerns about poverty and habitat destruction in every corner of the country.

It was fitting that Maximo Kalaw, Jr., who was the leading force in the Philippine movement, became the Earth Council's principal facilitator and coordinator in crafting the global consensus that has become the Earth Charter. Kalaw passed away in November 2001, but the Philippine process continues to deepen the Principles of the Earth Charter in the nation's consciousness, preserving them in ritual symbol and practical action.

Since the launch of the Earth Charter in 2000, Philippine efforts to embed the principles of the Charter in the Filipino psyche and in memories of the historical events in Philippine history have evoked the most fervent national emotions. There has also been theoretical exploration, with work of economists and social scientists, in re-examining the enterprise paradigm and advocating an ecosystem-based, and community-centred, management praxis. A new perception of nature has provided the design for both strategy and structure.

Understanding the roots of problems in the Philippines may give an inkling of their causes elsewhere on the planet as well. The strategy for addressing the crises in the Philippines may help us understand what is necessary to meet them globally. ●

Irene Dankelman, The Netherlands. A thematic essay which speaks to Principle 11 on the human rights and active participation of women and girls

# Gender Equality and Equity: At the Heart of the Earth Charter

Principle 11. Affirm gender equality as prerequisites to sustainable development and ensure universal access to education, health care, and economic opportunity.

**Irene Dankelman** has specialized in environment and sustainable development, with a special focus on gender issues. She works with national and international non governmental organizations, governmental and United Nations agencies, and with academia. The book, *Women and the Environment in the Third World: Alliance for the Future*, co-authored with Joan Davidson in 1988, became a pioneering publication. Irene was involved in organizing the first United Nations Environment Program women's assembly on the environment, Women as the Voice for the Environment in 2004. Dr. Dankelman is a university lecturer at the Radboud University in Nijmegen, The Netherlands, a consultant and a board member of several organizations, including the Women's Environment and Development Organisation, the Nature College and Women in Europe for a Common Future. The principles of the Earth Charter form an important source of inspiration for her work and life which she translates into practical initiatives.

Principle 11 of the Earth Charter calls for us to "Affirm gender equality and equity as prerequisites to sustainable development and ensure universal access to education, health care, and economic opportunity." With this Principle, the Earth Charter emphasizes, as a central element of its vision, the need to not only provide well-being and equal opportunities for women and men, but it also incorporates the equal and inalienable rights of all women and men.[1] Principle 11 has three Subprinciples: "Secure the human rights of women and girls and end all violence against them" (Subprinciple 11.a); "Promote the active participation of women in all aspects of economic, political, civil, social, and cultural life as full and equal partners, decision makers, leaders, and beneficiaries" (Subprinciple 11.b); and "Strengthen families and ensure the safety and loving nurture of all family members" (Subprinciple 11.c).

This year not only marks the five years since the launch of the Earth Charter in The Hague, it coincides with the Ten Years Review of the World Conference on Women in Beijing. The Beijing Platform for Action focused on many aspects of women's

lives, and as Bella Abzug mentioned in the Plenary Speech on 12 September 1995, "The Beijing Platform for Action is the strongest statement of consensus on women's equality, empowerment, and justice ever produced by the world's governments." She saw it is a vision of transformation – of what the world can be for women and men, for this and future generations.

The Beijing Platform for Action inspired the Earth Charter and was reaffirmed during the special session of the Commission on the Status of Women, 28 February - 11 March 2005 in New York. It identifies as one of its critical areas of concern "Women and the Environment." Other sections of the Beijing Platform for Action deal with women's human rights, the need to end all violence against women, and women's active participation in all spheres of life, including at decision-making levels.

Five years ago, at the Millennium Summit in New York in 2000, all 189 United Nations Member States committed themselves to establishing a better, healthier, and more just world in 2015. The Millennium Declaration promises "to promote gender equality and the empowerment of women as effective ways to combat poverty, hunger and diseases and to stimulate development that is truly sustainable" (Goal III.20). The Declaration includes Millennium Development Goal III.19, eradication of extreme poverty and hunger; and Goal IV., ensuring environmental sustainability.

Principle 11 of the Earth Charter, therefore, seems to be a reconfirmation of major international insights and commitments in the area of gender equality and environment. As the Earth Charter is a declaration of fundamental values and principles, it also offers an holistic ethical framework to inspire the effort of those working to achieve sustainable development that embraces the gender component and women's roles in sustainable development. As United Nations Secretary General Kofi Annan stressed at the opening of the Commission on the Status of Women meeting, 28 February 2005 in New York: "... Above all, I would urge the entire community to remember that promoting gender equality is not only women's responsibility; it is the responsibility of all of us....Study after study has taught us that no tool for development is more effective than the empowerment of women."[2]

Therefore, all organizations that have endorsed the Earth Charter, be it at local, national, or international levels, are committing themselves to secure the human rights of women and girls, and to promote their active participation in all sectors of society. It indicates an intention to use the Earth Charter to promote gender equality, equity, and social change, and to cooperate with others for the implementation of Principle 11.

The Earth Charter itself has been endorsed by many women's organisations or women's groups, such as the Medical Mission Sisters, Saint Mary's College, and the Women's Environment and Development Organisation. For some groups, such as the indigenous Tawo Seed Carriers in the Philippines, the Earth Charter has particular relevance. They have been made grateful recipients of the positive attitudes emanating from the media dissemination of information regarding respect for Mother Earth. On 10 March 2005, Lilia Adecer Cajilog (Firefly), a Tawo Seed Carrier, stated:

> The genuine Tawo has been always respectful to all natural phenomena as handed down to us by our Elders. (…). There is a hole in our Earth ship and it is the utmost urgent responsibility of all women to nurture love and compassion to the hearts from our self-generated poisons of ignorance (delusion), greed (cravings) and hatred (violence) (…). We commend your much needed work on the Earth Charter to educate and promote respect for all natural creation of Mother Earth. Women, wake up!

In their March 2005 newsletter, the Bioneers organisation, a non governmental organisation promoting practical environmental solutions and strategies, endorsed the Earth Charter, and honoured women's leadership in environmental protection. Bioneers emphasizes that one of the most promising trends in recent years has been the emergence around the world of grassroots, women-led movements that are developing solutions to social and environmental problems by reconnecting relationships. In that same newsletter, Sue Zipp further defined the organisation stating, "Encouraging a convergence between women and the environment holds great potential to engage many more women around restoring the Earth and our communities.

For the international Women's Environment and Development Organisation (WEDO), endorsing the Earth Charter was a natural step. In reflecting principles of respect and care for the community of life, ecological integrity, social and economic justice, democracy, non-violence and peace, the Charter clearly offered a holistic ethical framework for implementation of its own Women's Action Agenda for a Peaceful and Healthy Planet 2000 and 2015. That agenda was developed through worldwide consultations amongst women's groups and focused on issues such as: peace and human rights, access and control of resources, environmental security, and health, globalization, and governance for sustainable development (WEDO, 2002).[3]

The representative of the Buddhist organisation Soka Gakkai International (SGI) to the NGO-Committee on the Status of Women, Mary Mack, reports (15 March 2005) that the SGI works closely with the Earth Charter Initiative sponsoring panels, films, and other educational activities. SGI has collaborated with the Earth Council in production of the video "A Quiet Revolution," an educational film highlighting three cases where an individual or group of individuals led a significant change in the area of sustainable development. SGI has also collaborated with the Earth Charter Secretariat in developing the "Seeds of Change" exhibition that has travelled throughout the world.

On Earth Day 2002, Saint Mary's College, a women's liberal arts institution in the USA, endorsed the Earth Charter. A visitor to the campus asked a simple question: "So what?" His point was that singing the Earth Charter was not sufficient. This inspired a group of faculty, staff, and students to form a Community Leadership Team that would begin investigating ways to implement the Charter's principles and encourage the College community to become pro-active in this respect. They have been doing this for two years and have just received College support for a third year. There have been some significant changes and the community is pleased with the results to date.[4]

Not only can the Earth Charter inspire gender equality and equity in the context of sustainable development, it also offers powerful tools for local and national governments, women's and environmental organisations, companies, and individuals to make these linkages in their work. There are major opportunities to translate Principle 11 into practical steps in education and in development planning.

As the initiatives in this essay have shown, the holistic character of the Earth Charter forms an invitation to women from very diverse cultural backgrounds to become dedicated carriers of the Earth Charter's messages, to have a voice in decisions that affect their lives, and to stand up for human rights. The Earth Charter's call for the enhancement of our collective "caring capacity" – ensuring humanity's well-being and the Earth's future – is an appeal that speaks to our minds, hearts, and souls. ●

**Notes**

1   Gender equality is equal visibility, empowerment, and participation of men and women in all spheres of public and private life; often guided by a vision of human rights, which incorporates acceptance of equal and inalienable rights of all women and men. Gender equity is a set of actions, attitudes, and assumptions that provide opportunities for both women and men; recognizes differences and accommodates them in order to prevent the continuation of an inequitable status quo; and, emphasizes fairness in process and outcome.

2   A complete copy of Annan's speech can be found at http://www.un.org/News/Press/docs/2005/sgsm9738.doc.htm.

3   For more information, see http://www.wedo.org/files/agenda2015_eng.htm.

4   According to R. Jensen, Saint Mary's College, on 17 March 2005.

Principle 12. Uphold the right of all, without discrimination, to a natural and social environment supportive of human dignity, bodily health, and spiritual well-being, with special attention to the rights of indigenous peoples and minorities.

Henriette Rasmussen, Greenland. A thematic essay which speaks to Principle 12 on indigenous thinking embedded in the Earth Charter

# Sustainable Greenland and Indigenous Ideals

 **Henriette Rasmussen** is Minister of Culture, Education, Science and Church of the Government of Greenland. She has served as a Member of the Parliament of Greenland from 1984-1995 and 2002 to the present. She was Minister of Social Affairs and Labour from 1991-1995. She served on the Nuuk City Council from 1983-1991. She has also been Manager of The Greenland Publishing House, Chief Technical Advisor to the International Labour Organization in Geneva, Switzerland, from 1996 to 2000, and a reporter for Greenland Public Broadcasting Company. She is an Earth Charter Commissioner and has been active in the Inuit Circumpolar Conference for many years. She is a member of the pro-independence political party, *Inuit Ataqatigiit* (Inuit Brotherhood).

*Sustainable use of nature is one thing.*
*Sustainable development is another.*

Politics in Greenland deal with practical day-to-day issues. What do we do when the ring seal is not there anymore because the sea ice melts? How many tons of shrimp can we catch? But the Earth Charter deals with fundamental attitudes behind such questions. Personally, I find that fascinating, indeed of paramount importance to us all. For it is our attitudes, our frame of mind, that, in the end, will determine the outcome of the concrete issues. But, as it turns out in this country, it takes a while to direct people's attention to fundamentals.

Until now, a sustainable use of the Arctic wildlife has been – and is – the main theme around which discussions revolve in Greenland. The Inuit culture is the most pure hunting culture in existence. Having adapted to the extreme living conditions in the High Arctic of the North American continent for at least four thousand years, Inuit are not even hunter-gatherers . Inuit are hunters, pure and simple.

Needless to say, a culture that depends on one single kind of expertise will have problems adapting to modern living conditions. And problems abound in Greenland, as they do every-

where in the Inuit homeland. But, we are catching on. Appearing on history's grand scene from a one hundred percent hunting background, the first logical choice among modern types of livelihood was fishing, and Greenland is now one of the leading fisheries nations in the North Atlantic. Also, coal and minerals have been mined for several generations. Our tiny people of 55,000 is growing in many respects, and a burgeoning political autonomy is the order of the day.

Optimistic as this may sound, we cannot evade the question of the sustainability of our living resources. The fishing industry is under pressure everywhere, and in that trade nobody can evade tough negotiations and unwelcome quotas. Even more so, our hunters bear the brunt of the dwindling of wildlife. Sure enough, there is no shortage of seals in our waters, and Greenland has the highest quota of large whales in the world, approved by the International Whaling Commission. Even so, the segment of our people that is able to make a reasonable livelihood by wildlife harvest alone is dwindling, and our hunters have to comply with laws, rules, and monitoring as never before. Our people are not accustomed to the idea that efforts be made to keep hunting and fishing on a sustainable level, thereby implying that it is not already so. Tradition says: yes, of course, that kind of activity *is* sustainable! It has sustained us for thousands of years, it will do so in our time as well, and in that of our children and grandchildren! What else?

What else?! That is the big question hurled at us all now. A most relevant question. Basically, there is no doubt; slowly, all of us are going to face a completely different type of situation. We are entering an age of growing uncertainty about our resources and the way we handle them – an unease mostly not displayed by our community planners and decision-makers. But that uncertainty is there. There is a future shock awaiting us. Many don't know it, most will not hear about it, and nobody is certain how to handle it—massive overpopulation of the Earth, to be felt in every corner of the globe; gross abuses in industrial waste-handling; systematic pollution of the water we drink and the air we breathe, pushing the climate balance over the brink for the sake of short-term profits.

The real problem here is that we don't feel we have the time and energy to deal with such issues. Our electorates don't believe that these matters have to do with their day-to-day situation. Yet, somebody must say something. Also in Greenland, we are, by no means, more safe than others in this world. These huge, intractable issues must be addressed, and there is only one way to do that. We have to deal with our situation bottom-up, asking ourselves, "What part do I play here, however small and insignificant. What can I do to push things in the right direction, however humbly?"

For the last few years, the Greenland government has sponsored a campaign aimed at the hunters, working on a new kind of awareness-raising with regard to the sustainability of a number of hunting practices. Traditionally, Inuit hunters are not used to exchange opinions that differ sharply with one another. The very sensible tradition is to reach an agreement in the assessment of the situation, as soon as possible. However, our day and age does require an ability to table widely different opinions. Our time is one of uncertainty – and caution. Wildlife stocks in the Arctic no longer abound. Sustainability in our wildlife harvest is no longer a matter of course. And that is now being understood in our communities.

Sustainable use of nature has become a catchword. But, not so "sustainable development"! That, one must admit, is a much more difficult concept to deal with. One moves to another storey in the building, so to speak, with another view through the window. Here, it is not just a matter of looking after the welfare of this bird or that seal. It has to do with confronting an entire life-style, taking seriously that in 1992, also we Greenlanders took part in the Rio gathering and have – publicly and formally in Oslo 1998 – endorsed the Agenda 21 together with the other countries represented in the Nordic Council of Ministers. This endorsement amounts to saying that we have agreed to take a close look at every detail of our day-to-day lives, identifying every unnecessary practice that is harmful to the environment…for the purpose of doing something about it!

2003 was the year when the Greenland Home Rule Parliament updated its legislation on the safeguard of nature. At that point in time, the overriding concern was the securing of international commitments, such as, among others, the Convention on Biological Diversity, which obliges the ratifying countries to safeguard all and any species of animals and plants within the range of their legislation. In this case, it was the matter of securing living conditions of all plants and animals on nothing less than Earth's biggest island.

Legislation on domestic animals; hunting and fishing; safeguard of the environment when dealing with mineral resources; laws concerning museums and archaeological sites; regulations regarding physical planning and the use of landlots; and, not the least, a general environmental legislation touching on potential problems ranging from drinking water to ocean pollu-tion—all these areas of our day-to-day lives have now been given a legislative framework, providing new tools with which to secure a better world for our children and grandchildren.

Importantly, the Earth Charter has been translated into the Inuit idiom of Greenland. I anticipate that for the schools, and for the public alike, this translation will be a high-profile tool for the United Nations' Decade for the Education on Sustainable Development in this country. In general terms, for the years ahead, we have decided to tackle Agenda 21 from two angles: from the top and from the bottom.

From all points of view, Greenland's dependence on petroleum for heating is a heavy burden, and a potentially dangerous one as well. It is not surprising that cutting back on precisely that kind of dependence on the outside world be seen as a priority. Now, in the north, in the fishermen's and hunters' town of Sisimiut, the Home Rule government has created an Institute for Arctic Technology specializing, among other things, in state-of-the-art low-energy heating systems and electricity generated by solar panels. In the north, our winter is dark most of the time from autumn to spring. But then, on the other hand, we have the sun around the clock in summertime. The Arctic is not deprived of sunshine! It is just distributed around the year in a different way. With good research into the question of how to store summer's solar energy for use in wintertime, much clean and durable energy can be secured for future development projects.

In the south, in the fishermen's and sheepfarmers' small town of Narsaq, a group of citizens have taken the initiative, together with the local municipality, to create a center, officially called simply "A-21," for the purpose of environmental awareness-raising at the grass-roots. Here, the public will be given an opportunity to collaborate in finding a solution to the almost untractable issue of waste-handling, a problem that is acute everywhere in the Arctic. Also, age-old traditions for the re-use of waste materials are now being revived, together with the growing interest among the general public for solar panel technology and renewable energy systems. Citizens connected to the A-21 project see it as a priority to collaborate with the locally-based Greenland college for healthy foods and good cooking, supporting existing initiatives in Arctic gardening.

In the sheepfarmers' district, people are no strangers to ecological planning. Artificial fertilizers are not allowed, and for number of years already, the farmers have collaborated with professional environmental advisers from the outside world. While on the hillsides and in the valleys, successful, small-scale experiments are conducted in the field of boreal forestry.

My own involvement with the Earth Charter meant a great deal to me. I feel the Earth Charter has been a success. It is a text about the safeguard of our common environment agreed upon by groups as different as Buddhists, Hindi, environmentalists, animal rights' groups, and hunter/gatherers. We are in a dialogue worldwide! I feel certain that in the end, sooner or later, the basic tenets of the Earth Charter will be seen and understood by the people. But, let's admit that it will take time. Meanwhile, we must let the Earth Charter work as leaven in the bread. I keep doing what I can to further it in the government and environmental organisations in our country and others dealing with the Arctic region, such as the Nordic Council of Ministers, European Union, Arctic Council, and others.

In Greenland, the general public is very much aware of recent developments with regard to the many serious predicaments of indigenous peoples around the world. The now formally-established Indigenous Peoples' Forum at the United Nations in New York has attracted people's attention. From that perspective, what we see now is an initiative that reflects a growing sentiment that indigenous peoples have an obligation to enter into, and visibly support, the visions we all so sorely need in order to see our world survive. As indigenous people, we will do what we can, and time will ripen for the Earth Charter vision. ●

Philip Osano, Kenya. A project descriptive essay which speaks to Principle 12 on honoring and supporting young people

# Shaping Our Common Future: Youth Campaigning for Sustainable Development Using the Earth Charter in East Africa

**Philip Osano** is a core team member of the Earth Charter Youth Initiative (ECYI) and has been active in campaigning for the Earth Charter and sustainable development with young people since 2001. He holds a bachelors degree in Environmental Science from Egerton University in Kenya, and a masters degree in conservation biology from the University of Cape Town in South Africa. He was recently awarded first prize at a global Student Conference on Conservation Science at Cambridge University in England. He served as a member of the African Civil Society and the Government of Kenya Steering Committees for the World Summit on Sustainable Development.

*Honor and support the young people of our communities, enabling them to fulfill their essential role in creating sustainable societies.*
Earth Charter, Principle 12.c

In the wake of the preparations for the World Summit on Sustainable Development (WSSD) in August/September 2002, hundreds of young people in Kenya, Uganda, and Tanzania were involved in a campaign for a more sustainable world, using the Earth Charter as a tool to lobby their respective governments and other interest groups. This dynamic group of young people were brought together to express their hopes for a better future under the Earth Charter inspired project

"Shaping Our Common Future."[1] The project aimed to provide young people with a platform to actively and substantively participate in the review of Agenda 21[2] and to share a broad and long-term view of the levels of development by identifying strategies for tackling sustainable development challenges in East Africa.

The project involved youth organizations and umbrella groups working at local, provincial, and national levels within different areas of environment, society, culture, economy, and technology, and with different foci of education, advocacy, lobbying, and policy. Through meetings and discussion forums, young people shared perspectives and insights on past and present initiatives for sustainable development in the three East African countries; and, they promoted new initiatives to provide the public with information on some of the pressing challenges facing the planet and humanity today.

The project basis stemmed from past declarations and commitments to empower young people to participate fully in shaping the development of societies at the local and global levels; and, therefore, took into consideration the following documents in its formulation: Agenda 21 (specifically Chapter 25) (1992); the United Nations World Programme of Action for Youth to the Year 2000 and Beyond (1995); The Lisbon Declaration (1998); The Braga Youth Action Plan (1999); and The Earth Charter (2000).

The marginalization of young people in decision-making in the East African countries has been exacerbated by lack of empowerment and the exclusive nature of the socio-political institutions of political parties, non governmental organizations, and religious and cultural associations. The WSSD process, therefore, provided a platform to mainstream youth issues and involvement at the core of planning, education, and participation using the Earth Charter as a framework for mobilizing and developing joint strategies for the youth in Kenya, Uganda, and Tanzania. Prior to undertaking activities targeted at promoting participatory involvement of young people in policy formulation and decision-making at the Johannesburg Summit in South Africa, there were open and extensive consultations with youth associations in Kenya, Uganda, and Tanzania to identify critical priorities for achieving sustainable development in East Africa. Some of the highlights included The Earth Charter: Unfinished Agenda; youth policy; participation and rights; poverty and food security; health (especially the HIV/AIDS pandemic); human settlements; forest loss; climate change; water management; biodiversity loss; and legal instruments (international conventions, protocols, and agreements) on sustainable development.

In order to address the above issues, and to develop lobbying strategies for promoting the involvement of young people in the sustainable development reviews, several activities were undertaken as part of the project. These included a high-profile East African Youth Conference and Training Seminar in March 2002 that brought together over forty delegates from Kenya, Uganda, and Tanzania; year-round discussions and actions on sustainable development by young people in schools and other institutions; research on youth involvement in sustainable development in Kenya; a national, student essay contest on sustainable development in Kenya to raise the public profile of the Earth Summit preparations; and radio programmes involving interviews with young people as part of publicity and awareness campaigns using the media.

In Kenya, the "Our Common Future" Project coordinated a national, student essay contest involving schools and colleges that gave students a chance to express their perspectives on what needs to be done to ensure sustainable development is achieved in the country. The main objectives of the essay contest were to sensitise and create awareness about the World Summit on Sustainable Development process amongst students and to act as an avenue through which young people can air their views on matters relating to sustainable development in Kenya. Over 2500 entries were received and judged by a panel of judges from Egerton University, Kenyatta University, Nairobi University, and the Kenya NGO Earth Summit 2002 Forum. Key themes that dominated the essay submissions, included, *inter alia*, the use of education as a vehicle for achieving a more sustainable future; cross cultural and religious tolerance; commitment to peace and non-violence; a need for a values framework to guide present and future societies; and, promotion of human rights, with an emphasis on inter-generational equity in the use of earth resources. These themes prominently echo some of the key principles embodied in the Earth Charter. On 17 May 2002, essay winners were awarded prizes at a glittering ceremony presided over by the deputy leader of the official opposition, later Vice-

President of Kenya, the late Hon. Michael Kijana Wamalwa.

The East African Youth Conference was held from 15-18 March 2002 in the Rift Valley town of Naivasha, Kenya. The conference brought together over forty youth leaders from Kenya, Uganda, and Tanzania to chart the youth position on sustainable development priorities in the sub-region level and to draft a joint statement for WSSD. In the "Naivasha Declaration," the delegates endorsed the Earth Charter and further affirmed their commitment to lobby their respective governments to endorse the Earth Charter and to promote the Charter in other international youth forums on sustainable development, especially the UNEP Global Youth Forum 2002 in Denmark[3]. The conference also included cultural and practical exhibitions from youth organizations, a training session on advocacy and campaigning conducted by the members of the Kenya NGO Earth Summit 2002 Forum, keynote speeches from government figures, and youth discussion platforms for exchanging ideas and promoting networking.

The outcomes from the "Our Common Future" project were disseminated in major global events, including UNEP Global Youth Forum in March 2002 in Denmark; WSSD Prep COM IV in May 2002 in Indonesia; and the World Summit on Sustainable Development in August/September 2002 in South Africa. One of the critical factors for the success of the project was the use of the strong network structure already established by the governments of Kenya, Uganda, and Tanzania, and the NGOs in East Africa, to effectively reach out to a majority of youth organizations and educational institutions. The project established strong ties and linkage to the Kenya NGO Earth Summit 2002 Forum, a civil society initiative on the preparations towards the Earth Summit 2002 and the Greenbelt Movement. There was also a close collaboration with the WSSD National Preparatory Committee of the Kenyan government.

Clearly, the involvement of youth in environmental protection, economic, and social development is very critical for any society that aspires for a better future. The "Our Common Future" project is a concrete example of inspiration that was drawn from the Earth Charter, empowering young people to participate creActively (creatively and actively) in the World Summit for Sustainable Development by identifying priorities for sustainable development in the region, and bringing these to the attention of the policy makers. It is a clear demonstration, that given the time, resources, and the opportunity, young people have the ability to take forward the sustainable development agenda that has been elusive since the Rio Summit in 1992. Indeed, it is my solid hope that the Earth Charter will continue to inspire young people in the quest for sustainable development, especially during the United Nations Decade on Education for Sustainable Development 2005 – 2014, for this is the generation that absolutely cannot afford to fail. ●

**Notes**

1    "Shaping Our Common Future" Project was supported by the Kenya NGO Earth Summit 2002 Forum, and endorsed by the United Nations Environment Programme (UNEP). The author acknowledges the contribution from Robert Ouma, Faith Mullumba and Muta Maathai (Kenya), Humphrey Polepole (Tanzania) and Joseph Mulindwa (Uganda)

2    Agenda 21 (http://www.un.org/esa/sustdev/documents/agenda21/index.htm)

3    The UNEP Global Youth Forum, 25 – 30 March 2002 in Denmark noted "Use the Earth Charter as an education tool and lobby our governments to adopt and endorse the document as a sustainable development framework" (UNEP Global Youth Forum 2002_Youth Action Plans: Small Steps in A Long Journey). See also UNEP Global Youth Forum 2002 Report (http://www.natur-og-ungdom.dk/pdf/gyf.pdf) and United Nations World Youth Programme of Action to the Year 2000 and Beyond (http://www.un.org/events/youth98/backinfo/ywpa2000.htm).

# A Test for the Maturity of Humankind

In 1999, **Sergey Shafarenko** initiated the online discussion of the Earth Charter draft in the Republic of Kazakhstan and lead public discussions of the draft in the southeast region of Kazakhstan with its capital, Ust-Kamenogorsk. In summer 1999, Dr. Shafarenko represented Kazakhstan at the first Earth Charter hearings in Central Asia and was elected a member of the Central Asian Earth Charter Council. He held national public hearings and consultations in the six major cities of his country. He organized the Earth Charter educational summer camp for high school students and young people. In 2003-2004, the Earth Charter National Committee of the Republic of Kazakhstan lead campaigns in support of the Earth Charter, and published brochures, produced T-shirts, held ecological song festivals, and collected thousands of letters in support of the Earth Charter.

In recent decades, civilization's technical progress has surged, and clearly demonstrated human interference in the processes of nature, both at local and global level. Recent research carried out by the World Wildlife Fund confirmed that due to the global climate change, the average temperature on the Earth would rise by 2° Celsius. The warming in the Arctic might be three times higher, ranging from 3.2° Celsius to 6.6° Celsius. A vitally important problem has emerged: how to save civilization and all the community of life on Earth? Present civilization, like a small child lacking experience and driven by self-interest, can only take and consume the treasures of our planet, and does that just for itself, not caring for nature and destroying the biosphere.

The very home where this child was born and is living now has started to fall apart; this childhood of humanity has lasted too long. It is time to mature beyond simply taking and grabbing without giving something back. The Bible teaches us: "There is the time of gathering stones and the time of throwing away stones" (Ecclesiastes 3:5). It is time to draw lessons from the tragic experience of natural disasters of the recent years. We cannot forget the latest tragedy in the Indian Ocean; it is impossible to violate endlessly the laws of the harmony of nature, as all the processes on this planet are interconnected. We have to build our lives on the principles of beauty and responsibility. The wave of natural disasters will continue to grow if we are not able to make the very model of our civilization more humane with respect to nature, if we do not live in harmony with nature. The most promising international document which can show us the way out of the dark tunnel and which identified the main principles of the life on this planet, is, undoubtedly, the Earth Charter.

For the first time in the history of humankind, an important international document was created and discussed by the population of the planet at various levels. I believe the approval of this important document should be made urgently and at the highest possible level, by the heads of the states and by the United Nations (UN). The UN has to establish the Department of the Earth Charter to promote and bring to life the principles of the document at the international level.

Some fifteen years ago there was a documentary film about the laws of the rise and fall of the civilizations. After the numerous comparisons of indicators of public life – political, economic and social – only one indicator emerged as essential: the level of humankind's moral and ethical development, which could be considered to be fundamental for the creation of harmonic relations with the surrounding world. These basic ethical principles can be found in the text of the Earth Charter.

The term "sustainable development" has become very popular in recent years. It comprises environmental, social, and economic notions. The term "the biosphere territory" is much wider though. Scientists look at biosphere territories as the model landscapes for the introduction of the long-term, environmentally-oriented way of life and activity that take into consideration economic, social, cultural, and ethnic aspects. However, without a basis of moral and ethical values, these notions are doomed, as only the concept of the noosphere embraces all the ingredients that can bring to life the principle of the

© PLAN NEDERLAND / JOHANNES ABELING

harmonic, sustainable development of civilization. A group of Russian scientists also organized a seminar, "Humanity for Noosphere," in Moscow, at which they discussed using the ideas of the noosphere in the fields of economy, ethics, and society.

In 2002, representatives of non governmental organizations, scientists, and parliamentary deputies from the four countries of Russia, China, Mongolia and Kazakhstan created the International Coordination Council: "Our mutual home – the Altai." The Council focuses its activities on creating sustainable association of adherents and new models for the development of civilization based on the values and principles of the Earth Charter. To realize such promising projects, there are favorable conditions, such as the historic, philosophic, and cultural heritage of the peoples of Asia and Europe; the materials of the interna-

tional discussion on the Earth Charter; and research conducted by our universities, such as the documents of the international conference "Altai-Cosmos-Microcosm," held in Barnaul, in the Altai region of Russia.

As suggested by the rise in popularity of the ideas of Pierre Teilhard de Chardin and Vladimir Vernadsky, scientific thought has turned its attention to finding a worthy solution to the ecological and social crisis. The roles of human thought, and of personal responsibility for it, have emerged as key elements of the reconstruction of life. ●

Michael Slaby, Germany. A project descriptive essay which speaks to Principle 12 on youth aspirations

# Making Ripples of Change: The Hopes of the Earth Charter Youth Initiative

**Michael Slaby** is a graduate student of religion, international law, and politics at Heidelberg University, Germany. He volunteers as the International Coordinator of the Earth Charter Youth Initiative. Having been actively involved in youth-led initiatives since 1996, Michael can look back on several years of volunteer work focussing on sustainable development, human rights, and refugee aid. Slaby has led several Amnesty International groups at both the local and regional level. In his studies, he concentrates on the religious, cultural, political, and legal dimensions of globalization and has written his master thesis on models of bridging religious differences in interfaith dialogue.

Following from the Earth Charter's emphasis on youth involvement in all strategies to create sustainable communities, the Earth Charter Youth Initiative (ECYI) was launched in 2000. The Earth Charter Youth Initiative (ECYI) disseminates the values and vision of the Earth Charter among young people. The ECYI also provides for youth participation in the national and global Earth Charter processes. With the initial help of staff at the International Secretariat in Costa Rica, an international network was established that brought together youth non governmental organizations (NGOs) and young activists from thirty countries. For the last two years, the

ECYI has been run exclusively by volunteers and coordinated by a core group of five young individuals from different parts of the world who dedicate their free time to serve as international facilitators.

From the very beginning of the ECYI, the internet has been used as the main means of communication, facilitating a sharing of ideas and experiences. The specific contribution of the ECYI is thus to give a human face to the abstract term of "interconnectedness." By using e-mail and internet facilities, youth are in contact with likeminded activists in other parts of the world. Hence, local activism and "global thinking" are combined.

The aims of the Youth Initiative are to encourage young people around the world to bring alive the values of sustainability, justice, and peace as they are outlined in the Earth Charter and to effect positive changes by using the Earth Charter as an ethical guideline. The underlying idea is that the more young people will adopt sustainable lifestyles and engage in projects concerned with sustainable development, the more they will influence their local communities. And, as the whole global society is nothing more than a conglomeration of local communities, by starting on the grassroots level, we can actually start changing the world!

The ECYI strives for a kind of ripple effect – like after someone throws a stone into a lake, each ripple creating

another one until the whole lake vibrates. The more stones are thrown into the water, the more the ripples can transform into waves – waves of healing water to wash the wounds of our fragmented societies and our tortured planet. Grassroots youth activities around the world form the backbone in this process.

Not being an NGO in itself, the ECYI benefits from its loose and creative structure, linking youth around the world who share the ethical vision of the Earth Charter and strive to make it a reality for their local and national communities. These youth have developed a remarkable range of ideas for bringing the Earth Charter into action and spreading its message among their peers: from the Armenian summer camps, focusing on environmental issues and distributing children's versions of the Earth Charter in three different languages; to the Costa Rican Earth Charter Concerts; to the Earth Scout movement, which guides youth through activities demonstrating each of the sixteen main Earth Charter principles and motivates them to earn badges for each.

Similarly, various countries have established Earth Charter Youth Groups (ECYGs) — organisations of youth who educate themselves about the Earth Charter and engage in projects that foster environmental protection, sustainable development, social justice, or a culture of peace. Some ECYGs also function as networks of youth organizations that foster synergy effects and joint activities. Since the program's launch in April 2003, ECYGs have attracted youth especially in developing countries such as Sierra Leone, Ethiopia, Jordan, and the Philippines.[1]

Several youth organisations endorsed the Charter and are today using it as an ethical guide in their struggle against HIV, poverty, and environmental degradation. In five different junior secondary schools in Ethiopia , ECYGs have been created to focus on poverty eradication, tree-planting campaigns, and waste collection. Furthermore, the Youth Employment Summits, the Youth Caucus to the United Nations Commission on Sustainable Development, the Youth Advisory Council of UNEP, and other national and international youth initiatives have endorsed the Earth Charter as their common vision, including it in their declarations.[2]

I know how hard it can sometimes be to keep up the motivation when there seems to be just a small group of people who cares about specific problems in one's own or foreign societies. Why bother? Why not do something else, something which is more "fun"? Sometimes, the problems and challenges against which one has to struggle seem overwhelming. The question comes to mind: "What can I, as a single individual, do against all this?"

The answer the Earth Charter provides is as striking as it is simple. Each single effort counts in creating a more sustainable, just, and peaceful future. Thousands of people across the planet care for the environment, work for social justice, and struggle for peace. These committed people have a lot in common. Consciously or not, they follow the ethics of the Earth Charter. So, there is a global partnership for the well-being of the human family and the larger living world; and this partnership is growing stronger each day. Each effort, no matter how small it might appear, makes a ripple. The ECYI

encourages youth around the world, both as leaders of tomorrow and as citizens of today, to join hands and hearts "to fulfill their essential role in creating sustainable societies," as the Earth Charter states in Subprinciple 12.c. The Earth Charter Youth Initiative strives to make this global partnership visible by reaching out to youth and empowering them to create synergy based on the Earth Charter's principles, locally and globally.

Events in the five years since the launching of the ECYI have confirmed youths' interest in establishing a sound, ethical foundation for the emerging global society – without any significant financial assistance, but rather nurturing the enthusiasm of dedicated young people ready to spend their free time striving to make the world a better place. Especially in developing countries, youth have demonstrated that the Earth Charter plants seeds of hope in the hearts of people. Young people from those countries, which are directly and adversely affected by economic globalisation, have realised how essential it is to find holistic solutions to these challenges.

Yet, in the Western world, this message still has to be spread. Involving youth of the developed world remains a foremost challenge facing the ECYI. If young people in countries suffering from poverty and the remnants of civil war are able to bring about sustainable changes, how much more should youth in the developed world be able to do?

As violent conflicts and terrorism create an atmosphere of anxiety, the gap between rich and poor constantly widens, and the human family continues committing geo-cide on the natural world, young people around the globe need to find common strategies to make their voices heard. The ECYI network serves as a platform for this process of communication. The more we young people work together, the more the ripples of change created around the world will unite into a wave of hope. ●

**Notes**

1   See also the youth contributions from Alamoosh, Murray, Yap, and Osano in this volume.
2   See also the youth contribution by Nyoni.

# Part IV. Democracy, Nonviolence, and Peace

# Principles

13. Strengthen democratic institutions at all levels, and provide transparency and accountability in governance, inclusive participation in decision making, and access to justice.
    a. Uphold the right of everyone to receive clear and timely information on environmental matters and all development plans and activities which are likely to affect them or in which they have an interest.
    b. Support local, regional and global civil society, and promote the meaningful participation of all interested individuals and organizations in decision making.
    c. Protect the rights to freedom of opinion, expression, peaceful assembly, association, and dissent.
    d. Institute effective and efficient access to administrative and independent judicial procedures, including remedies and redress for environmental harm and the threat of such harm.
    e. Eliminate corruption in all public and private institutions.
    f. Strengthen local communities, enabling them to care for their environments, and assign environmental responsibilities to the levels of government where they can be carried out most effectively.

14. Integrate into formal education and life-long learning the knowledge, values, and skills needed for a sustainable way of life.
    a. Provide all, especially children and youth, with educational opportunities that empower them to contribute actively to sustainable development.
    b. Promote the contribution of the arts and humanities as well as the sciences in sustainability education.
    c. Enhance the role of the mass media in raising awareness of ecological and social challenges.
    d. Recognize the importance of moral and spiritual education for sustainable living.

15. Treat all living beings with respect and consideration.
    a. Prevent cruelty to animals kept in human societies and protect them from suffering.
    b. Protect wild animals from methods of hunting, trapping, and fishing that cause extreme, prolonged, or avoidable suffering.
    c. Avoid or eliminate to the full extent possible the taking or destruction of non-targeted species.

16. Promote a culture of tolerance, nonviolence, and peace.
    a. Encourage and support mutual understanding, solidarity, and cooperation among all peoples and within and among nations.
    b. Implement comprehensive strategies to prevent violent conflict and use collaborative problem solving to manage and resolve environmental conflicts and other disputes.
    c. Demilitarize national security systems to the level of a non-provocative defense posture, and convert military resources to peaceful purposes, including ecological restoration.
    d. Eliminate nuclear, biological, and toxic weapons and other weapons of mass destruction.
    e. Ensure that the use of orbital and outer space supports environmental protection and peace.
    f. Recognize that peace is the wholeness created by right relationships with oneself, other persons, other cultures, other life, Earth, and the larger whole of which all are a part.

*The text of the Earth Charter continues with 'The Way Forward' on page 164.*

# Democracy, Nonviolence, and Peace

 **Federico Mayor** has been Member of the Spanish and European Parliaments and Spain's Minister for Education and Science. Mayor is a member of the Earth Charter Commission. He was particularly active in the drafting of thePreamble, Part IV, and The Way Forward. Founder of the International Foundation for a Culture of Peace, he has promoted the dissemination of the Charter and its importance not only at the school and university levels but to town halls, councils, parliaments, and decision-makers of all kinds. Mayor is the author of many scientific papers, of several essays, and three collections of poetry.

*As never before in history, common destiny beckons us to seek a new beginning.*
The Earth Charter, The Way Forward, paragraph one

This "new beginning," this new phase in the history of humanity, "requires a change of mind and heart.... a new sense of global interdependence and universal responsibility.... Our cultural diversity is a precious heritage.... we must find ways to harmonize diversity with unity... Every individual, family, organization, and community has a vital role to play ... In order to build a sustainable global community, the nations of the world must renew their commitment to the United Nations" (The Way Forward, paragraphs two, three, and four). These are some of the paths to the future that will allow us to rectify some of the current directions that are filled with somber horizons. It is time for action. We can no longer delay making decisions, especially since, in the eighties, ideologies and ideals were substituted – in a historical abdication of political responsibilities – by "market" laws. And, in order to rectify, in order to correct current tendencies, it is vital to have the protagonist appear on the scene, the object of all the efforts made for humanity's progress and the betterment of the quality of life for all inhabitants of the Earth, without exclusion. For centuries, the power held by a few has imposed their design on the majority who, resigned, fearful, and confused, has – with brief periods of resistance – acquiesced. Today, we have reasonable hope that, finally, the twenty-first century will be the century of the people, of the emancipation of the citizens, of the voice of the people, of the change from imperceptible and anonymous subjects to interlocutors and actors, of new governance.

Thus starts the Charter's preamble: "We stand at a critical moment in Earth's history, a time when humanity must choose its future .... In the midst of a magnificent diversity of cultures and life forms we are one human family and one Earth community with a *common destiny*. We must join together to bring forth a sustainable global society founded on respect for nature, universal human rights, economic justice, and a culture of peace" (paragraph one). Similarly to the Preamble of the United Nations Charter (San Francisco, 1945), the focus is unmistakably directed at future generations, those who are a step behind us, those who will be doing it in a few years. On them depends the future, a future that they will have to design freely and responsibly. For ourselves, with our vision and courage, we must ensure that no one disturbs or predetermines the shape or appearance of tomorrow. This is our supreme commitment: from the past we have to extract lessons and apply them. And I never tire of repeating this – the past cannot be changed. It is the way it was. We can only describe it. And we have to do it truthfully. The future we can and we should change. It is our essential task. Our challenge. We cannot distract ourselves and look elsewhere. The eyes of our descendants are already watching us.

"Fundamental changes are needed in our values, institutions, and ways of living. We must realize that, when basic needs have been met, human development is primarily about being more, not having more" (Preamble, paragraph four). The global situation shows a growing environmental pathology at the same time that the gap between the rich and poor countries grows rather than wanes. "Injustice, poverty, ignorance, and violent conflicts are widespread and the cause of great suffering." All of this, as it is described in paragraph three of the Preamble, urgently requires, as I was arguing before, the appearance of civil society and the organizations in which it is integrated so that, from now on, civil society becomes an indispensable interlocutor, and an active participant in the construction of a "democratic and humane" world. In order to put into practice these aspirations, we need to strengthen the sense of solidarity, of fraternity, as it is proclaimed in Article 1 of the Human Rights Declaration. All free, all equal, all endowed with reason, all fraternally united. All different. To the point of uniqueness, each human being unique, creator. This distinctive capacity of the human species allows us to divert the fatal direction of our trajectory. To have deciphered the language of life – the spatial complementarity of molecules that governs from genetic transference to its translation into structural and dynamic components in all beings – allows us consequently to inexorably predict its behavior. With one exception, the one that endows each human life with boundless creative drive, the exception that allows, even at the edge of light and shadow, of certainty and uncertainty, the freedom to elaborate its own answers, to decide for itself, to "directing with meaning its own life", a definition of education difficult to improve upon, in the words of D. Francisco Giner de los Ríos. To have time to reflect, to think, to be oneself, to not just be a passive viewer, a receptacle that lets others decide in his/her name, that lets others—sometimes through different mediatic instances—determine the course of his/her behavior.

We, as creators, free, without attachments, with wide wings without weight for high flight, can "provide ethical principles to the emerging global community." Of the four Principles which initiate the Earth Charter, Principle 3 specifically refers to "Build[ing] democratic societies that are just, participatory, sustainable, and peaceful." The supporting Subprinciple 3.a states that we need to "Ensure that communities at all levels guarantee human rights and fundamental freedoms and provide everyone an opportunity to realize his or her full potential." I think this is a particularly relevant aspect. Some are busy tending to their needs, which many times allows them to barely survive; others are distracted by entertainment that prevents them from having time to think; others are obfuscated by fears, superstitions, and individualistic impulses that do not only show their ignorance, but often lead them to adopt intransigent, extremist, and fanatic positions; it is only a few who can steal away from daily routine and inertia in order to think what they say and say what they think. We run the risk of being led by immense gusts of mass media, of being molded by this omnipresent mediating power, of being engulfed by a great whirlwind of selected events – some magnified, others downplayed. This happens in such a way that we no longer know what we should know. These manipulations fill our gardens, many times to the most private corners, with foreign and undesired plants and trees.

The construction of democracy requires us to reclaim the right to transparent information and to express, without hindrance, our views and, with the help of modern technology, progressively incorporate multiple voices so that they can become a real popular clamor – one that victoriously confronts hegemony and plutocracy in such a way that silence is broken. To break a silence that has allowed so many injustices, so that an ethical-legal framework can pacifically and strongly be implemented at local and international levels, so that the word of the citizens –

for this constitutes real democracy – illuminates the paths of governance towards a brighter future; so that the "swords become plows," and we move from a culture of imposition and force to a culture of dialogue and peace.

Time to think, to listen, to be one's self. There is no strong and sustainable democracy without citizens who care for others and are capable of arguing in favor of their proposals. There is no democracy in silence, nor in submission or in fear.

Violence has no justification. Never. But, we need to try to explain why it occurs, why it is generated; why it emerges, fierce, to the point of, at times, involving the sacrifice of one's own life. As Part III of the Earth Charter establishes, we need to look for the roots of hostility, frustration, radicalization, and aversion in living conditions that are hard to make compatible with human dignity, in the once and again unfulfilled promises, in the abandonment, in the neglect, in the forgetfulness. To attain social and economic justice, it is indispensable to "eradicate poverty as an ethical, social, and environmental imperative . . . Guarantee the right to potable water, clean air, food security, uncontaminated soil, shelter, and safe sanitation, allocating the national and international resources required" (Principle 9 and Subprinciple 9.a) And these resources will not be attained if civil society continues to accept that "things are as they are and cannot be anything else," and that "there is no remedy." The age of silence is over. The age of genuine democracy starts where it should – with the voice of the people, with the never violent but always firm expression of their rights, of their projects, wishes, and dreams.

Integral, endogenous, sustainable human development for an adequate distribution of resources of all kinds – including, naturally, knowledge – for the good of all. The reduction of the present imbalances is a *sine qua non* condition; in the prosperous areas of the global village, only twenty percent of the world's population enjoys eighty percent of the goods, of the fruits of innovation, of discoveries, of technological applications. Its spiritual richness, however, is going astray. It needs to open windows and doors in order to meet and understand those who live, many times in crowded conditions, in poor and impoverished neighborhoods. So that "to live together," as the commission presided by Jacques Delors, recommended in its *Education for the 21st Century: Issues and Prospects*, becomes a reality and a cornerstone of the building of democracy in a new world. For this, it is necessary that, with a true willingness of conciliation, normalization, and pacification, and, without delay, measures be taken to alleviate the situation of billions of people. Measures to end the shamefulness of tax havens, where money coming from the most horrific trafficking (drugs, arms, people!) is "laundered." Measures that will immediately reduce facts like the following: United States and European Union agricultural subsidies reach 375 billion dollars a year. That is to say, a little more than one billion dollars daily. Weapons spending, which grew in the last few years as it corresponds to a war economy, has reached

2.6 billion dollars a day. It would be enough to start a progressive reduction of these investments and divert them to supporting endogenous global development, the financing of the new social and economic contract that is indispensable for a sustainable Earth and habitability; for a new environmental contract which would stop degradation, climate change, ocean pollution, that would permit, in all cases, the ability to act with scientific rigor through transdisciplinary commissions; to safeguard the diversity and identity of all cultures and languages avoiding progressive uniformity, the erosion of the identities of civilizations that could recognize the many bridges that unite them instead of the aspects that separate them; so that solidarity would be inspired in ethical principles universally accepted.

It is urgent that these transformations begin and that the disparities that the current economic system has widened, creating tensions and a generalized feeling of inability to straighten the paths that fill us with ignominy and hopelessness, be reduced. It cannot be that each day 40,000 people should die of hunger. It cannot be that the military-industrial complex should be producing weaponry for conventional confrontation of armies in different countries, when what it is needed now, in the face of terrorism, is to strengthen personal security, and to encourage the collaboration of all citizens – of which the great majority are on the side of life and against those who machinate atrocities from the shadows – and to use technological and human resources in order to, on a cooperative world scale, end violence, at the same time that misery, exclusion, poverty, and malnutrition are reduced and eradicated.

The Earth Charter claims that gender equality be assured, another condition for the establishment, at the local, regional, and global level, of peace and democracy. If the general principle is the complete equality of all human beings, how can we explain the discrimination that affects some ethnic groups, some indigenous communities, and women? How can we continue to accept a society that is essentially masculine in which the progress of the last decades is that men make ninety-six percent of decisions and represent eighty-eight percent of the voice of the Earth?

Democracy and nonviolence require the security of peace and not the peace of security; not the peace of imposition, of fear, of silence. As I stated before, the key to any democratic system is interaction, listening, and participation. Education for all throughout one's life so that the growing presence of citizens in governance can be assured. So that institutions – in particular universities – become, through interdisciplinarity, advisers to democratic institutions (parliaments, municipal councils, mass media) and watchtowers of anticipation and prevention. Prevention is the great victory. Only a democratic system in which it is the people who shape the content and tone of governance allows the full exercise of human rights without exception.

Democracy, nonviolence, and peace. The Declaration and Pro-

gramme of Action on a Culture of Peace, adopted by the United Nations General Assembly on the 13 September 1999, establishes that "civil society has to be fully engaged in the development of a culture of peace ... A key role in the promotion of a culture of peace belongs to parents, teachers, politicians, journalists, religious bodies and groups, intellectuals, those engaged in scientific, philosophical and creative and artistic activities, health and humanitarian workers, social workers, managers at various levels, as well as to non governmental organizations." In order to carry out Principle 16 of the Earth Charter, "Promote a culture of tolerance, nonviolence, and peace," it is especially useful to apply the measures indicated by the action program of the aforementioned declaration: education for all and throughout their whole lives, without any obstacles to access; promote sustainable economic and social development; promote respect of all human rights; ensure equality between women and men; foster democratic participation; advance understanding, tolerance and solidarity; support participatory communication, and the free flow of information and knowledge; and promote international peace and security.

The current contradiction between democracies at the local level, and oligocracy and hegemony at the international level, cannot continue to exist. As it is stated in the Earth Charter, cooperation among all peoples, disarmament, and the elimination of weapons of mass destruction, implies that the United Nations should have moral authority over financial, human, and technical resources that are essential for the fulfillment of its mission. "We, the people, have decided to save the succeeding generations from the horror of war." A United Nations system – with specialized international institutions on aspects related to labor, food, education, culture, science, finances, trade – broadly utilized, at the service of the whole world, with the adaptations advised by reality and a perspective vision.

The Subprinciple 16.f of the Earth Charter declares that "peace is the wholeness created by right relationships with oneself, other persons, other cultures, other life, Earth, and the larger whole of which all are a part." Today, we celebrate sixty years of the founding of the United Nations in San Francisco, and UNESCO in London, and the fifth anniversary of the launching of the Earth Charter in Amsterdam in the year 2000. This constitutes a framework, an indispensable and desirable background as it provides the Earth Charter with validity, authenticity, and a demand for very concrete commitments. Therefore, we need to promote its diffusion, so that all institutions of learning, all government agencies, all mass media, know and put in practice the major reference points, especially in the current circumstances of confusion and dismay.

All different, all equal, united, with hope due to the unique capacity to create, we commit to disseminate and observe the Earth Charter, to contribute to the Objectives of the Millennium. "That no one who can talk remains silent / that all join in that cry." ●

Edgar González-Gaudiano, Mexico. A thematic essay which speaks to Principle 13 on citizen participation in environmental education

# The Earth Charter in Action: Experiences and Perspectives for Education in Values in Mexico

Until December 2000, **Edgar Gonzalez-Gaudiano** served as Director General of the Centre of Education and Training for Sustainable Development at the Secretariat of Environment, Natural Resources and Fisheries of the Mexican Federal Government. Today is advisor to the Secretariat of Public Education in matters of environmental education and education for sustainable development. He is a member of the Commission of Education and Communication of IUCN and Regional President for Mesoamerica since 2001. He has been member of Board of Directors at the North American Association for Environmental Education. He has written six books and more than one hundred articles in several specialized journals about environmental education. Edgar is the main editor of the iberoamerican journal *Tópicos en Educación Ambiental*. His immediate objectives are to strengthen environmental education, particularly with the Earth Charter, in formal education at the Secretariat of Public Education and to promote it in different spheres of public life.

In Mexico, substantial progress has been made since the Earth Charter was launched. Numerous institutions and organizations have signed it and are involved in working programs to adopt it as a basic moral code. Many organizations of environmental educators have made an open commitment, but such is not the case of the broad community of education professionals, especially teachers. Therefore, there has been slow, but eventful, progress in the application of the Earth Charter as a well-defined part of the educational materials used throughout the school system.

Numerous intensive courses have been given by teachers in a growing number of states in the country, and versions suitable for young people and children have been written. Of course, the dynamism of the National Committee has played a part. For example, on a national level we have managed to have the Earth Charter included in several teacher training refresher course programs offered to elementary school teachers. Specifically, the principles of Part II, Ecological Integrity, form an important part of a module on biodiversity in the general course "The environmental problem from the school and the classroom".[1] Furthermore, the Earth Charter has been worked into the Science and Technology Program[2] as well as Civil and Ethics Education in the new secondary education syllabus. But, this is insufficient; more solid and consistent progress is required. We are working on the definition of a strategy to begin to raise the awareness of education specialists in values with respect to the Earth Charter. In our judgment, this is the most effective way of giving the Earth Charter the impulse we seek.

In an extremely short time, education in values has undergone radical changes in the context of Mexican elementary education. Two decades ago, the approach taken in civic education was still, from an excessively normative and prescriptive standpoint, terribly removed from the many problems affecting children. The program focused on the communication of a set of behavioral norms based on conventionally-accepted wisdom taught in a terribly boring way. Because of the teaching methodology used, and the fact that there was no text book, the subject slowly lost its relative weighting within the school syllabus and the course content received occasional, unsystematic treatment. The teaching of values has been constantly deemphasized in elementary schooling with the result that nowadays children are capable of processing huge amounts of information and understanding the underlying logic in a computer program almost instantaneously, but they are not so quick to pick up on the implications that this newly acquired information has for their own lives.

However, each historical moment has its own characteristics and the time that it has been our fortune to live in is, among many other things, a moment of crisis; one of the many crises that have recurred with such frequency that they have become almost permanent–environmental crises, economic crises, and assuredly, crises of values. The change of millennium has forced us, as humankind, to face a dark image of ourselves, an image that reveals us to ourselves as half-empty, lacking discourse of possibility or hope, and without direction and a sense of the future. Some of the utopias of yore have become reality and have revealed their limitations.

The numerous current problems and our perception of ourselves have once again given the issue of values importance in educational systems, but this time from a different perspective – one more in touch with the complexity of our times, thereby recovering human rights; respect for differences; multi-cultural aspects; democracy; gender; artistic appreciation; the preservation of environmental quality; and the defense of life, among many other issues left behind by the civilization of the modern world. What is now under discussion is the education of a citizenry capable of living together and showing solidarity and respect for each other's individuality. However, it is apparent that this perspective is still too fragmented; it has not managed to find a way of coordinating issues which, although independently dealt with by individual initiatives and social movements, are nonetheless closely related.

Values are grouped in complex codes, variously, and even contradictorily, linked on various levels; but these, in one way or another, indicate the profile of the person that one wishes to become, which is to say a somewhat improved version of oneself. But these codes are shifting structures which are realigned through experience and the social practices in which we, as individuals, engage. Today we observe very rapid changes in this realignment of identities and subjectivities; people no longer make definitive, permanent commitments even in their affective lives, and far less with regard to membership of political or social militancy groups. On the contrary, a wide spectrum of blurred, shifting interests is apparent, especially among young people, causing them to jump rapidly from one commitment to another in a process that some writers (Arditi, 2000) have called nomadic or "intermittent intervention."

This makes it very difficult to teach values; although we have to recognize that, at the end of the day, all school programs have an implicit moral code, manifest or otherwise, which achieves full expression throughout the entire education establishment[3] and in the set of school rituals and teaching practices. In this sense, the Earth Charter is revealed as a timely proposal for the articulation, in terms of four basic principles, of some of the major issues of our times. However, methodological and didactic problems persist, especially considering the nature of the institutional environment in which we operate and the weakening of stable identities.

One proposal that we are looking into with a view to complementing the work done of those whose research into education in values is to use the dramatic effect of the cinema for the analysis of some of the Earth Charter's contents. The idea is to make use of the large number of topics dealing with the four Parts of the Earth Charter already available in world cinema in order to intensify the learning experience by provoking strong emotions when interpreting the message. The debate's importance lies neither in convincing nor in negotiating interpretations, but in giving free rein to subjectivity when exposed to an aesthetic experience that consists of reconfiguring one's own experience.[4]

The importance of using aesthetic experience for teaching is that it detaches our entrenched individual referents and uproots us; in other words, it dislocates the discourses that have become part of our nature by questioning their certainty and their perceptive matrix, which is a basic consideration for getting in touch with values. On this subject, Gianni Vattimo (2000, 21) states: "The aesthetic experience gives us a view of other possible worlds, and in so doing reveals the relative contingency and the undefined character of the 'real' world to which we have limited ourselves."

Finally, we seek to take advantage of the deep meaning of the Earth Charter by transcending conventional pedagogic activities, not with a view to supplying more information or getting involved in some fun activities – not a bad idea in itself – but principally to try to dissolve the unfortunate, protective shell that the process of modern civilization has burdened us with, making us more and more insensitive, and less and less sympathetic, to the whole of life's value and beauty. ●

### References

Ortigosa L., S. (2002). Education in values through the cinema and the arts. In the *Ibero-American Education Journal No. 29*. OEI (May-August)

Vattimo, G. (2000). Postmodern: A transparent society? In Arditi, B. *The opposite of the difference. Identity and politics*. Caracas, Nueva Sociedad.

### Notes

1   The general courses are intensive, 40 hours in length, and are taken by teachers between academic cycles. They usually have credit value as a teacher training course.
2   The science and technology program is responsible for the physics, chemistry, and biology course materials in the basic education syllabus.
3   This includes the sciences, which claim objectivity.
4   Different didactic techniques have been used to this end, such as role playing, team teaching, etc.

Principle 13. Strengthen democratic institutions at all levels, and provide transparency and accountability in governance, inclusive participation in decision making and access to justice.

Alexander Likhotal, Russia. A thematic essay which speaks to Principle 13 on creating global dialogue on sustainable development

# The Earth Charter as a Vehicle of Transformation

**Alexander Likhotal** has been President and CEO of Green Cross International since 1996. Dr. Likhotal started his academic career as a lecturer at the Moscow State Institute for International Affairs, and later became a Senior Research Fellow, Professor of Political Science and International Relations, and Vice Rector. During the spell of Gorbachev's perestroika, he became the Head of the European security desk at the International Department of the Central Committee of the Communist Party of the Soviet Union. In 1991 Mr. Likhotal was appointed Deputy Spokesman and Adviser to the President of the USSR. He has stayed with President Gorbachev after his resignation as his adviser and spokesman and worked at the Gorbachev Foundation as the International and Media Director. He is the author of several books and numerous articles.

*The problems that exist in the world today cannot be solved by the level of thinking that created them.*
Albert Einstein

Twenty years after the end of the Cold War seemed to herald a new era of peace, security concerns are once more at the top of the world's agenda. A heightened sense of insecurity, reflected as much in headlines as in opinion polls worldwide, is palpable. Increasing tensions on the world scene, escalating terrorism, religious intolerance, relentless environmental degradation, and the systematic violation of human rights all demonstrate, now more than ever, the need to understand the diverse roots of conflicts, as well as the links between peace and security, poverty, and environmental deterioration.

Unlike traditional threats emanating from an adversary, new challenges are better understood as shared risks and vulnerabilities. Raising military expenditures or dispatching troops cannot resolve them. Nor can sealing borders or maintaining the status quo in a highly unequal world contain them. These "problems without passports" are likely to worsen in the years ahead unless the world arrives at a new global vision of common val-

ues, which must underlie the new forms of dialogue and cooperation needed among nations and civilizations.

As a first important step, we must replace the overriding culture of violence and conflict with a new culture of peace. This means not just strengthening and democratising our institutions of peace and security to better respond to and prevent violence, war, and conflict; it means developing, at all levels and in all spheres of life, a complex of attitudes, values, beliefs, and patterns of behaviour that promote not just the peaceful settlement of conflict, but, as well, the quest for mutual understanding, and opportunity for individuals to live harmoniously with each other and the larger community of life. Above all, it means promoting a new global security and sustainability ethic.

At Green Cross, the Earth Dialogues Forums initiated by Mikhail Gorbachev, Chair of Green Cross International, and Maurice Strong, Chair of the Earth Council, are a series of public forums on ethics and sustainable development. We have adopted the following definition to guide our analysis of ethics: a system of accepted beliefs, principles or values which guide human behaviour; a set of rules of conduct or morals of an individual or a group. In building upon this general definition of ethics, we can go further to define "universal ethics" as values and principles that apply across all levels of human diversity.

Much of the world has already accepted ethical principles that are considered "universal." These include the ethical treatment of civilians during war, and the ethical treatment of prisoners of war as found in the Geneva Convention; and the prohibition of slavery, and the prohibition of torture as found in the Universal Declaration of Human Rights.

For several years, a number of prominent civil and political leaders have gone to great lengths to develop moral frameworks for sustainable development. These efforts bore fruition in the form of the Earth Charter, a code of ethics for the planet. The Earth Charter has become an important document in the sustainable development field. Today, the Earth Charter is endorsed by more than two thousand organisations that represent hundreds of millions of people. Yet new environmental principles which should be universal, including the precautionary principle or the polluter-pays principle which were presented in the Rio Declaration in 1992, still await their adoption. Under current circumstances, it is becoming an extremely pressing task to have this code of basic moral principles observed by governments, business, and NGOs, simply in order to give future generations and our planet a chance to survive.

The recommendations below are built on the findings of the Green Cross International Earth Dialogue Forum that took place in Lyon in February 2002, and in Barcelona in February 2004. These gathered two hundred speakers and over two thousand participants as part of the process of promoting an understanding of the principles of the Earth Charter.

Both forums stimulated process of thinking differently about three interrelated challenges— sustainable development, eradication of poverty, and conditions for peace and security. They were designed as interactive platforms to facilitate dialogue between a wide range of stakeholders, including official decision-makers from civil society, business and industry, religious and spiritual leaders, as well as representatives from international institutions. The key conclusions are focused on the assumption that achieving lasting peace, prosperity, stability and sustainability, will require fundamental changes in the way that the international community addresses and responds to the multi-dimensional root causes of instability and insecurity.

It was found that ethics must serve as a foundation for sustainability. While certain ethical principles are already enshrined in national and international law, it is necessary to ensure that all universal values enjoy the same recognition and status, and that universal principles are universally applied. While ethical values are culturally relative and these differences must be respected and protected, there exist certain universal ethical principles that are beyond diversity. These must be identified and codified into law. Universal ethical principles supporting sustainability must be enforceable by law.

In response to the realities of globalisation, there must be a shift in the perception of national sovereignty. Specifically, there must be greater acceptance of global responsibility that stretches beyond traditional borders. As problems have become trans- and inter-national, so must the solutions. National and international security increasingly depend on sustainable and ethical approaches. Problems such as transboundary pollution, poverty, and social injustice are international sustainability and security issues that can only be resolved through united and cooperative international efforts.

There is an urgent need to change the priorities that promote material wealth over personal well-being and justice. These principles must be effectively reflected by changes in local, national, and international law, and by changes in the regulations and policies of global institutions, businesses, and govern-ments. For example, there must be a real change in the present measurements of country performance based primarily on economic indicators to include more holistic measures such as health, poverty levels, biological diversity, and social justice.

Only freedom and democracy can cope with the new challenges. No other system of government can claim more legitimacy, and through no other system can political grievances be addressed more effectively. We must support the growth of democratic movements in every nation, on the basis of our commitment to solidarity, inclusiveness, and cultural diversity, abstaining from any attempts of "exporting" democracy. Citizens are actors, not spectators. They embody the principles and values of democracy. A vibrant civil society that plays a strategic role in protecting local communities, countering extremist ideologies and dealing with political violence, can be only legitimate one.

Structural inequalities within societies must be reduced by eliminating group discrimination and barriers to socio-economic mobility; and promoting women's education, employment, and empowerment. The impact of rapid socio-economic change must be mitigated by integrating weak globalisers into the world economy using duty-free regimes, membership in international trade organisations, and transfer of key technology by designing long-term aid and investment policies that contribute to sustainable development, help empower marginalized groups, and promote participation. Developing educational systems must be linked to job opportunities. Radical ideology must be countered by promoting the growth of civil society organizations and increasing favourable exposure to democratic societies and thought by exchange and dialogue programs.

Earth Dialogues also stressed that the escalation of global problems is in many ways attributable to world politics lagging behind the real processes unfolding in the world. World politics is skidding, proving to be incapable of responding to the challenges of globalization. It is disappointing that, more than a decade after it was given a new lease of life with the end of the Cold War, multilateralism is foundering.

The world needs leaders who understand that, in the words of the Earth Charter, "when basic needs have been met, human development is primarily about being more, not having more" (Preamble, paragraph four). In a world increasingly besieged by corruption, greed, and self-interest, we need leaders who have the moral courage to ground their decisions in this new global ethic.

Modern world politics is not to be based on the conventional principle of balance of powers, but rather on the balance of interests, and that dialogue between cultures and civilizations must become its primary tool. Politics should concentrate on avenues of cooperation and ways to break through deadlocks by promoting just and long-term real-world solutions, not quick fixes or inequitable compromises.

We believe this will require global cooperation in population dynamics, including striving to reach a stable population with high human and social cohesive capacity; consumption patterns that will induce the production of goods and services based on less material-intensive, renewable and recyclable resources; renewable and clean sources of energy; low-waste and low-polluting commodities and services; goods and services that use little space and land area; products and services based on socially- and environmentally-friendly clean technology; delivery of the Millennium Development Goals with equity; policy measures to correct global market and policy failures; consolidating multilateral institutions, such as the United Nations, and the triangle of partnership among governments, businesses, and civil society.

We do understand the challenge. We have to translate it into action. In order to achieve this we need a Global Glasnost – openness, transparency, and public dialogue – on the part of nations, governments, and citizens to build consensus around these challenges. And we need a policy of Preventive Engagement – international and individual responsibility and action to meet the challenges of poverty, disease, environmental degradation, and conflict in an early, preventive, and non-violent way so that military force must not become the only option.

The Earth Charter, which provides a blueprint of relevant ethical principles is perhaps not a panacea, and has never been conceived as such. It is a bold and creative attempt to stimulate the world's transformation in the direction of safe, just, and inclusive future. ●

# Living the Earth Charter in The Netherlands

Alide Roerink, The Netherlands. A project descriptive essay on uses of the Earth Charter in The Netherlands as they relate to Principle 13

**Alide Roerink** is anthropologist and has been involved over the years in networking, advocacy and policy development for gender justice, international solidarity and global governance. Since 2000 she is with NCDO, the National Committee for International Cooperation and Sustainable Development in the Netherlands. Among other programmes with a focus on public education on international development cooperation, NCDO acts as national focal point to the Earth Charter Initiative.
As 'Advisor International Relations' Roerink is member of the NCDO Management Team. Roerink is Senior Advisor to the international Earth Charter Initiative.

Major events of 2005 provide evidence of a growing feeling of global commitment to solving global problems. The tsunami that caused such catastrophic devastation at the end of 2004 created an unprecedented response, not just from governments and agencies, but also from individuals all around the world. The build-up to the G8 in July and to the UN Millennium Summit in September 2005 saw the biggest ever international campaign against poverty and for sustainable development. This campaign mobilized millions of citizens around the world in support of policies for a just and fair division of the world's resources.

Can this energy also be harnessed to achieve the goals of the Earth Charter

and to promote its values? What is the contribution of the Netherlands in developing this global sense of responsibility?

The Netherlands has a long and strong tradition of international engagement and global solidarity. This is reflected in the level of the aid budget, the priorities of the policies for international cooperation and the nature of Dutch political engagement. Strengthening of the international rule of law is anchored in the national constitution. In 1974, the Netherlands reached the United Nations target of earmarking 0.7 percent of Gross National Income (GNI) for official development aid (ODA). Since 1997 the ODA has been fixed at 0.8 per cent of Gross National Product (GNP). Until recently, the Netherlands has continued to be a strong international advocate, leading by example, calling upon other rich countries to do the same.

Funding for awareness raising on global issues in the Netherlands is high. Spending on global education remains consistently among the highest in Europe. There is also a tradition in the Netherlands of government support for the work of different constituencies from differing faiths, the humanist tradition, and nonreligious people from different political backgrounds – on the basis that these diverse civil society actors should be supported to engage diverse segments of the public.

At the basis of this tradition is, among other things, the founding of the National Committee for International Cooperation and Sustainable Development (NCDO), thirty-five years ago.

It started as "Committee Claus" as the Dutch answer to the UN's call that all rich countries install national committees to promote international solidarity in their societies. Prince Claus, the late husband of Queen Beatrix of The Netherlands, reached out as chair of the national committee to a wide audience in the Netherlands. With his love of Africa and his passion for development cooperation he brought the message that international cooperation is of concern to everyone in powerful and innovative ways. Although Prince Claus performed this function for a relatively short period of time, his influence was enormous and is still felt. The mission of NCDO, to strengthen public support in Dutch society for international cooperation and sustainable development, is still relevant and has not changed. It is still essential today to realize the Earth Charter principle to "promote meaningful participation of all interested individuals and organizations in decision making" (Subprinciple 13.b) .

Prince Claus acknowledged the relevance of broad public support in society to influence the political agenda. He believed a democratic Netherlands with actively engaged citizens would give high priority to international solidarity and development cooperation. And indeed, the Netherlands developed as one of the countries that actually met its promises with respect to global financial agreements and development cooperation promises.

The first encounter of the Netherlands with the Earth Charter goes back to 1992, the process for the World Conference on

Principle 13. Strengthen democratic institutions at all levels, and provide transparency and accountability in governance, inclusive participation in decision making and access to justice.

Environment and Development in Rio de Janeiro—the Earth Summit. The first attempt to arrive at an Earth Charter failed in Rio. The initiative was continued in following years and taken outside the United Nations arena, thanks to, among others, Ruud Lubbers - in those years Prime Minister of The Netherlands. Her Majesty Queen Beatrix expressed her interest in the Earth Charter. She was present at the start of the worldwide participatory consultation on the structure and content of the Earth Charter. Five years later, in June, 2000, the Earth Charter was internationally launched and the first copy was presented to Queen Beatrix in the Peace Palace in The Hague. In 2005 the Queen of the Netherlands participated in the celebration of the first Earth Charter lustrum in Amsterdam, linked to the celebration of her being twenty-five years on the throne.

Since 2002, NCDO has taken up the task of serving as the focal point to the ECI in the Netherlands. The National Committee of NCDO endorsed the Earth Charter and integrated it into its policy framework (2002-2006), thereby providing NCDO funds for civil society activities and Dutch projects related to the Earth Charter. In 2002, the Earth Charter document was translated into Dutch and has since then been widely distributed as a flyer, at special meetings such as United World College Youth Action Summit, summer 2002, and via internet. All municipalities received the Earth Charter flyer as a result of cooperation with the Dutch Association of Municipalities.

The National Platform Johannesburg 2002 – a broad coalition of 450 non governmental organizations – selected the Earth Charter as one of the priorities. The Platform endorsed the Earth Charter unanimously. This resulted in a dialogue on the Earth Charter with the Dutch governmental delegation for Johannesburg. As Minister for the Environment, Jan Pronk wrote to his colleagues all over the world with the suggestion that they place the Earth Charter on the Johannesburg agenda. The Dutch position in the WSSD was finally decided by the new

cabinet of Prime Minister Balkenende. The Netherlands contributed to the development of the Earth Charter, but with the chances of UN endorsement or adoption low – perhaps because of a perception of the Earth Charter as a "people's document" – a more reserved attitude emerged. Only if other countries proposed acknowledging the Earth Charter was the Netherlands prepared to join.

Dutch members of the cabinet in Johannesburg did show interest in the Earth Charter. Agnes van Ardenne, Minister for Development Cooperation, attended an important Earth Charter meeting. Prime Minister Balkenende spoke on the Earth Charter in his speech to the world leaders assembled. He called upon the business community to be inspired by the Earth Charter.

In the run-up to the celebration of five years Earth Charter in 2005, there were several organisations who worked together to lend the Earth Charter further momentum. NCDO, Plan Netherlands and the Royal Tropical Institute (KIT) worked together to facilitate the celebration of the fifth anniversary of the Earth Charter. An Earth Charter youth version was developed and distributed to all primary schools in the Netherlands. The Ark of Hope found a temporary home in the Tropenmuseum Junior. Children in the Netherlands have expressed their dreams for the future and added them to the Ark of Hope. Queen Beatrix received the twenty-five most beautiful pages from the children and brought them together in a vessel that she created and decorated herself to be offered to the Ark of Hope.

The Earth Charter provides a framework and source of inspiration for organisations and individuals who want to contribute each in their own way to international solidarity, sustainable development, and building an inclusive multicultural society. The Earth Charter isn't a faraway dream. Five years after the launch, support can be demonstrated in living the Earth Charter in the Netherlands. Yet, public support is not

automatically translated into a higher priority in policies and politics for solidarity and sustainability. The Netherlands' internationally renowned reputation for tolerance, engagement, and contributions to healthcare, welfare, and education has come under pressure. Attempts to establish real transitions towards sustainable development are still of marginal influence. Dutch energy consumption is still increasing and initiatives for sustainable investment funds and organic agriculture are not yet mainstream. A breakthrough will entail finding new ways to link practical innovative experiences to higher priorities in policies and politics. For The Netherlands, which is changing and in confusion – partly as a result of the increased fear and vulnerability for terrorism, globalisation, and cultural alienation – the Earth Charter can help provide such a breakthrough.

To really make the difference, more people will have to serve as examples. Research shows that a new engagement is coming up, characterized by a "common shared ethical inspiration." This movement represents the cross-cultural ideal of access for every person to ethical-spiritual self creation. And since this affects people's lives as a whole, it involves as much ownership over one's own life as possible. The new engagement knows no blueprints.

These findings match the NCDO's experience with a growing group of youth in the Netherlands who call themselves "practical idealists."
They discover concrete possibilities for responsible consumption and production. They engage others in sustainable lifestyles and practical forms of global solidarity. They do not do this with a moral call to refrain or by threatening with doom scenarios; but by showing with flair that 'clean clothes" are beautiful; that fair food is smart; that you can create a new and positive identity based on a combination of elements from different cultural and ethnic backgrounds. They show that you can be more by having less. ●

Karine Danielyan, Armenia. A project descriptive essay which speaks to Principle 13 on strengthening democratic institutions at all levels

# Five Years with the Earth Charter in Armenia: The Development of Democratic Institutions

 **Karine Danielyan** was a candidate of biological sciences, and is a Doctor of Geographic Sciences, and an academician at the International Academy of Ecology. She is Professor of Yerevan State University. Dr. Danielyan is Chairperson of the Association for Sustainable Human Development of the United Nations Environment Program National Committee of Armenia, and of the Earth Charter National Committee of Armenia. She has also served as Minister of Environment in Armenia.

*Dedicated to the memory of Maximo Kalaw*

In Armenia, the Earth Charter is perceived as a document closely connected with people because Armenian citizens actively participated in discussions of the very first drafts of the document, argued, presented their recommendations, and saw their ideas incorporated in the new versions of the Earth Charter. Consequently, those students who studied the Earth Charter at Yerevan State University deliver lectures on the Earth Charter today. For more than five years, the youth section of the Association for Sustainable Human Development has worked with schools and organizes summer eco-camps; and the Earth Charter always has its special place at all lectures, discussions, and contests of compositions, paintings, and posters.

The Association published the Earth Charter four times, including the brochures that, along with the text of the Charter, contained articles and essays about it written by famous political and public figures and Armenian reporters. The brochures also contained Armenian translation of articles by two of the Co-chairs of the Earth Charter Steering Committee, Professor Steven C. Rockefeller and Mrs. Kamla Chowdhry. For the past eight years, the Association has conducted numerous seminars, conferences, and roundtables dedicated to sustainable development issues at local, national, regional, and international levels, and almost always the theme of the Earth Charter was built into the agenda.

The version of the Earth Charter for children developed by the Association was republished thrice; the last booklet was published in the form of the message of the Association. In addition, children have performed a play about the Earth Charter.

At the end of 2004, we prepared an Earth Charter poster aimed at demonstrating the close connection of the document with the people. Indeed, we see the Earth Charter process as a unique "bottom-up" experience: from discussions at local communities, local and national NGOs, University departments up to the Johannesburg Summit; then, witnessing its adoption by United Nations Educational, Scientific and Cultural Organization (UNESCO) and the World Conservation Union (IUCN); and, finally, watching its inclusion into the plan of implementation for the UN Decade of Education for Sustainable Development as one of the key tools of such education.

Principle 13 reads, "Strengthen democratic institutions at all levels, and provide transparency and accountability in governance, inclusive participation in decision making, and access to justice." The period of disseminating this ideology of the Earth Charter in Newly Independent States coincided with the transition period of the early 1990s when our countries became independent from the Soviet Union and democratization processes establishing human rights principles raised the awareness and participation of civil society. These processes have unfolded with great difficulty.

Among the documents influenced by the ideas and principles of the Charter are "Sustainable Development Concept of the Republic of Armenia, 2002"; "Main Principles and Approaches of the Sustainable Development Concept for South Caucasus, 2002"; as well as "Guidelines on Local Agendas 21 for Cities of Countries in Transition," including the example of Armenia, Azerbaijan, and Georgia, 2003. All three documents, which are significantly focused on formation and role of the civil society and public participation in decision-making, are broadly dissemi-

© COUNTERPART

general rights on information and freedom of speech. This represents a major shift in the content of our constitution, which will be reflected at many other levels. It was a more participatory process than ever before, though not yet a perfect one.

For some years, we have used the Earth Charter as an instrument to raise awareness among our youth to help them understand the challenges we face. As a consequence, their generation thinks more freely, and they are more ready to endorse democratic values, in general, and environmental democracy, in particular.

At the same time, the chaos of the transitional period poses significant hurdles toward establishing sustainable development principles. Socio-economic problems, drastic income polarization of the population, and absolute power of the newly-emerged oligarchs do not promote development of democratic institutions at all, and often democratization processes and formation of a valid civil society are merely imitative. Economists explain this phenomenon with the specificity of the transitional period related to initial accumulation of capital. Thus, I would like to hope that this complicated and difficult period will soon be over and we will manage to activate democratic reforms and ensure a real transition to sustainable development. It is certain that education will play a key role in this challenging process of building an enduring democratic post-Soviet Union Armenia.

In 1991 when Armenia declared its independence and sovereign state, we found ourselves in a situation which we had to start from the scratch but with an advantage of highly educated citizens. Independent Armenia entered a transition period in 1992, which gradually brought about significant changes in the country in economic, social, political, institutional, and psychological realms. With the aim of developing an open and democratic society and free market economy,

nated in Armenia and in the region of South Caucasus in general, and are actively used.

Provisions of Principle 13 of the Earth Charter are accordant with the pillars of the Aarhus Convention. In 2003-2004, a European Union Program dedicated to implementation of the aforementioned Convention was conducted in six post-Soviet countries, including Armenia. The Association actively participated in the Program; and during the trainings conducted in the framework of the Program, we distributed the Charter and allotted time to its presentation. Finally, in October 2004, the Association organized a roundtable in the Parliament on issues related to sustainable development. Members and experts of Parliament received brochures with the text of the Charter and posters.

Modest but tangible results have already manifested with the Razdan city local government, the second city in Armenia, where we conducted a roundtable on the Earth Charter in 2000. The city government has become our good partner in all subsequent events and programs in the sphere of sustainable development. A course of lectures on

Sustainable Development has been delivered over the last four years at Ruzdan University (based on textbooks published by the Association and Yerevan State University). In the framework of the course, students study the Earth Charter as well. It is appropriate that Razdan city is the only city in Armenia, and the first one in South Caucasus, to officially join the European Union of Sustainable Cities, as well as the International Council of Local Environmental Initiatives (ICLEI).

Currently, Armenia is preparing a new version of a constitution for the country. There have been discussions within the commissions involving the civil society representatives. There are ongoing the discussions in the Parliament. After Parliamentary approval of the project, it will be put to public referendum at the end of 2005. Owing to active lobbying by the non governmental organizations sector, we managed to include, in the constitution draft, provisions on sustainable development and articles that reflect environmental rights of citizens, including their right to access environmental information. These articles are absent in the current Constitution; it contains only articles on

Armenia undertook important political, economic, and institutional reforms. The establishment of democratic institutions, the adoption of a legal framework and constitutional guarantees for human rights and fundamental freedoms, and the creation of a modern public administration were prerequisites for breaking from the old system and building a new, democratic society.

However, the pace of democratisation is rather slow and in many instances Armenia still falls short of internationally accepted democratic principles. The civil society of Armenia has a long way to go to become a "hefty watchdog" controlling the distribution of powers in the country. On the other hand, the successive governments of Independent Armenia have failed so far to identify the country's priorities and development strategies in all spheres.

In 1999, in the framework of the project "Lobbying the forming of sustainable development policy of Armenia," we issued a two-volume edition of "Towards Sustainable Development of Armenia," in which the draft Earth Charter was published for the first time in Armenian. After that the Association participated in the online conference on the Earth Charter consultation and held national consultations on the Earth Charter, among many others activities. We have conducted a number of seminars in Yerevan and in various regions in our country. I have included the Earth Charter in my university lectures on sustainable development.

I share a quite interesting reaction of one of my students: "It will be dangerous to our nation to take [the] Earth Charter in faith and put it in action at once. As we have bitter experience: we were the first nation to adopt Christianity as an official religion and two thousand years we have paid for it – for ages we have been slaughtered with requirements to deny the Christian faith. We were longing for the world to recognize the genocide of 1915; we never heard from our butchers, nor from their offspring: "we were wrong, excuse me." We did not get even moral satisfaction. How can it be possible having such heavy and aggrieved heart to feel ourselves as an equal part of the united world community? And yet, this is not only our problem – it is a moral problem of all humanity. The same idea is expressed by famous film director Taron Kaplanyan: "We have still a serious problem with world community…" I understand my students, understand my friend Taron, but I hope we shall surmount this obstacle also, and when we get rid of this pain, shall sense ourselves as an equal part of modern humanity.

I am certain that the upcoming United Nations Decade of Education for Sustainable Development should play an essential role in positive transformations for our country. Under the coordination of our Association, NGOs of Armenia, Azerbaijan, and Georgia have developed an Action Plan for this Decade in which the Earth Charter has a special role in the system of formal and informal education.

Jointly with the Center of Constitutional Rights and Aarhus Center, the Association intends to organize a roundtable on sustainable development with the support of the Organization for Security and Cooperation in Europe. The roundtable will be held at the hall of the Constitutional Court for members and experts of the Court, as well as judges of the Republic of Armenia. Special attention, in presentations and discussions, will be drawn to issues related to public participation and access to justice.

Indeed, the Earth Charter faces many obstacles, primarily of moral nature. Nevertheless, I am certain that everything depends on us, each inhabitant of the Earth. Further preservation of our remarkable planet in its unbelievable harmony for our next generations is conditioned by our level of morality. So will we succeed in this objective, or will we destroy the bases of our existence and disappear as a kind? The biosphere will remain, of course, it will recover and continue its development, but without us.

It is difficult to estimate or measure the role and the significance of the Earth Charter, but in Armenia it has generated significant impact. I am very happy the Earth Charter proclaims "Earth, our home, is alive with a unique community of life" (Preamble, paragraph two). We are obliged to take the path outlined by the Earth Charter; there is no other alternative. And may God help us to overcome all impediments on the way. ●

# Earth Charter Imperatives: Linking the Global and the Local in Developing Countries

**Chamniern Paul Vorratnchaiphan** brings more than thirty years of experience in community organizing, social and environmental research, teaching, consulting, and project team leading to his current position as Director of the Grassroots Action Program at Thailand Environment Institute. He works with implementation mechanisms such as Local Agenda 21, Sustainable and Healthy Cities, Earth Charter principles, Millennium Development Goals, and ISO 14001. He strongly supports the participation of local communities and local authorities, particularly in areas of local development and physical planning processes. Mr. Chamniern promotes spiritual maturity as an essence of the principle of deep ecology and the balance and integration of yin and yang as important strategies for understanding the Earth Charter.

Local governments have been asked to endorse the Earth Charter as a means to inspire transformation hopefully leading to developing a deeper culture of sustainability, respect, and equity in their cities and localities. The Local Government Declaration to the World Summit on Sustainable Development was one such step closer to localizing commitments to sustainable development. However, to be successfully implemented, these commitments must result in sustainable, integrated planning, investment in and management of resources, promoting public health and clean energy, as well as adopting socially and environmentally sound procurement policies.

A challenge therefore exists on how to translate the lofty statements of the Earth Charter into concrete local actions. An even greater challenge exists to formulate a "local charter" that truly embodies all the spirit and principles of the overarching document. While some progress has been made by localities in developed countries, the Earth Charter must not become only for those who can afford it, and "exported" as another by-product of globalization. Ways and means are needed for the Earth Charter to establish effective linkages between the good thoughts, ideas, and principles of global sustainability balanced against the reality at the local level, in all parts of the world,

dealing with people's specific conditions, aspirations, and culture. In the case of developing countries, the Earth Charter needs to be flexible enough to recognize and promote strategic priorities that cannot only be stated at the local level, but also be realistically transformed from a vision into meaningful action.

When looking to the Greater Mekong Subregion, a number of countries are making significant advances in decentralization, bureaucratic reforms and other advances that give increasing responsibility to the local level. Many of these reforms are being driven by a growing demand from communities and other civil society members for action on deteriorating environmental quality and declining health and safety conditions. For example, in 1997 Thailand adopted a new and modern constitution along with a number of organic laws[1] and supporting legislation for decentralization and major administrative reforms. These changes facilitate devolution of authority and resources to local government units and encourage greater public participation in the local management of natural resources and the local environment[2]. As a result, many local authorities are seizing the opportunity presented them and are now defining and implementing their own vision and development priorities that better reflect and address local conditions and needs.

While Thailand is perhaps one of the most economically and democratically developed of countries in the region, similar processes are emerging in many of its neighbouring countries. However, local governments in all these countries remain challenged by deficits in capacity, processes, and tools. These deficits must be overcome to allow local governments to make the transition from centrally controlled units, to being truly devolved entities that can pursue locally-decided development in a balanced, sustainable, and equitable manner. Additionally, as in many developing countries, local development is also influenced by other factors such as globalization, loss of traditional wisdoms, ongoing client-patron relationships, and corruption that threatens the identity and culture of the place by only emphasising economic development at the cost of all other aspects.

While having a relation to the wider Earth Charter, the framework and challenges described above have a mutual impact on the opportunities and challenges for pursuing Principle 13 on strengthening democratic institutions. Its subprinciples, on access to information, 13.a; on meaningful participation, 13.b; and, on strengthening local environmental management, 13.f; are largely being pursued by Thai and other local authorities and have good potential for adoption and implementation under the various decentralization and reform initiatives. However, when attempting to pursue the remaining subprinciples on protecting freedom of expression, 13.c; on access to administrative and independent judicial procedures vis-à-vis environmental harm, 13.d; and on eliminating corruption, 13.e; it must be recognized that significant work is still required. It is the internalization of all components of Principle 13, more than any other, that will promote sustainable development at the local level in developing countries.

These challenges do not mean that integrating principles and components of the Earth Charter cannot be initiated in such countries. Rather, it is becoming increasingly imperative that the principles and ideologies as expressed in the Earth Charter, and especially Principle 13, must now find a way to seize the opportunities presented by ongoing change in these countries and become meaningful to the local level in concrete terms in order to bring balance to the development process.

A number of important initiatives are underway in many countries in the subregion that promote sustainable development at the local level and can subsequently reinforce the localization of the Earth Charter principles. In Thailand, municipal governments have come together through a grassroots formulation process to establish a set of forty-seven "Sustainable City Indicators" that they are currently using to guide their investment decisions in an integrated and balanced approach, which offers a means of evaluating their progress towards achieving a more liveable and sustainable city. This initiative complemented the national work of Thailand to revise their Sustainable Development Indicators.[3] Like all countries, Thailand is required to report annually to the Sustainable Development Committee on its progress.

Other initiatives have sought to introduce strategic management principles[4] to local Thai governments to support them taking a more holistic and integrated approach to their development planning and management. Supporting frameworks and networks[5] are being reinforced and energized for local governments both in Thailand and the subregion. Significant work is also being undertaken to localize Millennium Development Goals at the provincial level.[6] While some of these initiatives are donor driven, there is an overall demonstrated interest by local governments to embrace such interventions and begin to internalize sustainable development principles.

In many ways, the local initiatives and demands emerging from developing countries can be viewed as a "challenge" to the Earth Council to find ways and means of bringing the Earth Charter to be relevant and workable for their local governments

without losing sight of the overall global objectives. Whether through linking with locally based Sustainable City Indicators, or offering ways to realistically transform the Earth Charter principles from local vision into meaningful action, work must be undertaken that can result in generating important lessons that others can learn from and begin to hopefully reverse much of the unsustainable development activity that is plaguing localities in the developing world.

These various ways and means for the Earth Charter to establish linkages that balance between the global and the local should not only inspire local governments, but should also result in their transformation from vision to meaningful action. In pursuing such transformation, a question emerges as to whether any of the resulting instruments, at any level, will be strong enough to protect nature and the rights, culture, and well-being of the people who inhabit it from human-induced degradation and destruction. In the course of attempting to answer this, significant discussion has been pursued that goes beyond scientific, technological, financial, and environmental frameworks by attempting to build an ethical foundation as a core principle to achieve greater sustainability. As a result, the Earth Charter speaks of ecological governance as well as other ethical imperatives to guide conduct at all levels. However, concepts such as governance and ethics tend to remain external to many traditional societies and by themselves cannot restore a lost identity – as is the case of many localities in the developing world. The point to be raised for further discussion is the issue of whether "building an ethical foundation" in society is sufficient to achieve a sustainable way of life. And, if it isn't, of how we go beyond strengthening ethics to regain a society's innate spirituality to be at the core of its actions. There is a need to reinforce spiritual maturity while it still exists in our societies and to rebuild spiritual maturity where it has long been lost. ●

### Notes

1   Subsidiary laws determining the fundamental political principles of the government.

2   Specifically sections 56, 78, 79, 282-284, and 290 of the 1997 Constitution

3   As the Thailand Environment Institute (TEI) was secretariat and advisor to both the local (SCI) and national (SDI) processes, significant linkages and synergies were able to be maintained between the two processes.

4   This TEI driven initiative was introduced to encourage and train municipalities to undertake a more strategic approach to local development planning that emphasized shifting from an incremental approach in the planning and budgeting process to one that establishes a vision and works to formulate action plans for achieving it.

5   TEI is working with SCP/UN-Habitat to establish a "Sustainable Cities Resource Centre" for training and other capacity building supports in Thailand and the Greater Mekong Subregion, as well as to formalize a Regional Learning Network (RLN) that brings together a range of locally and nationally based resources that provide technical and other support for local authorities as they attempt to deal with increasingly complex urban issues.

6   With donor support from UNDP and NESDB (2004-2005), TEI is implementing pilot activities to elaborate Provincial Millennium Development Goal Reports and integrate the outputs within the provincial development plan for implementation.

Principle 13. Strengthen democratic institutions at all levels, and provide transparency and accountability in governance, inclusive participation in decision making and access to justice.

Rustem Khairov, Russia. A project descriptive essay on Earth Charter endorsement by three Russian Republics as it relates to Principle 13

# The Earth Charter in Russia since 1994

**Rustem Khairov** is Executive Director of the International Public Foundation for Survival and Development of Humanity. Before that for twenty years he worked in the Institute for Control Sciences and International Research Institute for Management Sciences of the Academy of Science of the USSR. Since 1994, he has participated in the Earth Charter project. Currently he is Earth Charter Project Coordinator for Green Cross International and is Deputy Chairman of the Earth Charter National Committee of the Russian Federation. Dr. Khairov is a member of the Commission for Sustainable Development of the State Duma of the Russian Federation and a member of the Expert Council for the Government of the Russian Federation. He is author is of more than fifty scientific presentations and articles in the fields of philosophy, psychology, sociology, global modeling, peace research, international cooperation, ecology, and sustainable development.

The birth of the Earth Charter project coincided with one of the most difficult periods of the new Russian history. In the 1990s, we witnessed tanks attacking Parliament, war in Chechnya, panic after dramatic dissipation of the USSR and collapse of communist ideals, breakdown of the ideological guideposts, and the search for a new framework for development.

When developing the Earth Charter was proposed in 1994, Russians took its humanitarian idea of an integrated global ethic for "an outstretched hand of God." From the first minutes of discussing that idea in The Hague Earth Charter meeting, it became clear that the document under debate could become not only the code of sustainable development principles, but even a strategic milestone on the way to building new society and new civilization.

It was at the same period of time that the Green Cross was founded – an international ecological organization headed by the first and last USSR President, Mikhail Gorbachev. I was authorized to coordinate the Earth Charter activities within the framework of that institution, while the International Foundation for Survival and Development of Humanity became the instrument to realize that work.[1] Green Cross International (GCI) worked closely with the Earth Council and other partners to develop and implement the Earth Charter.

Activities relevant to the Earth Charter in Russia can be divided into two five-year stages. The first one, 1995-2000, deals with development of the Earth Charter principles; the second one, 2000-2005, with the dissemination and implementation of the principles in the regions of the Russian Federation, as well as on the federal level. Within the framework of the first stage, our efforts, first and foremost, focused on integrating the latest scientific discoveries in the theory of biota regulation to make the basis for

necessary laws in biosphere development that were to be taken into consideration. Many eminent Russian scientists were involved, including V. Gorshkov, K. Losev, V. Danilov-Danilian, and others. The scientific theories of these Russian researchers laid the foundation for many Earth Charter principles, especially in Part II, the section on Ecological Integrity.

Parallel to that effort, cooperation was established with the leaders of the main religions of Russian Federation, as well as scientists and experts on "culture of peace and tolerance" such as F. Mayor, I. Galtung, T. Heyerdahl, at The Institute of Culture of Peace in Kazan, and others Within this first phase, we hosted many round tables for discussing and publicizing the Earth Charter project. Public hearings were held in Moscow with participation of the Earth Council and over 150 representatives of governmental institutions and non governmental organizations. There were also workshops and conferences in Kamchatka, in the countries of Central Asia, Altai, the City of Nizhny-Novgorod, St. Petersburg, among others. Publications included compilations of the Earth Charter papers and documentation of public hearings (over 40,000 copies). Endorsement of the Earth Charter was included in some resolutions, memoranda, and other final documents of the many events that took place in different regions of the Russian Federation.

The second stage of our focus was to embed the Earth Charter in the regions of the Russian Federation and to promote the document at the federal level as much as possible. Three regions in the rank of republics were selected: Tatarstan, Kalmykia and Kabardino-Balkaria. The choice of those regions was precipitated by the republics having constitutions similar in tone and principle to the the Earth Charter, and by the openness of their leaders to the ideas of sustainable development, on the one hand, and by the diversity of natural, economic, and social parameters on the other hand.

Of the three republics, Tartarstan is the largest, with a highly diverse population of about fifty percent Muslim Tartar peoples, forty percent Orthodox Russians, and the remainder a variety of other ethnic groups. It has become a leading oil and gas producer and contributes financially to the Russian Federation. Kalmykia is, for the most part, an agricultural country where the main religion is Buddhism. Kabardino-Balkaria is one of the most naturally beautiful countries in the North Caucasus.

At that second stage, the work was very intense. Serious consultations were held at all levels of NGOs, Parliamentary leadership, and ministries. Three key challenges faced Tatarstan: balancing development with environmental protection, ensuring peaceful coexistence among differing ethnic and religious groups, and sustaining national identity. In the face of these challenges, Tatarstan's progressive, yet assertive political leadership, especially in the person of President Shaimiev, saw the Earth Charter as a vital instrument for achieving its goals.
The attempts to apply every Earth Charter principle to the specifics of the region were worked out in detail, as well as the legal issues of concordance with the constitutions of the republics concerned and the Russian Federation Constitution.

The greatest bulk of the preparatory work was carried out in the Republic of Tatarstan. By June 2000, in the Palace of Peace in the Hague, it became possible to acquaint all those present with President Shaimiev's proposal regarding "the Republic's readiness to become an experimental territory for implementation and testing the Earth Charter principles." In April 2001, the Parliament of Tatarstan endorsed the Earth Charter as a guide for action, witnessed by members of the international Commission on the Earth Charter, delegations of the GCI, Earth Council, representatives of the Earth Charter national committees of the Commonwealth of Independent States, the USA, Australia, Europe, and India. Thus, the Tatarstan became the first republic in the world to have initiated the practical implementation of the Earth Charter principles.[2]

With the support of Green Cross International and the International Public Foundation for Survival and Development of Humanity, Tatarstan has actively engaged the Earth Charter as a guide for sustainable development. The government of Tatarstan has also analyzed, in detail, how well its key laws and policies stand up against Earth Charter principles. These efforts culminated with the Parliament of Tatarstan's vote to endorse the Earth Charter. Plans are under way to use the Earth Charter in school curricula.

The next region of the Russian Federation to affirm the Earth Charter was the Republic of Kalmykia. On October 24, 2002, the Earth Charter was endorsed at the 29th session of the Peoples Hural (No. 798-?). Then, it was the turn of the Republic of Kabardino-Balkaria, where on April 24, 2003, the Earth Charter was endorsed at the sitting of the Parliament (No. 607-?-?). At present, work is under way to promote the Earth Charter's principles in eleven regions of the Russian Federation situated along its central artery – the Volga River, where over one-half of the Russian population lives.

Regarding the federal level, the Earth Charter was included in Parliamentary hearings of the State Duma of the Russian Federation in October 2001; it was included in the official report of the Chairman of the Parliamentary Delegation of the Russian Federation in Johannesburg in 2002; and, it was reported and passed over to the President of the Russian Federation, V. Putin. More than once, it was discussed in the central mass media and relevant ministries, agencies, higher educational establishments, and public institutions. At present, the main work to promote the Earth Charter is being carried on in educational establishments of Russia;[3] and, it is being considered as a network element of the international television channel, WorldMade[4], located in and broadcasting from Amsterdam.

A tough ten years have passed. Life on Earth has not become better or easier. Wars go on in different regions of the world. Absolute poverty still exists. Terrorism continues. The world has not yet accepted (far from it) the principles of an equitable, sustainable, and peaceful global community for the twenty-first century as proclaimed by the Earth Charter. But, these ideals are increasingly discussed in the Russian public – at schools, higher educational establishments, among scientists, and on the municipal level. The Kyoto Protocol is coming into force, having recently been endorsed by the Russian Federation Parliament.

What is the future of the Earth Charter, in my opinion? What is its role and mission? Given the momentous speed of objective realities in global climate change, demographic shifts, new information technologies, terrorism, changes in the political map of the world, limits of global resources, to name but a few, the Earth Charter is, on the one hand, a universal code of principles for sustainable development in a modern world – an authentic "people's" document that has absorbed hundreds of recommendations from many countries of the world. On the other hand, it is a "living," flexible document

Principle 13. Strengthen democratic institutions at all levels, and provide transparency and accountability in governance, inclusive participation in decision making and access to justice.

closely associated with existing problems of modern society. Earth Charter provides a necessary ethical framework to develop new values landmarks and new realities. I am delighted that, since its first days, it has been my good fortune to take part in this humanitarian project, together with the outstanding people of our time. Tartarstan, Kalmykia, Kabardino-Balkaria and the Earth Charter movement now enter an exciting new period when the ethical foundation described in the Earth Charter will not only be discussed, at all levels of government and society, but implemented. ●

### Notes

1    Since 1997 together with the National Committee on Earth Charter in the Russian Federation.
2    I will not dwell on the results of the practical implementation of the Earth Charter principles and ideas adopted by the Parliament of the Republic of Tartarstan, because they are dealt with in a special book devoted to the Earth Charter which I hope will be published in English very soon. It will be a good supplement to this collection of essays.
3    See the website of the Earth Charter in Russia at www.earthcharter.ru
4    Located in and broadcasting from Amsterdam. See also, www.worldmadechannel.tv

Angela Antunes and Moacir Gadotti, Brazil. A thematic essay which speaks to Principle 14 on incorporating the values of the Earth Charter into education

# Eco-pedagogy as the Appropriate Pedagogy to the Earth Charter Process

**Angela Antunes** is Executive Secretary of Paulo Freire Institute, Doctor of Education from the University of Sao Paulo and author of many books. Her Ph.D. thesis for the School of Education at the University of Sao Paulo was on "Sustainability Pedagogy", using the Earth Charter as one of the philosophical keystone documents upon which to build that pedagogy. At the Paulo Freire Institute, she has coordinated several projects that have the Earth Charter as a reference point: "Project Youth Peace" (2002-2003), Budget for the Participating Child: Exercising Citizenship from Childhood (2003-2004), Participating Budget for the City of Guarulhos (2005).

**Moacir Gadotti** is Professor at the University of Sao Paulo, the Director of the Paulo Freire Institute, and author of many widely-read and translated books, among others: *Education Against Education* (1979); *Invitation to Read Paulo Freire* (1988); *History of Pedagogical Ideas* (1993); *Praxis Pedagogy* (1994); and *Current Issues on Education* (2000). This thematic essay is the fruit of several debates that took place at workshops and congresses, particularly at the Continental Conference of the Americas, in December 1998, in Cuiaba, Mato Grosso, and during the Earth Charter 's First International Meeting on Educational Issues organized by the Paulo Freire Institute in Sao Paulo in 1999. At the Rio Global Forum in 1992, Dr. Gadotti with others produced the "Treaty on Environmental Education for Sustainable Societies and Global Responsibilities". This thematic essay also re-examines ideas discussed in the book *Earth Pedagogy* (2000).

S everal decades of debates about "our common future" left some "ecological footprints" not only in the economic field, but also in the ethical, political, and educational ones, to guide us on a possible path to face the challenges of the twenty-first century. Sustainability has become the dominant issue in the beginning of this century, with impact not only on our planet but also on the ability to re-educate our thinking and all our senses, with further possibility to rekindle our hope of a future with dignity for all. The Earth Charter is found among these footprints.

The sustainability values promoted by the Earth Charter have terrific educational potential: the preservation of the environment depends on an ecological conscience and shaping this conscience depends on education. It is here that eco-pedagogy, or Earth pedagogy, comes into play. It is a pedagogy to promote learning as the "meaning of the things from everyday life," as stated by Francisco Gutierrez and Cruz Prado.[1] We develop this sense as we go, experiencing our context, and in this process we open new trails – we do not merely observe the journey. It is then a democratic and understanding pedagogy, a pedagogy for everyday life.

Education is connected with space and time where relationships between the human being and the environment actually take place. They happen primarily at the emotional level, much more than at the conscious level. Thus, they happen much more in our subconscious; we do not realize them, and many times we do not know how they happen. So, eco-education is necessary to bring them to the conscious level. And eco-education requires a pedagogy. As emphasized by Gaston Pineau,[2] a series of references are associated with this: the Bacherladian experience; studies on the imaginary; the trans-versatility, trans-disciplinarian, and inter-cultural approach; as well as constructivism and alternative pedagogy. These days, we need an eco-pedagogy and eco-education. We need an Earth pedagogy precisely because without this pedagogy to re-educate men and women, we can no longer speak of Earth as a home, as a burrow for the "animal-man", as Paulo Freire said. Without a proliferation of sustainable education, Earth will be perceived as nothing more than the space for our sustenance and for technical-technological domination, the object of our research, essays, and sometimes of our contemplation. But, it will not be a living space, a space giving us "solace" and requiring from us "care".[3]

It is in the context of the evolution of ecology itself that eco-pedagogy appeared – and is still in its infancy today – having been

Principle 14. Integrate into formal education and life-long learning the knowledge, values, and skills needed for a sustainable way of life.

initially called "pedagogy for sustainable development," but which has now gone beyond its initial purpose. Eco-pedagogy is in development either as a pedagogical movement[4] or as a curriculum approach. Eco-pedagogy implies redirecting curricula to incorporate values and principles defended by the Earth Charter. These principles should guide content, concepts, and the preparation of didactic books. Jean Piaget taught us that curricula must reflect what is important for students. We know this is correct, but incomplete. Curricular contents must also be meaningful for students, and they will be only meaningful to students if their contents are also meaningful to the health of the planet and to a context greater than that of the individual student.

Understood in this light, eco-pedagogy is not just another pedagogy among many other pedagogies. It not only has meaning as an alternative global project concerned with nature preservation (Natural Ecology) and the impact made by human societies on the natural environment (Social Ecology), but also as a new model for sustainable civilization from the ecological point of view (Integral Ecology), which implies making changes on economic, social, and cultural structures. Therefore, it is connected to a *utopian project* – one to change current human, social, and environmental relationships. Therein lies the deep meaning of eco-pedagogy, or the *Earth pedagogy* as we call it.

Eco-pedagogy is not opposed to environmental pedagogy. On the contrary, for eco-pedagogy environmental education is a premise. Eco-pedagogy enables environmental pedagogy with strategies, guidelines, and means to make it a reality. It was at the Rio Global Forum in 1992, during which environmental education was much discussed, that the importance of eco-pedagogy was underlined as a sustainable development pedagogy. This Global Forum was one of the most important events in the last days of the twentieth century. Since then, the debate about the Earth Charter has become a significant factor in the creation of a planetary citizenship. Any pedagogy designed outside of globalization and the ecological movement will have serious problems with legitimacy.

The sustainability culture presumes that sustainability pedagogy can handle the great task of educating planetary citizens. This is an on-going process. Education for planetary citizenship is taking root thanks to numerous experiences. Even though many of these experiences are local, they succeed in educating us to feel not only like members of Earth, but also beyond that – to live as cosmic citizens.

Classic pedagogies were anthropocentric. Eco-pedagogy is based upon a planetary understanding of gender, species, kingdoms, formal, informal, and non-formal education. Our point of view is more comprehensive – from man to planet, beyond genders, species, kingdoms – evolving from an anthropocentric vision to a planetary understanding, to practicing planetary citizenship, and to a new ethical and social reference—planetary civilization.

Eco-pedagogy is a fitting pedagogy for these times of paradigmatic reconstruction, fitting to a culture of sustainability and peace, and, therefore, adequate for the Earth Charter process. It has been gradually growing, benefiting from much input originated in recent decades, principally inside the ecologic movement. It is based upon a philosophical paradigm supported by Paulo Freire, Fritjof Capra, Leonardo Boff, Sebastiao Salgado, Boaventura de Sousa Santos, and Milton Santos; arising from education and offering an ensemble of interdependent knowledge and values. Among them, we would like to mention the following: educate to think globally; educate feelings; teach about the Earth's identity as essential to the human condition; shape the planetary conscience; educate for understanding; and educate for simplicity, care, and peacefulness. In the midst of that, we consider the Earth Charter not only a code for planetary ethics – it is also a call for action.[5] In this sense, we would like to mention some of the real examples where the Earth Charter was used as an instrument for real action.[6]

With the support of the Paulo Freire Institute, Sao Paulo City (2001-2004) used the Earth Charter to train education managers for the Unified Educational Centers dedicated to developing educational, cultural, sport, and leisure activities. Education leaders were trained on the principles of the culture of peace and sustainability so that they can incorporate them in their educational projects and in their decision-making. The Earth Charter was submitted as an educational project during this process. Training education, in the fullest meaning of the words, is a very fertile field to promote the principles and values of the Earth Charter.

The preparation of social studies teachers is another strategy to practice the principles and values of the Earth Charter. Some examples include: the "Youth Peace Project,"[7] which took place in three cities of the state of Sao Paulo and included 225 social studies teachers; the "Citizen School Project," which used the "reading of the world" methodology of Paulo Freire and addressed co-existence principles based on the Earth Charter's values for developing the Political-Pedagogical Project of the schools[8]; the "MOVE-Brazil" adult education project which purpose is to teach literacy to forty thousand young people and adults in six Brazilian states within three years, and includes the Earth Charter as a reference for education; the "Budget for Participating Child"; and, "Exercising Citizenship from Childhood," which involved all children of elementary education in the Sao Paulo city network schools of five hundred educational units, promoting child and youth participation and a direct participation in priorities for education and for the city. The Paulo Freire Institute was responsible for the direct education of 2,500 teachers and ten thousand children involved in the project. The Earth Charter was one of the documents used as a basis for reflecting on education and on the city, and it also guided the education of children. The project to develop as many as five hundred people as social leaders was included in the Participating Budget for the city of Guarulhos, a municipality which also used the Earth

Charter as a reference. Based upon the Earth Charter, social and environmental issues related to the city were discussed as well as priorities for the budget, which included the direct participation of the population.

Eco-pedagogy is a pedagogy centered on life: it includes people, cultures, *modus vivendi*, respect for identity, and diversity. It understands the human being in evolution, as an "incomplete, unfinished, and non-conclusive" being, as stated by Paulo Freire – a being in continuous development, interacting with others and the world. The prevailing pedagogy is centered on tradition, on what is already concluded, on what oppresses students by the way they are tested. With eco-pedagogy educators must welcome students. Their welcome and care are the basis for sustainability education.

The Earth Charter has contributed to the development of sustainability initiatives in schools and, principally, in communities. But, we still need to broaden the Earth Charter's recognition and acceptance around the world as a mobilizing force toward a culture of peace and sustainability, as a way to celebrate diversity. As a call for unity, it can be used to develop the meaning of responsibility with respect for quality of life and to become a force to fight terrorism based on a global consensus.

Faced with the possibility of planetary extermination, the Earth Charter presents alternatives based on a culture of peace and sustainability. Sustainability does not imply only biology, economy, and ecology. Sustainability has to do with the relationship we have with ourselves, with others, and with nature. Pedagogy should begin, above all else, by teaching how to read the world, as Paulo Freire taught us – a world which is the universe, because the world is our first teacher. Our first education is an emotional education, which places us before the mystery of the universe, in close contact with it, producing in us the feeling of being a part of this sacred, living being, in continuous evolution. ●

policies. Moreover, the inclusion of the Earth Charter in the agenda of the Global Social Forum and the Global Education Forum was very important. In January 2003, more than 5,000 people participated in two workshops on the Earth Charter, in Porto Alegre. These workshops had the participation of Angela Antunes, Peter Blaze Corcoran, Moacir Gadotti, Mohit Mukherjee, Leonardo Boff, Rick Clugston, among others.

6    In a small article such as this it is impossible to list all the good experiences which are taking place in Brazil connected with the Earth Charter. We would like to point out however the School of International Education in Salvador (Bahia), which centers its entire school curriculum on the Earth Charter, and the "Earth Harmony" Project in Florianopolis (Santa Catarina), which created its own educational material following eco-pedagogy. The Earth Charter guides the entire work of that group in educating teachers. At the University of Sao Paulo, an Eco-pedagogy Workshop Group was established at the Education School of USP (GRUTEUSP). This Group has been giving seminars and conferences on the Earth Charter. The Blue Planet NGO (Sao Paulo) has been developing projects with public schools, having among its references the Earth Charter. Its director, Professor Luiz Carlos de Oliveira, defended his master's thesis at the Sao Paulo Catholic University on "Eco-pedagogy in the school work."

7    This project has the purpose of educating teachers and social studies teachers (youth and adults) to build a culture of peace and sustainability. By getting together virtually and physically present with "culture circles" twice a month, participants discuss theoretical ideas and experiences based on three basic underpinnings: 1. Culture for peace and sustainability; 2. The Earth Charter and Agenda 21; 3. Culture, communication, and politics. In addition, they receive information on community radio, school newspaper, and student union. This project was concluded in 2004 with the publication of a book containing its results: *The Education of Social Studies Teachers*.

8    Series of books from the Paulo Freire Institute under the title "Guide for a School Citizen" guides the implementation of this project which began in 1992. In 2004, Elisabeth M. Ferrero and Joe Holland's book was translated and published in this collection: *Earth Charter: Thoughts for Action*.

## Notes

1    Prado, F.G. *Eco-pedagogy and planetary citizenship*. Sao Paulo: IPF/Cortez.

2    Pineau, G. *De l'air: essai sur l'ecoformation*. Paris: Paideia.

3    Boff, L. *Know how to care*. Petropolis: Vozes.

4    The Movement for Eco-pedagogy gained force in particular after the First International Meeting on the Earth Charter and Education Perspectives, organized by the Paulo Freire Institute, with the support of Earth Council and UNESCO, between August 23-26, 1999 in Sao Paulo and the First International Forum on Eco-pedagogy, which took place at the School of Psychology and Education Sciences of the University of Porto, Portugal, between March 24-26, 2000. Guiding principles for this movement came from these meetings enclosed in the "Eco-pedagogy Charter"

5    In terms of real action, an important victory in Brazil was the introduction of the Earth Charter among the 21 action goals for *Brazilian Agenda 21* and the creation of an "Earth Charter" Workshop during the *Brazilian Forum for NGOs and Social Movements for the Environment and Development*. In addition, the Minister for the Environment, Marina Silva, adopted the Earth Charter as an ethical guideline for her environmental

Principle 14. Integrate into formal education and life-long learning the knowledge, values, and skills needed for a sustainable way of life.

# South African Initiatives that Draw on the Earth Charter

**Razeena Wagiet** takes a keen interest in monitoring trends, shifts, and debates on environment and education, including policies and implementation issues, and has been a central role player in environment and education national developments in South Africa for a number of years. She holds academic and professional qualifications in the areas of botany, zoology, ecology, education and a PhD degree in Environmental Education. Dr. Waiget was Environmental Adviser to the previous Minister of Education, Professor Kader Asmal for four years. Her work in the Ministry of Education included establishing the National Environmental Education Programme (NEEP), which resulted in environment being recognised as a key issue in all education and training programmes. She is currently the Executive Director, People and Conservation at South African National Parks. In both these two positions Razeena has drawn on the Earth Charter to strengthen the values dimension of the programmes that she has been implementing.

Today, most South Africans value the privileges of living in a country with a very high regard for human rights, which are enshrined in a Constitution that permeates all policies and legislation. It is difficult to believe that only a decade ago, the majority of South Africans were disadvantaged by a myriad of injustices that included a lack of access to natural resources, adverse impacts of environmental degradation, and unhealthy work and living areas which alienated most people from the environment.

Over the past ten years as the country grappled with the birth of a new democracy and the formulation of policies and legislation, the relationship between social justice and ecological sustainability became clearer, so too did the connectedness between sustainable development and care for natural resources. Linking environmental issues to human rights and social justice, and incorporating these into our Constitution, signaled a national commitment to environmental protection, for which environmental education is crucial. Environmental education is critical to achieve environmental and ethical awareness, and to develop the values, attitudes, skills, and behaviour to change the basic relationships that people have with the Earth and with each other. Briefly discussed here are two environmental education projects, located within the Ministry of Education and South African National Parks respectively, which draw on the values and principles of the Earth Charter.

At the World Summit on Sustainable Development held in South Africa in 2002, several participating South African environmental educators recognized the Earth Charter as a means to incorporate the values and principles that translated the goals of our young democracy into environmental education endeavors. Included were staff members involved in the National Environmental Education Programme for General Education and Training (NEEP-GET), who embarked on a process to employ the principles outlined in the Earth Charter into curriculum supporting activities. The curriculum, which underscores human rights, inclusivity, and a healthy environment, aspires to develop environmentally literate, active, competent, and committed citizens. The Earth Charter proved to be a very useful mechanism in the NEEP-GET programme to develop the values dimension that is often a neglected component in environmental education endeavours. The principles and values of the Earth charter were integrated into all four components of the NEEP-GET, namely curriculum policy, materials resource development, professional development, and school-based implementation.

The values and principles outlined in the Earth Charter are also being integrated into environmental education programmes in South African National Parks (SANParks) over the past two years. SANParks, after 1994, has undergone major changes with regard to philosophy, policy, and organisational structure to reflect the new political, economic, and social realities of South Africa. Two years ago, SANParks established the Directorate of People and Conservation, as one of the three lead Divisions in the organisation, to further a "people-centred" approach to

© SAMSAM

conserving South Africa's natural and cultural heritage. The goal of the People and Conservation Directorate is to enable people to take responsibility for the conservation of our national heritage and contribute to the socio-economic development of neighbouring park communities. In essence, People and Conservation ensures that SANParks deliver on a people-centred conservation and tourism mandate.

Through the environmental education projects and programmes, staff strive to develop a conservation ethic by responding to environmental issues in ways that produce mutual benefits for people and parks. The programmes further aspire to enhance access for learners and teachers from disadvantaged backgrounds, by enhancing their access to South African National Parks. Concomitantly, the environmental education programme provides learners and teachers the opportunities to expand their learning environment in a National Park; for many of our disadvantaged learners, this entails a first-time point of access to some of our most prized national assets.

The Earth Charter forms an overarching framework for school teachers and National Parks staff to develop a cadre of educators, learners, and their communities that will respect and value our national heritage. The values are contributing to mould students and programme participants from different heritages together, and encapsulate what South Africans have desired for generations - a non-racial, non-sexist society based on equality, freedom, and social justice. Through engaging with the principles and values outlined in the Earth Charter, programmes of value allow the talent of the nation's youth, in all its diversity, to thrive and flourish. ●

Principle 14. Integrate into formal education and life-longlearning the knowledge, values, and skills needed for a sustainable way of life.

Louise Erbacher, Ben Glass, and Kendon Glass, Australia. An Earth Charter project descriptive essay which speaks to Principle 14 on education for sustainable development and sustainable living

# Taking it to the Brink: The Story of the Brink Expedition

**Louise Erbacher** has always incorporated global issues into her work as a primary school teacher. She was inspired upon discovering the Earth Charter at the Asia Pacific Conference in Brisbane, Australia in 2001. She then joined the local Queensland Earth Charter Committee (QEEC). Since 2002, she has worked with QECC while simultaneously volunteering as the Education Co-ordinater for the Brink Expedition. These roles continually remind her of the empowering nature of the Earth Charter — how the story of one person trying to make a difference can inspire others to take action to create a more sustainable future.

**Ben Glass** is a young Australian adventurer and student of film and television. He is Media Liaison Officer for the Brink Organisation and has travelled on the Brink Expedition from 2002-2004 before returning to Australia to organize the final leg of the Expedition through Australia. Like his older brother Kendon, Ben has a keen interest in social and environmental issues and his honours thesis explored how the media could be used as a tool to motivate young people to take action on such issues. He plans to use some of the experiences to produce a documentary to raise awareness of the issues of social and environmental concern.

**Kendon Glass** is a young Australian adventurer and media professional. He is the Project Director for the Brink Organisation and will be cycling and sailing around the world as part of the Brink Expedition until the end of 2006. It is a worldwide journey that spans over thirty countries in a quest to highlight a range of social and environmental issues, or Hotspots. The Brink Expedition provides Kendon with an opportunity to combine his love of travel and adventure with his instructional technology skills in the form of an interactive website that tracks the story of the journey. While developing a curriculum that would give schools an opportunity to share the adventure, Kendon discovered the Earth Charter.

The challenges that lie ahead for our planet and its people are many and varied. The future will depend on our ability to equip the next generation with, in the words of Principle 14, "the knowledge, values, and skills needed for a sustainable way of life."

There are many educators in our world who are passionate about issues of peace, justice, democracy, and the environment. Their philosophy reflects the values and principles of the Earth Charter and their curriculum provides the opportunities for students to play an active role in developing a sustainable way of life. There are many more educators, however, who lack this same motivation and who struggle to find a catalyst for change, a stimulus to inspire them when integrated into the formal education system.

So how do we empower educators and their students to contribute to the realisation of an optimistic future vision? How do we truly engage educators and their students to take up the responsibility of becoming more active global citizens? How can we create a model for learning that will excite, entertain, inspire, and transform both students and educators alike?

During 2002, a group of like-minded volunteers came together to create a project that would soon capture the hearts and minds of educators and students, promoting "the knowledge, values, and skills needed for a sustainable way of life" (Principle 14). The Brink Expedition (http://www.brinkx.org) has proven itself to be an inspirational model for learning. It is an unpredictable journey across land and ocean, made all the more challenging by the Brink Expedition Team's determination to travel using natural sources of energy. A powerful example of human agency, the Brink Expedition is a global odyssey of epic proportions, exploring the Earth's amazing diversity of culture and environment. It is the spirit of the Earth Charter in action around the world.

When the Brink Expedition Team visits a community, they communicate the message of the Earth Charter and spend

time in schools to discuss the Earth Charter and the Brink hotspots. All schools registering with the Brink School Room receive a school pack, containing the Earth Charter, a children's adaptation of the Earth Charter, and the UNESCO CD Rom – *Teaching and Learning for a Sustainable Future*, as well as other Brink Expedition materials.

Using the Earth Charter as a framework for the creation of environmental and social justice curriculum modules, the Brink project provides educators and students with a real life adventure that energises the learning process. Teresa McNamara, a teacher from Toowong, Brisbane, Australia, used the Brink Curriculum and the Earth Charter to help her students to examine the way in which they had an effect on the Earth. She writes, "After exploring the principles of the Earth Charter, the students engaged in serious discussion about the extent of their ecological footprint and what that might mean for their future" (Personal communication).

Now in its fourth year, the project continues to grow, with new social and

environmental issues to investigate and new lands to explore. The journey continues through Europe as the Brink Expedition Team focus on the issue of global warming, before it continues on to the Middle East to look at understanding cultures. Across Asia, the Brink Expedition Team will investigate fairer trade and endangered species, and the final leg through Australia during 2006 will provide an opportunity to consider the issues of disappearing forests and indigenous Australians.

The boundless adventures of Brink's various expedition members are presented on the World Wide Web through intimate personal accounts and breathtaking photographic images. These provide a looking-glass through which young people can view a world rarely seen within mainstream media. Argentina, Chile, Bolivia, Brazil, Venezuela, Barbados, the Atlantic Ocean, Spain, and the Isle of Mallorca are some of the places that have been cycled and sailed, so far on the Brink adventure, and shared online with a global audience. Educators and students have been able to connect with the Brink

Expedition Team through school visits and satellite phone calls, providing them with a global perspective. The Brink Expedition is a live adventure across space and time that breaks down the barriers of formal education to enhance students' learning experiences and to assist educators to meet the challenge set out in Principle 14 of the Earth Charter.

Emails sent to the Brink Expedition Team from students around the world Australia describe a fascination with the journey and many have expressed a desire to travel the world themselves one day, to see everything with their own eyes. From Rio Grande, Argentina, Liliana says "I'm browsing the Brink website and it's so interesting! I admire you for taking on this task!"

While it can be said that the essence of the Brink Expedition is the Earth Charter in action, it is the Brink "Hotspot" issues of social and environmental concern, as presented in the online Curriculum Modules, that truly reflect the values and principles of the Earth Charter. The introductory module explores the inspiration

Principle 14. Integrate into formal education and life-long learning the knowledge, values, and skills needed for a sustainable way of life.

behind the Brink Expedition and the Earth Charter and investigates the role of media in raising the profile of social and environmental issues. Each of the curriculum modules provides students with an opportunity to take on the role of media presenter to raise awareness of each particular Hotspot issue.

Perhaps the most telling evidence of the success of the Brink Expedition is the interaction with the students themselves. Kendon Glass, Brink Expedition Team Member and the inspiration behind the whole project, described a visit to school in Mallorca, Spain, where a group of sixteen-year old students remained captivated for over an hour as they listened to the experiences of the Brink adventure.

Similar situations have occurred in Australia with students who have interacted with the Brink Expedition Team via satellite phone. Here are some comments from students in Brisbane, Australia:

*"I was really excited the first time we called the Brink Team on their satellite phone. I couldn't believe that we were talking to them while they were in the Amazon Jungle."* (Brigette, age 10)

*"I remember when Ben came in to see us at school and he talked about the Tasmanian tiger and how it was extinct and how we needed to do everything that we could to stop that from happening to other animals. These guys really care about what they're doing – they're fighting for Planet Earth."* (Kelly, age 9)

*"The Brink Expedition Team is travelling without using fossil fuels, so we had to make a support vehicle for them that would use a fuel that was safe for the environment. I made a model of a solar-powered bus to help carry all their supplies. I can't believe that they carry everything with them on their bikes!"* (Rebecca, age 9)

*"I think the Brink Expedition is so cool. These guys are risking their lives to use environmentally friendly transport to travel around the world. Riding their bikes is so much harder than driving a car, but they are doing this so that they can help people to understand the issues. If we don't take care of our Earth, there will be nothing left! I think the Brink Expedition Team have the best jobs in the world!"* (Mary, age 10)

Children from all around the world are excited by adventure. If we can inspire them with the story of the Brink Expedition, then they will begin to think of ways that they can make a difference in their own lives and contribute to the creation of a better future. They will begin to understand how everything is connected and how their actions today will impact upon tomorrow. They will begin to transform the values and principles of the Earth Charter into *action.* ●

Yunhua Liu, China. A project descriptive essay on the Earth Charter as an inspiration for environmental education as it relates to Principle 14

# The Earth Charter and Development of China's National Guidelines for Environmental Education in the School Curriculum

**Yunhua Liu** began teaching in rural primary and middle schools in remote areas of China during the Cultural Revolution, then teaching overseas after graduation from Guangzhou Institute of Foreign Languages. In 1996, she joined WWF and spear-headed the China Environmental Educators' Initiative (EEI), which formed a partnership with twenty-one teachers' universities. She is advising the Shangri-la Sustainable Community Initiative, which empowers local Tibetan communities to participate in decision-making for natural resource management and cultural restoration. She finds the Earth Charter to be an inspiration in her work, providing an ethical framework and a model for building consensus to achieve a common vision.

The Earth Charter has been inspirational in China as a framework and tool for people striving for a sustainable future. A major example is the experience of working on the national programme "Education for Sustainability." World Wide Fund for Nature China Programme Office began its Environmental Educators' Initiative (EEI) in 1996 as a joint initiative with the State Ministry of Education supported by the British Petroleum Company. The goal of EEI is to incorporate education for sustainability in the curricula of China's primary and secondary schools. The program has created a national network of Education for Sustainability centres across the country in twenty-one teacher training universities; it has trained a core team of practitioners within these universities. These expert practitioners, in turn, have provided training for hundreds of thousands of teachers throughout the country, including three thousand teacher advisors who are on the staff of provincial education bureaus.

One important achievement of the EEI has been development of China's National Guidelines for Environmental Education for primary and middle schools. The development of this document took four years, during which time the developers were greatly inspired by the Earth Charter. This inspiration can be seen from two specific aspects.

First, the framework of the National Guidelines was developed through a long process of consultation between government officials, non governmental organizations, teachers, and students. The Earth Charter helped all those involved to clarify the ethical framework of sustainability. Secondly, the process of the Earth Charter's formulation provided a model for the process of achieving goals for environmental education, and specifically provided inspiration to overcome difficulties that at times seemed insurmountable.

Principle 14. Integrate into formal education and life-long learning the knowledge, values, and skills needed for a sustainable way of life.

© BETH HENNESSEY

In fact, sometimes during the four-year process of developing the Guidelines, it seemed impossible that a consensus would ever be achieved among the thousands of stakeholders for an approach to building sustainability. The ideas about the purpose, scope, approach, specific contents, and implementation mechanism for the guidelines initially put forward by more traditional practitioners was quite different from those proposed by reformers. One major objective of the national curriculum reform was for China's students to master more scientific knowledge in order to make China more competitive in the global economic market. This, at first, seemed quite different from, and almost irreconcilable with, the stated goals of Education for Sustainability – to empower students to become informed and active citizens of an ecologically sustainable, socially just, and democratic society. The traditional content of the curriculum focused on scientific knowledge and the mastery of facts about the environment, whereas the focus of environmental sustainability was to help students to obtain a more holistic view of their world, including social, economic, and political understanding in addition to knowledge of the physical and natural world. Instead of the traditional approach of students being passive recipients of instruction, the reformers planned for the guidelines to promote a new way of learning that was inquiry-based, student-centered, interactive, relevant to the lives of the students, and linked to their cultural traditions. Given the ambitious goals for reform, the challenges were understandable, making development of the Guidelines a long and difficult process.

In the end, the partners reached agreement on the Guidelines through a process of compromise and consensus-building. For the first time, China has guidelines for national environmental education that are actually being implemented across the country, benefiting two hundred million students. It is also the first time that a non governmental organization has had a leading role in development of such an important government policy.

The ethical framework that the Earth Charter represents, and the road that was taken to formulate the environmental education document, have been an inspiration for many of those involved in the process in China. The Earth Charter will remain an inspiration for future work as people in the field of education in China come together to revise the guidelines and bring them even more in line with the concepts and approaches of education for sustainable development. ●

# Testimonials and Experiences from the Balearic Islands, Spain

**Guillem Ramis** was an elementary school teacher on the Mediterranean island of Mallorca, Spain for most of his life. He noticed racism and growing xenophobia and realized that there was a need for multicultural education. When he came upon the Earth Charter, he felt he held the blueprint to address these issues, as well as many more. Guillem worked on a children's adaptation of the Earth Charter in order to make the language accessible to his young learners. He coordinated several translations of the adaptation. Under his guidance, there are about seventy schools in the Balearic Islands that have incorporated multicultural education philosophy based upon the Earth Charter.

Since the 1980's, increasing immigrant population flows into the Balearic Islands of Spain from Northern and Eastern Europe, Africa, and the Americas were causing important changes in the ethnic composition of the islands. I was a third grade teacher at Blanquerna Public School, on the island of Mallorca, and aware of the need for an educational response to the situation.

In the year 2000, the Ministry of Education of the Balearic Islands established a multicultural education programme for peace and co-operation. The programme, called Vivim Plegats, or Living Together, was initiated to counter the growing racism and xenophobia in the Balearic Islands due to the arrival of the new immigrants mentioned. As I had already taken steps in that direction, the Ministry decided to relieve me of my teaching duties, allowing me to dedicate myself full-time to create, organize, and coordinate the Vivim Plegats programme, a position I was glad to accept.

The small Vivim Plegats team decided to work with two documents as an ideological basis for this programme – the Convention of the Rights of the Child and the Earth Charter, which in addition to addressing issues of human rights, the central problem we were facing, offered a very broad vision of peaceful living. As an initial step, in order to make the language of the Earth Charter more accessible to young learners, we put together three children's adaptations of the Charter, each targeting different age groups. These adaptations were then translated into a number of languages including Catalan, Spanish, Gallego, and Euskara – the four languages of Spain; French; English; Russian; Portuguese; Greek; Japanese; German; and Arabic to facilitate its accessibility by students and the families of recent immigrants. The children's adaptations of the Charter became the inspiration and starting point for a number of activities in the programme.

During the years from 2000 to 2004, over seventy schools in the Balearic Islands put into practice the principles of the Earth Charter, with students working on themes related to multiculturalism, education for peace, and co-operation. A team of teachers developed a methodology to help incorporate the Earth Charter's values into the existing curriculum. Each teacher was then encouraged to develop his or her own personal vision. Children as young as three years old learnt about the Charter through simple illustrations showing the Earth as our common home. For older children, suggested activities ranged from cultural-exchange workshops to a photography project based on illustrating the Earth Charter's principles through photos taken by children.

As part of the programme, a multicultural team, known as monitors, visited the schools regularly and gave performances about their cultures so children learnt about life in different immigrant communities. The monitors reflected the multicultural nature of the new society, the challenges that different groups experienced on the islands, and the political and cultural situation in the world. The programme further encouraged inter-school collaboration - they shared the Earth Charter with the other schools, thereby establishing a common link between them all, and then exchanged letters and e-mail correspondence. The programme also involved the community, from parent participation to cultural performances, exhibitions, and essay competitions. Due to a change in government, the Vivim Plegats programme is no longer supported by the Ministry, but the

Principle 14. Integrate into formal education and life-longlearning the knowledge, values, and skills needed for a sustainable way of life.

Principle 14. Integrate into formal education and life-longlearning the knowledge, values, and skills needed for a sustainable way of life.

majority of the participating schools continue to be committed to the vision of the programme. In May 2005, for the second year, Mallorca hosted the Children's Social Forum, which incorporated the principles of the Earth Charter.

Adults know that today's children will be the ones responsible for our society of tomorrow, and I believe the children of Mallorca should have their own environment in which to grow and relate to each other. They also have their own "little forum" where, with ideas and resources appropriate to their ages – games, stories, dialogues, drawings, and songs – they learn to talk, live, and have fun together. In this way, we work towards the defense and construction of a more just, responsible, kind, and happy society. In this process, the "Fòrum d'Infants," as a basis for its formation, incorporated the Earth Charter. Its principles were developed in a reflective, active and playful way: "The Earth is our house. We are part of an immense universe. What we can accomplish. Respect and care for living beings. In life, all is connected. Each person should have what they need to be able to live. No to war, yes to peace."

Eventually, the children of today will be responsible for our society tomorrow; therefore, children have to be educated as citizens of the planet Earth and inheritors of all its values and riches. With the Earth Charter, children learn that "another world is possible" – and another Mallorca too! ●

Sally Linder and Cameron Davis, USA. A project descriptive essay which speaks to Principle 14 on promoting the arts in sustainability education

# The Ark of Hope and The Temenos Books

**Sally Linder** is an artist/painter. She designed and painted the Ark of Hope and co-created the Temenos Books Project and the Earth Charter celebratory event For Love of Earth. Accompanying the Ark of Hope on its memorable 350 mile walking journey to the United Nations, she continues to travel with it around the world, exposing educators and lay citizens to the Earth Charter through Temenos Bookmaking. Since returning from the 2002 World Summit on Sustainable Development, Sally has been painting the luminous people and land of Johannesburg, South Africa's informal settlements. Exhibitions of her art have been held in Indonesia, Africa, the United States, India, Canada, and The Netherlands.

**Cameron Davis** is an artist/painter who co-created the community arts project Temenos Books, Images for Global Healing, Peace and Gratitude, and the event For Love of Earth: A Celebration of the Earth Charter, September 9, 2001, Shelburne Farms, Vermont, USA. Davis is on the faculty of Department of Art and Environmental Program at the University of Vermont in Burlington, Vermont. She has worked with graduate students developing curricula reflecting the Earth Charter principles, and continues to utilize the Earth Charter as a framework for content and assignments in her undergraduate interdisciplinary course, Painting and Issues of Ecological Perception.

Migrating butterflies rest on the Ark of Hope, their fragile wings covering the paintings on the large wooden chest; pictures of a bodhi tree wafting in the breeze, Nigerian yam beetles crawling underground, a blue hilal casting a shadow on the bowed head of a Vietnamese girl in a wheelchair. Whether in brushstrokes of spiraling spring waters, or vivid summer colors, the Ark's painted flora and fauna portray a harmony that reflects the Earth Charter's vision.

Lifting the Ark's lid reveals the Charter hand-scripted on papyrus paper. The papyrus ripples from the moisture of the rivers followed by people conveying the 500-pound Ark to the United Nations. Inside the Ark lie handmade Temenos Books of painted prayers and affirmations for a hopeful future. The Earth Charter story is enacted in these interwoven relationships of butterflies and Ark, Nigeria and Vietnam, rivers and people.

Hundreds of lap-sized Temenos Books nestled in the Ark form an imaginatively diverse community. The project title, "Temenos," indicates a protected circle where the extraordinary can occur. Each book, crafted from wood or cloth, wire or paper, holds pages of images and text reflecting each contributor's personal and tactile response to the Earth Charter. Together, the Ark of Hope and Temenos Books have awakened more than ten thousand people around the world to the promise of the Charter, warming their hearts to its principles and energizing their imaginations with its tremendous potential.

The community art projects of Temenos Books, Images for Global Healing, Peace and Gratitude, and the Temenos Earth Masks, emerged from the conviction that envisioning an act of compassion is the first step to living it. From our experience, we knew that art has the capacity to engage inner dialogue with the external issues of the world. We facilitated contemplative gatherings using meditation bells, silence, ceremonies of deep time, and ecological awareness games. The Earth Charter principles guided the content as project participants worked with paints, scraps of colored papers, feathers, leaves, and pebbles to create images on individual pages, entire art books, or giant masks. Indeed, the extraordinary occurred. Deepest desires and dreams are embodied in each Temenos Book. The principles of the Earth Charter aided participants' emerging understanding of an interdependent world, generating a collective hope in attaining a sustainable and peacefully-shared Earth home.

Teachers from Indiana, USA, to Johannesburg, South Africa, embraced the project as a means to relate their curriculums to a global expression of sustainability and non-violence. One Temenos Book's accordion pages unfold in long trains of painted oceans and jungles teeming with endangered species; another has paintings of trees watered by clouds while birds fly amongst sari-, chador-, and jean-clad

Principle 14. Integrate into formal education and life-longlearning the knowledge, values, and skills needed for a sustainable way of life.

children skipping rope. Its last page displays a huge hand touching big red lips with the caption, "Let Our Smiles Touch One Another." Crafting hand-dyed, felt-covered books, 900 children in one Vermont school witnessed their connection with farmers, sheep, wool, vegetables, and the world community. Older students added another link by using their Temenos Books to educate local governments about the Earth Charter, encouraging its endorsement by twenty-two Vermont towns. University students unleashed their own creative ways to introduce the Earth Charter – beating drums, wearing costumes, and zooming into schools and cafes on roller blades.

On September 9, 2001, the largest Temenos gathering took place at Shelburne Farms, Vermont. For over a year we planned the event, For Love of Earth, A Celebration of the Earth Charter. The day opened in silence as a half-mile ribbon of 2000 people followed a well-worn cow path in the early morning mist. We walked slowly, deliberately, tracing Earth's contours with our steps. Arriving at the massive barn, we entered a protected circle, fecund with scents of timber and hay. A parade of three hundred children surrounded us with giant Temenos Earth Masks of stars and sunflowers, bears and bumblebees. Musicians, speakers, dancers, and singers brought forth the Earth Charter principles. Cascading rice kernels "fed the world," yards of floating gossamer cloth brushed overhead, and large snow geese puppets called as peace gently sifted down and settled into our hearts. On tables graced with art supplies, participants painted their hopes onto Temenos pages. Nestled in a circle of straw lit by late afternoon light, the Ark of Hope was unveiled and the tiny book gifted to it. The Ark was envisioned as a protective holding place for a copy of the Earth Charter and the precious cargo of Temenos Books. When all had been sung and said and given, people returned home with an enriched under-standing of the Earth Charter.

Two days later, 9/11 stunned the world. Grabbed by a powerful instinct, three of us picked up the weighty Ark of Hope and began a two-month, 350-mile walking journey to the United Nations. The simple act of walking, the strain of intention, and the depth of commitment grounded the thousands who joined the pilgrimage. Sweating hands left a golden patina on the carved wooden unicorn horns used as carrying poles. Traveling at three miles per hour gave plenty of time to discuss the Charter with farmers over fences, and car salesmen in parking lots. People can be wary of political brochures; yet walking a beautiful box filled with something unknown picqued curiosity, softened hearts, and initiated conversations. Through the power of grassroots' networking, families, schools, and faith centers hosted the Ark. Sidewalks and river banks provided ample surface for interested folk to color new Temenos pages. Four months later the United Nations opened its doors – exhibiting the Ark of Hope and Temenos Books.

In the summer of 2002, several of the Ark walkers traveled to South Africa to share the Ark of Hope and create more Temenos Books with youth from Johan-nesburg's informal settlements. In an official event at the World Summit on Sustainable Development, the youth gifted the Ark of Hope to the world.

Grass-roots' networking and the website, www.arkofhope.org, continue the momentum of the Ark of Hope and Temenos Books by informing the public of the opportunity to host the Ark of Hope in their country's communities, thereby promoting a hands-on intro-duction to the Earth Charter. Website instructions on Temenos Bookmaking encourage organizations, schools, and individuals to create their own Temenos Books to add to the growing collection of books housed in the Ark.

Whether it is women of India twisting strands of silk into visual prayers of hope or Dutch families paddling the Ark down Amsterdam's canals, the Ark of Hope and Temenos Books are a living testament to a collective understanding of interdependence and shared respon-sibility. They carry hope, inspiration, and courage for the possibilities of the Earth Charter. ●

Richard M. Clugston and John A. Hoyt, USA. A thematic essay which speaks to
Principle 15 on humane animal treatment and humane sustainable development

# The Earth Charter and Animals

**Rick Clugston** is Executive Director of the Center for Respect of Life and Environment, and publisher and editor of *Earth Ethics*. He is Vice President for Higher Education of the Humane Society of the United States. He directs the Secretariat of University Leaders for a Sustainable Future and the Secretariat for the Earth Charter USA Campaign. Dr. Clugston currently serves as the Chair of the Global Higher Education for Sustainability Partnership, and is the Deputy Editor of *The International Journal of Sustainability in Higher Education*. He serves on the Steering Committee of the Earth Charter Initiative.

**John A. Hoyt**, former President and Chief Executive Officer of The Humane Society of the United States, has been a member of the Earth Charter Commission since its formation in 1994. As President of one of the largest animal protection organizations in the world, Mr. Hoyt's principal contribution to the Earth Charter document was a concern for the respect and protection of individual non-human creatures. Mr. Hoyt, in concert with Rick Clugston, through the Center for Respect of Life and Environment of the Humane Society of the United States, has been one of the major financial contributors to the advancement of the Earth Charter internationally. Mr. Hoyt has spoken widely throughout the United States in advancing the acceptance and utilization of the Earth Charter.

While most people would agree that we should treat all animals well, concern for our fellow sentient beings is not present in high-level discussions about development policy. Over the past twenty years there have been intense national and international debates over the limits of the dominant economic model and the meaning of a possibly more effective alternative called sustainable development. A major problem in the current approach to fostering global economic development is the assumption that nonhuman animals and nature are "objects" which have no intrinsic worth or moral claim on us, and which human societies can exploit for even trivial humans ends. Our economic, legal, and political systems embody this anthropocentric and mechanistic premise in their principles and practices.

The worldviews, of both modern science and European Christianity, that shaped our globalizing economies have encouraged human beings to exploit animals with little regard for their suffering. Francis Bacon and René Descartes, founders of modern science, believed that only humans have souls and that nature is just a great machine. Descartes regarded the screams of animals being vivisected as no more than the noise a machine makes as it breaks down, a mere grinding of gears. So, too, has the Christian church emphasized human dominion over the Earth and all its creatures. Too often dominion has been interpreted to mean domination – implying that the only value of the rest of creation is its utility to humans. Hence, our economic task is only to exploit these natural resources efficiently.

Such worldviews must change if we are to create a sustainable future. Scientists, religious leaders, educators, and politicians must begin to recognize that the community of life on Earth, as Thomas Berry says, is a "communion of subjects, not a collection of objects." With such a shift in worldviews, our economics, science, and education would cultivate compassion for all sentient beings and contribute to lifestyles and business practices that are ecologically sound, socially just, and humane, as well as economically beneficial.

As Steven Rockefeller states:

> A major objective of the Earth Charter is to promote a fundamental change in the attitudes toward nature that have been predominant in industrial-technological civilization, leading to a transformation in the way people interact with Earth's ecological systems, animals, and other nonhuman species. Humanity must, of course, use natural resources in order to survive and develop. However, the Earth Charter rejects the widespread modern view that the larger natural world is merely a collection of resources that exists to be exploited by human beings. It endeavors to inspire in all peoples commitment to a new ethic of respect and care for the community of life.[1]

The Earth Charter is the first major international document that makes the humane treatment of individual animals a necessary condition for sustainable development. As a past president, and a current vice president of The Humane Society of the United States, we are committed to the preservation and protection of animals – not just species, but particular animals subjected to unwarranted and unjustified abuse and suffering. Happily, the Earth Charter, for the first time in any international document of this sort, recognizes and embraces this concern.

Principle 1.a reads, "Recognize that all beings are interdependent and every form of life has value regardless of its worth to human beings." What this principle acknowledges is that sustainability is not exclusively about the human situation, but must address all beings and acknowledge our mutual interdependence with all living beings and ecological systems.

In addition to its general affirmation of a non-anthropocentric worldview, the Earth Charter also includes a major principle and three sub-principles focused on animal protection, 15.a, b, and c. Unfortunately, from the authors' point of view, the subprinciples for Principle 15 do not reflect a coherent agenda for animal protection. Rather they reflect what the drafting committee members could agree upon. A fuller development of an animal protection agenda foundered with major disagreements about whether the Earth Charter should condone the use of animals for food or medical research under any circumstance. Inuit hunters, Hindus, and Jains advocating nonviolence toward animals, representatives of a major animal protection organization, and others could not find much common ground. So proposed principles were dropped to guide appropriate laboratory tests on animals, or the conditions for raising and slaughtering cattle, chickens, and hogs for food.

Thus, Subprinciple 15.a is only an assertion that domesticated animals should be treated humanely, without mentioning specific contexts. Subprinciples 15.b and 15.c. address wild animals, asserting that methods of hunting, trapping, and fishing should neither cause unnecessary suffering to the target animals, nor be so inexact that non-targeted animals are killed.

Clearly, more fully developed animal protection principles would need to set guidelines for direct and indirect human impacts on the lives of animals. The Humane Society of the United States describes some of these challenges:

> Humans have exploited some animal species to the point of extinction. Research animals suffer pain and distress in laboratory tests considered necessary for human health or well-being. Animals killed for fur fashions endure unimaginable agony in inhumane traps or on fur 'ranches.' Animals used by the food industry live on factory farms where they are treated as unfeeling commodities rather than as sentient beings. The use of animal parts for traditional medicines has contributed to the disappearance of some species worldwide.

Animals raised as pets, or used in circuses, or for other forms of entertainment often suffer. Development decisions rarely consider the impact on individual animals. In factory farming, millions of animals are crammed into small cages and pens, never seeing the light of day in an attempt to reduce the costs per unit of production. This development approach creates terrible consequences: cruelty toward farmed animals; the environmental impact of their wastes; worker safety and health; public health concerns from antibiotics and contaminated meat; and the quality and viability of rural life. Factory farming – with all these negatives – may be an issue that helps wake up the public to the need for a new political economy that values rural communities, animals, Earth, and future generations. It shows the inhumaneness of the current economic and political system underlying globalization, which discounts future generations, externalizes social and environmental costs, and fails to recognize the sentience of animals, or ecological integrity. There is a better way. The path toward food security for all and enduring well-being of rural communities, animals, and Earth is being articulated and practiced by a wide range of groups. The Earth Charter as a guide to sustainable development can help shape a new economy and a new agriculture that respects and cares for the community of life.

A major task to be completed in the future is to refine what the principles and sub-principles of the Earth Charter statements will mean ultimately in, as "The Way Forward" section states, "an international legally binding instrument on environment and development" (paragraph four). The Earth Charter presents a consensus vision of an integrated agenda for the pursuit of peace, social and economic justice, and the protection of cultural and biological diversity. It affirms that each of these important goals can only be achieved if all are achieved. Justice, peace, and ecological integrity are inextricably intertwined. We can only care for people if we care for the planet. We can only protect ecosystems if we care for people by providing freedom, eradicating poverty, and promoting good governance. The Earth Charter identifies, in a succinct and inspiring way, the necessary and sufficient conditions for promoting a just and sustainable future.

The remarkable contribution of the Earth Charter is to make respect for and the protection of individual animals a necessary condition for sustainable development. It also challenges those of us focused on our particular interests to work together with others for a larger integrated agenda. We, as animal protectionists, must recognize that our agenda cannot be achieved without alleviating poverty, empowering women, and protecting ecosystems. So, too, must those who care primarily about poverty alleviation, women's health, climate change, and other issues recognize that animal protection is an essential dimension of a sustainable future. ●

**Note**

1    Rockefeller, S.C. (2004). "Earth Charter ethics and animals." *Earth Ethics*, Spring 2004, p. 5.

Sylvannus Murray, Sierra Leone. A project descriptive essay which speaks to Principle 16 on encouraging and supporting mutual understanding, solidarity, and cooperation

# Using the Earth Charter with Ex-combatants in Sierra Leone

**Sylvanus Murray** is a graphic designer, presently working with the United Nations Mission in Sierra Leone as an Information Assistant. He he has taken on youth leadership roles in his church and community as early as 1992. Since then, he has been actively involved in youth work at national and international levels. Mr. Murray founded the Youth Empowerment for Development Ministries in 1998. It is a non-profit, non-governmental, non-partisan umbrella youth organisation seeking to address the welfare of young people in Sierra Leone and beyond. Mr. Murray works with the Earth Charter Youth Initiative and coordinates the Earth Charter Youth Group in Sierra Leone.

S ierra Leone currently faces the challenge of social reconstruction after enduring a decade-long war that was concluded in 2002. It claimed some 50,000 victims and left thousands of people injured and traumatized. The women and youths were mostly affected. Deeply perceived in their traditional roles as housekeepers and child-bearers, women were relegated to the back in all aspects of socio- political and community discourses. The outbreak of war further worsened their conditions. They were largely left to protect themselves and their children as most men departed the villages and towns to hide in the bushes while others joined the

government troops, the civil defence militia, or the rebel force of the Revolutionary United Front (RUF). Hence women became vulnerable to all the warring factions. Most of them were raped, brutally assaulted, or even maimed and amputated.

The Sierra Leonean youth faced a similar situation. In the pre-war period, young people formed an alarming percentage of the uneducated and unemployed portion of the population and had no significant influence upon policy formulation or decision-making. The devastating economic situation made many of them join the armed groups. Others were forcibly conscripted. Thus, young people largely comprised the bulk of the warring factions, whereas only a very small number of them were among the decision-makers. They took instructions from their commanders to loot, burn, maim, rape, and kill. According to testimonies from the Truth and Reconciliation Commission (TRC), youths serving as soldiers were drugged and ill- trained and forced to commit the cruellest human rights violations against innocent civilians of their communities. Some of them were even forced to commit atrocities against their own parents. Thus, the issue of reconciling ex-combatants with their local communities is imperative in our current post-war situation. Here, the Earth Charter comes into play as its ethical vision of sustainability, non-violence and peace can serve as a guideline in the effort of promoting a culture of peace and toleration.

Therefore, we held several meetings with leaders of various youth organizations at which the Earth Charter was discussed in the light of our major concerns of post-war reconstruction and economic development. The meetings culminated in the establishment of a committee of twenty representatives drawn from different, umbrella youth organizations and community based organizations which is called Earth Charter Youth Group – Sierra Leone (ECYG-SL). The group pinpointed on Principle 16 which elaborates the components of a global society at peace, including tolerance and non-violence. The group was conscious of the fact that tolerance is indispensable for understanding, solidarity, and cooperation in the post-war reconstruction efforts of the Sierra Leonean youth.

In one of our major early activities, we participated in a week-long workshop at the second capital city of Bo and introduced the Earth Charter to the other 350 participants. The result was great –

*Principle 16. Promote a culture of tolerance, nonviolence and peace.*

giving birth to two further Earth Charter Youth Groups in Bo. Another group of twenty youth leaders was established in the east-end of the capital, Freetown. The creation of this second group in Freetown enabled young people from that part of the city to work together in not only incorporating the principles of the Earth Charter and practicing them, but to also take the Charter to other members of their groups and communities.

The ECYG-SL used the tenets of Earth Charter Principle 16 to encourage and support mutual understanding, solidarity, and cooperation between the ex-combatants and other members of the community. This is mostly done through organizing community meetings and conducting sensitization sessions aimed at fostering dialogues and discussions about the values of sustainable development and peace among the participants. In one of these sessions, we addressed ex-combatants who were trainees of the vocational training centre of Peacelinks. One of our main points was that, as young men who are currently being disarmed, demobilized and are now on the verge of been reintegrated into society, it is of vital importance that the former fighters are informed about issues that are happening around them, both at national and international levels. The main cause for one of the most brutal conflicts in the history of the country was the lack of true information. When people are well-informed, they can be also empowered to participate in projects that can help to develop and

safeguard their communities. It was further emphasized that if we want to find better ecological, economic, political, cultural, and even spiritual ways of protecting human societies, we need to demilitarize our minds and support mutual understanding, solidarity, and cooperation among all peoples and within and among nations. The concluding discussion about the possibilities for future collaboration and the presentation of a series of publications about the Earth Charter formed the highpoints of the sensitization.

Among the groups which endorse the Charter and partner with the ECYG-SL is the Firestone Cultural Community Development Organization (FCCDO,). The FCCDO has not only introduced the Earth Charter to youth and children of the community, but it has also been using the Earth Charter as a comprehensive strategy to prevent violent conflict and to manage and resolve environmental conflicts and other disputes. One of such comprehensive strategies that takes heed to the interrelation of ecological, economic, and security concerns is the introduction of home-garbage collection for members of the Firestone Community. Initially, members of the community sent their children, or wards, to dispose of their garbage in a nearby Nicol Stream, which is used by many as a source of drinking water and other domestic purposes. This engendered frequent quarrels among members of the community which sometimes resulted in violent conflicts

and police matters. The ECYG-SL, comprising members from FCCDO, introduced the collection of garbage from the homes of community residents. Using principles of the Earth Charter, the members were able to persuade community members to join the program. This created some form of employment for young people, helped to create conducive sanitary conditions in the community, and also reduced the number of conflicts about the pollution of the river as the garbage is now deposited at the government-approved dump site at Bomeh.

This activity gives proof to the fact that environmental protection, economic development, and peace are inextricably linked. In search of a new vision that promotes economic stability, respect for all forms of life, good governance, human rights, and democracy, the youths in our country have found the Earth Charter as a guiding document. Inadequate shelter, food, health care, and education are widely considered as some of causes that led to the ten-year war and have the potential of dragging the country into another round of social turmoil. Therefore, these issues must be addressed in an integrated approach, as it is outlined in the Earth Charter. ●

Martin Lees, Scotland. A project descriptive essay which speaks to Principle 16 on education at the University for Peace

# The Earth Charter as a Guide to Building a Culture of Peace and Sustainable Development

After some years as a manager in industry, **Martin Lees** started a thirty-year international career at the Organisation for Economic Co-operation and Development where he was responsible for programmes on Cooperation in Science and Technology, on the Procedures and Structures of Government, and the "InterFutures Project" on the long-term future of the world economy. He then served at the United Nations in several capacities and in 1982, he was appointed Assistant Secretary General for Science and Technology for Development. He has also been responsible for several high level programmes of international cooperation with China. From 1991 to 1996, he developed and implemented programmes of cooperation with the Newly Independent States of the Former Soviet Union, as Director General of the International Committee for Economic Reform and Cooperation. For two years, he assisted in the revitalization of the University for Peace as Director for Programme Development, leading to his appointment as Rector, 2001-2005.

In spite of undoubted progress, we will leave to our successors a difficult and dangerous world which still suffers from injustice, threats to peace, and abiding poverty for millions. There is, consequently, an intense and deep public concern about the state of our world, about relations between peoples and ethnic and religious groups, and about the prospects for peace and equitable development for future generations.

We can no longer rely on the concepts and policies which have guided us since the Second World War. We need a transformation of thinking, new strategies, and the mobilization of public support and commitment to address the threats to peace and progress in the twenty-first century.

Here, the stated mission of the Earth Charter takes on a profound importance: "to establish a sound ethical foundation for the emerging global society and to help build a sustainable world based on respect for nature, universal human rights, economic justice, and a culture of peace." Representing the accumulated wisdom of a wide diversity of groups and interests brought together over an extended period through a worldwide process of consultation, the Earth Charter serves as a basis for dialogue and the evolution of new values and approaches adapted to the needs of the twenty-first century.

Over the past five years, the Earth Charter has demonstrated its value as an educational tool, as a catalyst for dialogue, as a framework of values, and as a call to action. For this reason, the Council of the University for Peace (UPEACE) has formally endorsed the Earth Charter, which has come to play an important role in the conception, design, and implementation of the newly developed academic programme of the University. UPEACE has oriented its programmes of education, training, and research for peace to focus on issues critical to the Earth Charter's four major themes: respect and care for the community of life; ecological integrity; social and economic justice; and democracy, nonviolence, and peace. Moreover, we are teaching in critical fields that contribute to a culture of peace. These include academic programs in: Human Rights; International Law; Peace and Conflict Studies; Peace Education; Gender and Peace Building; Environmental Security; Media and Peace; Economic Development, Peace and Security; and Disarmament and Non-Proliferation.

To develop a global strategy to achieve a culture of peace, we must clarify the causes of violence and conflict in the modern world. In the past, conflict occurred principally between sovereign states. However, in recent decades, the nature of most conflict has changed. Today, the overwhelming majority of armed conflicts take place within, not between, states. One tragic consequence of this mutation in the nature of conflict is that approximately ninety percent of all those now killed in conflict are civilians – most often women, children, and the elderly.

Establishing a culture of peace depends on the many motivated and expert men and women in, and from, the countries concerned who can work to achieve reconciliation and reconstruct equitable societies. And, peace and progress can

Principle 16. Promote a culture of tolerance, nonviolence and peace.

The Earth Charter in Action

Part IV: Democracy, Nonviolence, and Peace   153

only be sustained if deeply-entrenched attitudes and behavior throughout society at large can be changed, away from hatred, intolerance, and violence and towards solidarity, respect for human rights, gender equity, and reconciliation. In both these vital respects, the role of education for peace, through many channels and at every level, is of fundamental importance, as reflected in the mission and programme of the University for Peace.

What is the meaning of "peace"? Peace is not simply the absence of conflict. Rather, think of peace in the same way as you think of health. Being truly healthy is much more than simply not being sick. True health means living an active, productive life; pursuing your aspirations; and even contributing to the happiness of others. Thus, when we wish for a culture of peace, we wish for a world of security, justice, dignity, solidarity, opportunity, progress, and hope for the vast majority of human kind. We wish in fact for a world to the measure of the high aims of the Earth Charter! We are far from this today.

We can, in fact, only achieve security for ourselves if the world around us is peaceful and prosperous. Our security and progress are, in the long term, indivisible from the security and progress of others. A pre-condition for peace in the twenty-first century is the creation, through national and international cooperation and action by governments and civil society, of conditions in which the vast majority of our fellow humans can feel secure and hopeful in their lives.

We do have the capacity to create a better world. It is not simply a question of resources – we have seen how vast resources can be rapidly made available for war. As made clear by the Earth Charter, it is a question of values, priorities, organization, and will.

The threats to the lives, security, and well-being of hundreds of millions of people in the coming century will not

arise only from the willful consequences of conflict – "man's inhumanity to man" – but also from economic and environmental pressures such as poverty, famine, pollution, and disease, and the collapse in "failed states" of the minimum social and political capabilities essential to preserve the framework of stable, peaceful societies. We are, in fact, challenged to manage systemic problems of increasing complexity and under conditions of dynamic change, substantial uncertainty, and risk. A more systematic, interdisciplinary approach must be developed which recognizes the key relationships between the issues we face and also between the strategies and policies to address them. This approach commands a new respect for international solidarity and cooperation and shared ethical principles. It must take full account of the diversity of ideas, aspirations, and approaches in our pluralist world. In all these respects, the Earth Charter provides a guide and a starting point.

If we are to manage our future problems, we will need a new generation of leaders, adapted to the conditions and challenges of the modern world. They will have longer-term vision and commitment to the future of humanity. They will be able to operate across disciplinary, sectoral, and institutional boundaries. And, they will not be prejudiced by narrow ideological or national views; they will be open to different cultural insights and opinions.

This is an immediate challenge to our academic institutions – to undertake the interdisciplinary and multicultural research and teaching on which new policies and leadership must be based. The new generation of leaders and teachers, if they are to function effectively in the modern world, must be willing to recognize their own limitations – to understand that they themselves have been conditioned by their own backgrounds and experience. They must not believe that their task is to impose on others their own opinions because they consider these to be unambigu-

ously correct. They may then be able to function successfully in a pluralist world, benefiting from and respecting diverse cultures and opinions while retaining a clear sense of purpose for the common good.

In our increasingly interdependent world, it will simply not be feasible in the longer term for the wealthy and privileged of the planet to defend their advantages by military means, or by vast expenditures of human ingenuity and material resources. We must renew our efforts to strengthen international solidarity and cooperation to build solid foundations for world peace.

Our planet is at risk of separating into two worlds within and between countries – a relatively safe world of wealth and privilege and a dangerous world of poverty and hunger, injustice, and misery. But, these two worlds are fundamentally interdependent – through environment and climate change; through the movement of people, through migration, and mass tourism; and in the face of rapidly spreading, deadly diseases which respect no national boundaries. We now understand that we are also obliged to face together the threats of international crime and terrorism which affect developed and developing countries alike.

In effect, the well-being and the security of all of us depend directly and indirectly on an intricate web of international relationships and cooperation, which, in turn, depend on good will, trust, and common interest among groups and nations – easily destroyed, very difficult to reconstitute. To achieve a culture of peace, we must explicitly strengthen international solidarity, trust, and cooperation. On the positive side, humanity has never had greater resources in terms of knowledge, skills, technological systems, and resources to address threats to peace, security, and development. But, these resources are not effectively applied on a significant scale to prevent conflict and build the foundations of solidarity and peace. The flows of resources to stimulate development remain small in relation to the needs and opportunities.

Our current policies, principally focused on reaction to specific and immediate problems, are not, in fact, laying the foundations for sustainable peace. In the absence of a renewed and concerted effort engaging the whole world community to prevent conflict and to build the foundations of peace and progress, the prospects for peace and security in the twenty-first century are limited, even for the most wealthy and powerful countries.

Committing ourselves in practice to sustainable peace requires new ideas, new policies, and new leadership, as so clearly set out in the Earth Charter. Education for peace can make a critical contribution. The developing countries and the countries in transition cannot be stable and cannot reduce poverty, illiteracy, hunger, and disease unless violence and conflict can be prevented and resolved. And, this can only be achieved if there are thousands of leaders, teachers, and professionals in these countries who work to prevent and mediate conflict and achieve reconciliation; teach non-violence, tolerance and human rights; build the basis of good governance, justice, and democracy; and undertake the programs needed to achieve equitable and sustainable development. To prevent conflict, it is essential to achieve a culture of peace in society as a whole by changing attitudes and behaviour away from intolerance, hatred, and violence, and towards tolerance, reconciliation, respect for human rights and gender equity, and mutual understanding among different ethnic, religious, and cultural groups. Such changes in deeply-held beliefs and attitudes can only be encouraged by education through many formal and informal channels and through a positive role of the media.

Strengthening educational capacities in developing and transition countries to provide teaching, training, and research on critical issues of peace and development at every level has emerged as an increasingly important means to build the foundations of peace and progress. Also important will be widely informing men, women, and children in the developed countries on world issues and peace education. Voters in these democracies must become aware of and understand the present and future realities of world affairs if they are to support the outward-looking, longer-term policies needed to achieve a secure and peaceful world for all.

By disseminating knowledge and supporting efforts throughout the world to educate a new generation of leaders, teachers, and experts on the critical issues of conflict prevention and the building of peace, we can contribute to a more peaceful and secure future for humanity. And in this global effort, the Earth Charter will play an important part. ●

Principle 16. Promote a culture of tolerance, nonviolence and peace.

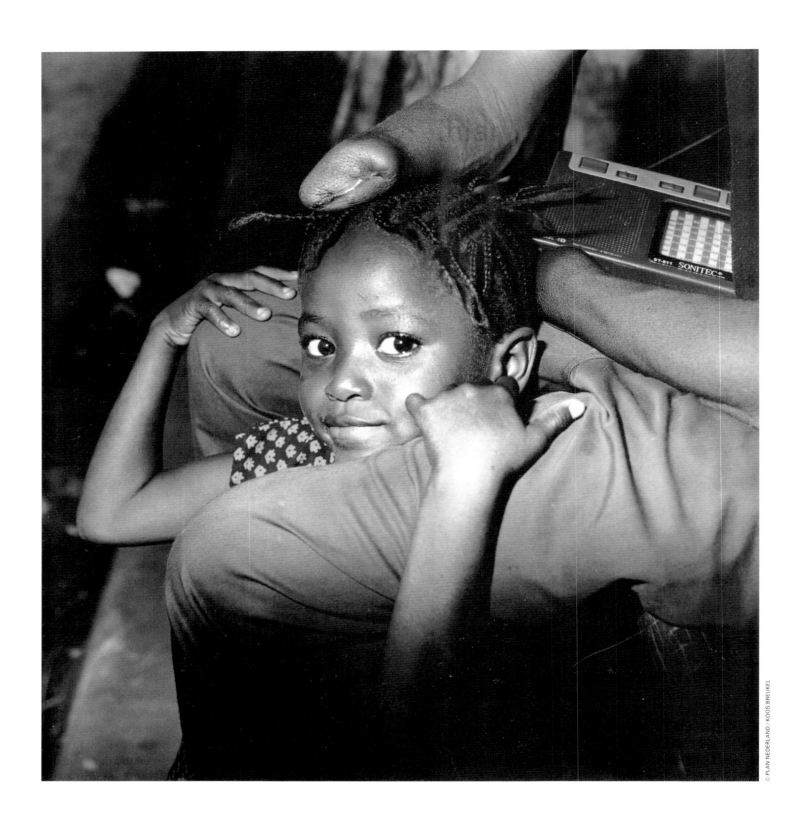

Mohamed Sahnoun, Algeria. A thematic essay which speaks to Principle 16 on using the Earth Charter to resolve the root causes of violent conflict in Africa

# Degradation of the Environment as the Cause of Violent Conflict

**Mohamed Sahnoun** has had a distinguished diplomatic career serving as Adviser to the President of Algeria on diplomatic affairs, Deputy Secretary-General of the Organization of African Unity (OAU), and Deputy Secretary-General of the League of Arab States in charge of the Arab-Africa dialogue. He has served as Algeria's Ambassador to the United States, France, Germany, and Morocco, as well as to the United Nations (UN). Mr. Sahnoun is currently Secretary General Kofi Annan's Special Adviser in the Horn of Africa region. Previously, he served as Special Adviser to the Director General of the United Nations Scientific and Cultural Organization (UNESCO) for the Culture of Peace Programme, Special Envoy of the Secretary-General on the Ethiopian/Eritrean conflict (1998-1999), Joint Representative of the UN and the OAU in the Great Lakes region (1997), Special Representative of the UN Secretary General to Somalia (1992). He was a member of the World Commission on Environment and Development (the Brundtland Commission) in the 1980s, as well as Senior Adviser to the Secretary General of the United Nations Conference on Environment and Development in 1992.

In Somalia there is a young boy. When he goes to the well to water his herd of sheep, he meets another Somali with his herd. They look at each other very suspiciously, and one says to the other, "Who are you?" And the other says, "I am the son of so-and-so, who is the son of so-and-so," and they go through the lineage of their fathers to determine if they are from the same clan. If they recognize that they are from the same great-grandfather, they shake hands and water the herds. But if they don't, then one will tell the other, "Why the hell are you coming here to water at this well? This well goes back to my grand-grandfather, why do you come here and take our water? This is our water, not yours." And so, they start fighting. This is a typical Somali example where the environment is a very important factor in violent conflict. The people there speak the same language, are of the same ethnic group, and are largely of the same religion. But in actuality, Somalis are divided into clans and sub-clans fighting each other over natural resources like

water and grazing land. Before, the fighting was with sticks; now it is with Kalashnikovs. That is the terrible thing about it. There is no difference there; they are the same people.

I am often a witness in my work of the linkage between the degradation of the environment and the spread of violent conflicts. We tend to underestimate the impact of degradation of the environment on human security everywhere. Repeated droughts, land erosion, desertification, and deforestation brought about by climate change and natural disasters compel large groups to move from one area to another, which, in turn, increases pressure on scarce resources, and provokes strong reaction from local populations. It is the issue of insecurity brought about by the prospect of exclusion from resources, or the perceived threat of starvation, that ignite most violent conflicts. This feeling of insecurity is often brought about by degradation of the environment.

It is my conviction that prevention, and prevention only, based on long-term common interests and solidarity, is the solution to the terrible tragedy brought about by violent conflicts across Africa. Prevention includes sustainable development. The Earth Charter will enable us to chart better the path to sustainable development. It calls us to "implement comprehensive strategies to prevent violent conflict and use collaborative problem solving to manage and resolve environmental conflicts and other disputes" (Subprinciple 16.b). The Earth Charter maps a path which minimizes the stress on our environment and encourages us to build democratic societies that are just, participatory, sustainable, and peaceful (Principle 4).

I began my career as an international civil servant as Deputy Secretary General of the Organization of African Unity. I began in the early 1960s in Adidas Ababa, Ethiopia, dealing with the nascent conflicts of that time, such as border conflicts, guerrilla wars, and internal conflicts. From the beginning, I saw the association of environment and security. I was struck clearly by the fact that most often, if not all the time, crises were direct consequences of the degradation of the environment, such as repeated droughts, deforestation, and erosion. When we were tackling the problem of violent conflict, we knew that what we

Principle 16. Promote a culture of tolerance, nonviolence and peace.

were doing in resolving this conflict was really only a temporary thing. We were able to get the parties of the conflict into a temporary agreement, but the root causes of insecurity were not tackled.

This insecurity was brought about by the uncertainty of the future. People were not sure what would happen to them in the years to come, in the months to come, and, sometimes, in the days to come. People were not sure about the children – whether they could send them to school, whether they could nourish them, or whether they could feed them. Therefore, because of that anguish and that insecurity, there was a tendency to join a tribal group or a clan to seek refuge and to defend the interest in that clan system or within that tribal system–even if that kind of logic was leading to war, or was not really leading to resolving or giving an answer to their problems. There is no rationale for people who are in that situation; they only look for survival.

Very early on I joined Maurice F. Strong in lobbying for Africa to join the 1972 United Nations Conference on the Human Environment in Stockholm, Sweden. The great thing which Maurice Strong did was to plead for the headquarters of the United Nations Environment Programme to be established in Nairobi, Kenya. It was the first time that an international organization had its headquarters in the developing world. Until then, the institutions were only in New York, Geneva, or Vienna. From Nairobi, people realized the conflicts are because there is environmental degradation.

The Earth Charter calls for the need to "eradicate poverty as an ethical, social, and environmental imperative" (Principle 9). To eradicate poverty is to address the root cause of the problem of security – through granting to people "the right to potable water, clean air, food, security, uncontaminated soil, shelter, and safe sanitation" (Subprinciple 9.a). That is a very, very important element which the Charter puts right at the beginning of Part III, Social and Economic Justice. That's one way of doing it, and, of course, Principle 3 is also a very, very essential call for the promotion of societies that are "just, participatory, sustainable, and peaceful," and, therefore, in a sense, tackle the root causes of conflict.

As United Nations Special Representative to the Secretary General on Somalia, and now as Special Advisor to the Horn of Africa, I do a lot of mediation, especially now on the Sudan peace process. A peace agreement was signed in January 2005. But this is the second agreement that was signed, as we had already signed an earlier agreement in 1972 when I was in Adidas Ababa. It was signed by the North and South leaders of Sudan, but it only held for eleven years. In 1983, war started again because we did not address the root causes. And now, even after we have signed a new peace agreement, there is no real lobbying and no real interest on the part of the part of the international community, on the part of the big powers of the

developed world, to see to it that some of the root causes of the conflict are resolved. For example, very often the Horn of Africa is subject to erosion and drought. In the high parts of Ethiopia, the rainy seasons can be very cold and people need a heating system. All they can do is cut the trees. The Horn of Africa has lost over fifty percent of its green corridor in just the last half century. Can you imagine the terrible loss of green corridor because, of course, people need wood? They have no alternative. If we don't attack the root causes of environmental degradation and insecurity, the peace agreement we just signed now in Sudan will be jeopardized in just a few years.

When I was dealing with the Great Lakes region of Africa, I said that if we want peace in the long-term, we need a mini-Marshall Plan–something as we did for Europe after the Second World War. In all the legacies of history, we forget that the Cold War was a terrible, terrible problem for the Third World and for developing countries in general. During the Cold War, the two big blocs fought each other through the people of the Third World. They did not encourage good governance and democracy – they were helping dictatorships. If the dictator was with you, that was the most important thing. "If you are with us, we don't care what you do to your people. You are our friend, and, therefore, we support you even if you are a dictator." Human rights and good governance were not at all a priority. It is only now, after the Cold War has ended, that there is really any kind of interest in human rights and good governance.

I believe that by upholding Earth Charter principles, such as "respect Earth and life in all its diversity" (Principle 1), "build democratic societies that are just, participatory, sustainable, and peaceful" (Principle 3), and "secure Earth's bounty and beauty for present and future generations" (Principle 4), we can respond. I believe the Earth Charter is a very adequate and comprehensive response to the call to resolve root causes of insecurity and violent conflict in Africa. It is my hope that the Charter is adopted and endorsed as widely as possible, so that it becomes like the Universal Declaration of Human Rights. In a sense, the Earth Charter is about Earth's rights. One cannot go without the other. We must complete what we have achieved so far in governance and in human rights through the international endorsement of Earth's rights. ●

Principle 16. Promote a culture of tolerance, nonviolence and peace.

158    Part IV: Democracy, Nonviolence, and Peace

The Earth Charter in Action

Muazama Burkhanova, Tajikistan. A thematic essay which speaks to Principle 16 on consultation and participation

# Environmental Problems and Sustainable Development in Tajikistan

**Muazama Burkhanova** is an energy-engineer, an economist, and an ecologist answering practically to all elements of sustainable development. She has worked long years in the Academy of Sciences of the Republic of Tajikistan as the head of Departments of Power and Water Problems, and Rational Environmental Management. Her desire to combine scientific ideas with their realization came through creation in 1995 of a public organization, Foundation to Support Civil Initiatives. It is the first nongovernmental organization of the Republic whose mission has been directed at development of democratic processes through the public sector and civil society. She has been the coordinator of initiatives of the Earth Charter in the Republic of Tajikistan since 1998.

Scientific-technical progress of the twentieth century, with its focus on the fast economic growth, has created abundant material wealth. At the same time, it has increased the pressure of the anthropogenic influence on the environment. As a result of the ruthless exploitation of natural resources, immense wealth is in the possession of a limited number of the world population, whereas the vast majority barely subsides in poverty on the rare humiliating hand-outs from the rich countries. Thus, unsustainable consumption leads humankind to unsustainable development.

The realization of the looming ecological catastrophe forced progressive people of the planet to seek ways of averting the global collapse. The reports of the Club of Rome, for example, made it possible to launch the world-level dialogues that were free from any political, religious, and nationalistic agendas and the influence of the rich states.

Tajikistan got involved in the consultation process in the end of the 1998, when the Fund for Support of Civil Initiatives of the Republic of Tajikistan became a focal point of the Earth Charter for Central Asia established by the Earth Council. In the fall of 2001, the Republican Conference "Tajikistan: The Way to Sustainable Development" was held in Dushanbe, the capital. The Earth Charter was one of the main issues of discussion at this conference. The event was organized by the Tajik National Commission on Sustainable Development and the Fund for Support of Civil Initiatives.[1]

The conference became the final stage in a series of national discussions and hearings held from 1999 to 2001 among governmental agencies, non governmental organizations, schools, universities, and local communities. The conference also adopted the comments and suggestions for the last draft of the Earth Charter on behalf of the Republic of Tajikistan, which were sent to the Earth Charter Secretariat. Among other comments on each paragraph of the last draft of the Earth Charter 2000, reasons were named for its slow dissemination. These included the need to simplify the text, so that it would be clear and accessible to every person, every family, regardless of their station in society, and not only for the specialists and the environmental activists. We felt the Earth Charter must not become yet another ecological initiative; it must reach the hearts of every lay person. Ways of using the Earth Charter principles in the everyday life of people should be developed. We said that besides the protection of the human rights and freedoms, declared in many international documents of the United Nations, the Earth Charter needed to make a stronger emphasis on the rights of Earth and the whole community of life, re-envisioning the environment as not simply an endless provider of natural resources, and protecting it from aggressive and thoughtless treatment.
We believed the text should include a passage about the particular moral responsibility of state leaders at the highest level for any grave ethical violations in the treatment of the Earth which might harm living and the future generations.

In the beginning of the twenty-first century, political will consolidated at a global level. The heads of states adopted in 2000 the United Nations Millennium Declaration and the eight main goals of the Millennium Development Goals (MDGs) that represent the agreed upon international indices by which to assess future results. It is worth noting that Goal 7 of the MDGs, "Ensure environmental sustainability," is a multi-sectoral task, and it plays the leading role in achieving all other the Millennium Development Goals.

In addition to global appeals, we see our personal call and input in the following expression: "think globally, act locally". The development and realization of the programs for sustainable development and environmental sustainability at the local level is one of the main directions of the work of the Republic of Tajikistan NGO, "Foundation to Support Civil Initiatives" (FSCI). The FSCI acts as a coordinator and the expert in the development and realization of the Local Environmental Action Plans (LEAPS). This program raises awareness of grave ecological distortions at the local level, thus influencing long-term national strategies by involving NGOs, scientists, independent experts, and other representatives of civil society.

Another important component of this program is its multi-sectoral approach to decision- making processes. The participation of governmental representatives in the meetings of The Multi-party Council signals that LEAPs are gaining official recognition. At the same time, traditional knowledge of local population is taken into serious consideration during the discussions in The Multiparty Council. They try to reach the decisions that will fully reflect the priorities of the different national districts, enhance the involvement of the local communities and local municipalities, and answer the needs of the local population.

The selected priorities of our LEAP program on the local level speak about the principles of sustainable development and Earth Chapter values. Part of this program conducts trainings corresponding to the aims of project. Our training reflects the following basic principles of the Earth Chapter: sustainable consumption of living, deepened awareness of environmental and economical issues, and empowering people to take concrete actions.

During the period of July 2004 to February 2005, the FSCI successfully carried out a concrete pilot project that resulted in consulting and training activities. Accomplished with the help of the network of the national territories interested in the LEAPs, this pilot project focused on the development of environmental governance for the country's capital, Dushanbe. The FSCI experts worked out the indicators for the detailed analysis of the situation, the potential of the terrain, the priorities for the given region, the results and the recommendations of the project and, finally, the development of the pilot projects for the integration of the environmental and socio-economic objectives facing the city.

As an outcome of this project, the FSCI presented a concise report and recommendations that were accepted by the authorities, approved by the city hall, and included into the plans for Dushanbe's urban development. Some of our urgent recommendations have already received financial support, for example, the approval and the financing of the building of a waste processing plant in Dushanbe.[2]

At the time of this writing, the FSCI has initiated an educational program focused on ways of resolving the multitude of problems facing the city council and the inhabitants of Dushanbe. This has opened a lot of opportunities for the propagation and dissemination of ideas and principles of the Earth Charter, particularly its ethical approach to the Earth – to the extent that the city council of Dushanbe is now considering taking up a long-term sustainable development program based on environmental priorities.

During the training seminars and presentations, it became clear that the development of short- and long-term programs of environmental governance is impossible without using the ethics and principles of the Earth Charter. The Earth Charter Education Toolkit can be used with young and adult persons, students, NGO's, civil board organizations, and is relevant to educators and policy makers for discussion devoted to Earth Charter implementation. ●

**Notes**

1    The materials of the Republican Conference "Tajikistan: The Way to Sustainable Development" can be obtained at the website of our NGO "Foundation to Support Civil Initiatives": http://fsci.freenet.tj/, section "Publications".
2    The Program of the Environmental Management of the Dushanbe city can be found at the websites: http://fsci.freenet.tj/, www.untj.org/library/, www.dushanbe.tj/.

Jan Pronk, The Netherlands. A thematic essay which speaks to Principle 16 in African diplomacy

# The Earth Charter as the Basis for a Comprehensive Approach to Conflicts in Sudan

**Jan Pronk** served for ten years as a member of the Dutch Parliament. Throughout his career, Jan Pronk has played a prominent role in promoting sustainable economic and environmental development. He served three times as Minister for Development Cooperation in the Government in The Netherlands, and as Minister of Environment. Two times he was Chairman of the Intergovernmental Group for Indonesia. He was also President of the United Nations Conference of Parties of the Convention on Climate Change held in The Hague. Mr. Pronk served as the Secretary-General's Special Envoy for the World Summit on Sustainable Development held in Johannesburg in 2002. He was formerly Deputy Secretary-General of the United Nations Conference on Trade and Development from 1980 to 1985, and Assistant Secretary-General of the United Nations from 1985 to 1986. In 1975, he chaired the Committee of the Whole of the 7th Special Session of the General Assembly of the United Nations. Upon his nomination in 2004 as Special Representative for Sudan, Mr. Jan Pronk laid down all positions to dedicate himself completely to the responsibilities and duties entrusted to him by the United Nations' Secretary-General. He is based in Khartoum.

The sixteenth and final principle of the Earth Charter calls for promoting "a culture of tolerance, nonviolence, and peace." Nowhere, at first sight, does the realization of this principle seem further away than in Sudan, with its conflicts in several parts of the country, especially in Darfur. And while the Earth Charter encompasses a broad and holistic approach to conflicts and other problems in the world, the strategy of the international community toward Sudan has been all but comprehensive. Too little was done too late. It was only humanitarian – help the victims, pick up the pieces. We did not learn the lessons of the conflicts of the 1990s.

Nevertheless, I see progress in Sudan. 2005 is the year in which Sudanese leaders, who have been fighting each other for years, became future-oriented. They looked forward, which is an essential element of The Earth Charter. The Charter bears a broad range of elements in it, all of which could be of use in Sudan. The Charter may have an environmental focus, but it also talks about governance, about social issues, about equal sharing in times of scarcity, about not overexploiting resources, and about taking care of future generations.

The Earth Charter could be a perfect guideline for negotiations in Sudan. In political talks, to solve a conflict one always needs a declaration of principles. The principles in the Charter could be used as a framework within which a specific conflict could be addressed. The values enshrined in the Charter could underpin a domestically – or internationally-shaped comprehensive approach. The Charter could provide a base and a guide to build such an approach and to find support for it among all stakeholders.

Such a comprehensive approach towards Sudan is essential and has been lacking until recently. It implies five dimensions: political, economic, social, cultural, and environmental. All should be addressed, and in time, to prevent escalation of the conflict. The approach toward Darfur was not timely. The conflict had burst into major violence and the international community was only giving humanitarian assistance. But to be comprehensive means that one also must deal with the causes of conflict, and not only with the consequences.

The historical root causes of the Darfur conflict are, in the first place, cultural and racial – different groups not seeing the others as equal, but as inferior, and themselves as superior. Secondly, there is a colonial dimension. The problems in the new state of Sudan after decolonization were also rooted in the way colonial powers drew the borders of the country, giving shape to power relations within the country and extending favors to specific groups and elites. A third root cause is related to the environment and resources. In Darfur, farmers and nomads compete over land and water. There are also other actual causes like poor economic governance – the country's ruling class allocating resources to their own people – and poor political governance. These greatly complicate solving the root causes.

An important aspect of the comprehensive approach is the

Principle 16. Promote a culture of tolerance, nonviolence and peace.

mechanism chosen by the people in a specific society for decision-making and leadership. Western systems may seem more effective to some, but if they are not accepted, they will not work. In Darfur, the leaders of the tribes and the government are going back to traditional forms of conflict resolution, combined with concepts such as better governance and democracy. These methods help solve problems between nomads and settlers, an important issue behind the conflicts in Darfur and other parts of Sudan. In Darfur, age-old camel tracks run from north to south and back. Traditional law says that camel drivers in conflict with landowning tribes have to pay for the use of, and any damage to, the camel tracks. They know exactly where to go and where not, but because of overpopulation, desertification, climate change, and scarcity, travel has become difficult. Meanwhile, the traditional conflict resolution schemes were suppressed when the central government imposed new procedures in the 1990s. I believe a sustainable end to the war, and reconciliation thereafter, can only be accomplished by sitting together again, in traditional ways. This includes compensation for damage against cattle, people, and houses. If not, there is always the possibility for revenge, which is included in the traditional rules in Darfur. This is not an unlimited right; retaliation has a deadline and is related to whom in the clan the damage has been done. Such elements and causes were not systematically confronted in the past. They weren't even studied comprehensively.

A complicating fact is the international dominance of the security paradigm. This, in practice, always concerns the security of actors, not of victims, of the population. Security is biased. Security is about stability, the absence of violence. But it does not at all address root causes. It is about the security of an internal and expatriate elite. Security may even be dangerous. Security kills because, as a paradigm, it is exclusive; it keeps people out; it creates a form of inequality. When people feel excluded and alienated, they don't accept it and they act against the system that excludes them. Security also considers people as being from a specific category – say as Moslems, Arabs, Palestinians. The alternative would be a new paradigm of human security. I prefer to think in terms of sustainability because it goes into the realm of promises. Whereas, security is exclusive, sustainability is holistic.

One important element of a comprehensive approach is cooperation between international actors. We need a unified system in which all elements of the United Nations and the international community work together. I think it is very important to see Sudan as a domestic problem, instead of an international problem. Of course, there are international dimensions like colonial heritage, arms trade, and economic ties. But the solution lies in a domestic, or African, approach. We have to support African and Sudanese players, not substitute for them. In 2005, we see this starting to happen. We see people starting to talk, in political (pre-) negotiations towards peace. They adopt declarations of principles, many of which are forward-looking and contain language which may not be directly quoting the Earth Charter, but are rooted in international discussions leading to declarations such as the Earth Charter. In globalized politics, there are now some commonalities, or basic references that are being shared by all people concerned, so that we know what we mean when we use specific language.

The Earth Charter says that a global partnership is needed, but it also calls for involvement of all stakeholders, including civil society. This, too, is a necessary element of a comprehensive approach. A sustainable solution can only be found if it is bottom-up and inclusive, with all social strata taking part.

Sudan is a very authoritarian, undemocratic, and, sometimes, dictatorial society. Before civil society can come in, one must first shape power by international pressure and by domestic pressure. Domestic pressure in Sudan could only be done with arms; the people of the South had no other choice. The power of ideas was not strong enough, so a liberation movement was needed, as in the struggle for decolonization. Civil society at its start is always elitist, but in the case of Sudan, the elite was in Khartoum in the North. In the South, a counter-elite was to be created. The Sudan People's Liberation Army was the vanguard of the exploited, neglected, marginalized, and oppressed. The problem is, in Sudan like in many other African countries, that after the liberation a countervailing power can make the same mistakes. So after the vanguard, one needs deeply-rooted counter-movements based in the middle and lower strata of society of the country. One can never realize sustainability without them carrying the process.

International pressure can follow one of two different paths. One way is regime change from the outside – military intervention – which I am against. The other way is changing the character of a regime using economic, political, and cultural means such as sanctions, diplomatic pressure, and values. It seems forgotten now that this worked in the struggle against Latin American and Iron Curtain dictatorships, and against the regime in South Africa. It is values-based; it is about human rights, freedom, the sharing of responsibilities, and the fruits of progress. These are global values, shared by people of different social classes and of different creeds – all the things that are in the Earth Charter. ●

# The Way Forward

## The Way Forward

As never before in history, common destiny beckons us to seek a new beginning. Such renewal is the promise of these Earth Charter principles. To fulfill this promise, we must commit ourselves to adopt and promote the values and objectives of the Charter.

This requires a change of mind and heart. It requires a new sense of global interdependence and universal responsibility. We must imaginatively develop and apply the vision of a sustainable way of life locally, nationally, regionally, and globally. Our cultural diversity is a precious heritage and different cultures will find their own distinctive ways to realize the vision. We must deepen and expand the global dialogue that generated the Earth Charter, for we have much to learn from the ongoing collaborative search for truth and wisdom.

Life often involves tensions between important values. This can mean difficult choices. However, we must find ways to harmonize diversity with unity, the exercise of freedom with the common good, short-term objectives with long-term goals. Every individual, family, organization, and community has a vital role to play. The arts, sciences, religions, educational institutions, media, businesses, nongovernmental organizations, and governments are all called to offer creative leadership. The partnership of government, civil society, and business is essential for effective governance.

In order to build a sustainable global community, the nations of the world must renew their commitment to the United Nations, fulfill their obligations under existing international agreements, and support the implementation of Earth Charter principles with an international legally binding instrument on environment and development.

Let ours be a time remembered for the awakening of a new reverence for life, the firm resolve to achieve sustainability, the quickening of the struggle for justice and peace, and the joyful celebration of life.

# The Transition to Sustainability

**Steven C. Rockefeller** is Professor Emeritus of Religion at Middlebury College, Vermont, where he taught for thirty years and served as Dean of the College and Chair of the Religion Department. He received his Master of Divinity from Union Theological Seminary in New York City and his Ph.D. in the philosophy of religion from Columbia University. Among his publications are *John Dewey: Religious Faith and Democratic Humanism* (Columbia, 1991), and *Spirit and Nature: Why the Environment is a Religious Issue* (Beacon, 1992). He chaired the international Earth Charter drafting committee and serves as a member of the Earth Charter Commission. Active in the field of philanthropy, he chairs the board of the Rockefeller Brothers Fund, an international grant making foundation based in New York City, and is a trustee of the Asian Cultural Council.

"As never before in human history, common destiny beckons us to seek a new beginning." These words introduce the concluding section of the Earth Charter, entitled "The Way Forward." The new beginning envisioned by the Earth Charter is the transition to a sustainable way of life, which involves as radical a shift in human thinking and behavior as the emergence of agriculture, the rise of the nation state, or the industrial revolution. One recent study aptly describes this shift as "The Great Transition."[1] The Earth Charter views the Great Transition to sustainable patterns of development locally and globally as essential to the survival and flourishing of human civilization in the twenty-first century. It also considers a sustainable future as a real possibility that human beings may achieve if they have the will, courage, and vision. This essay endeavors to clarify the distinctive contribution of the Earth Charter to the Great Transition, and it explores the Earth Charter's vision of the way forward and the progress being made.

The Earth Charter is designed to focus attention on the fundamental importance of ethical values and choices in the process of social change and the achievement of sustainability. Ethical values are concerned with what people determine to be right or wrong, good or bad in human conduct and relations. They form a community's sense of social responsibility and reflect a concern with the common good, the well-being of the whole community. Ethical values have a profound impact on human behavior, especially those values to which a people feel deeply bound. Scientific knowledge can inform our ethical choices by clarifying the consequences of different courses of action. However, science cannot determine, in the final analysis, what is right and wrong. That is the domain of the imagination, the heart, and the will. As stated in the Earth Charter Preamble, "When basic needs have been met, human development is primarily about being more, not having more" (paragraph four). Our ethical commitments reflect what kind of persons we choose to be as well as what quality of relations we choose to maintain in our communities.

A major social transformation involves a change in a people's ethical values. Ending slavery and discrimination on the basis of race or ending discrimination against women are prime modern examples. The Great Transition requires that a new ethical vision take hold of the imagination and heart of the world's peoples. The ethical reasons for a shift to sustainability are, of course, not the only reasons. There are many economic, health, and other practical considerations that appeal to individual, corporate, and national self-interest and that provide strong arguments for the shift. These practical considerations do often generate progress in the movement toward sustainable development, and that is well and good. However, appeals to self-interest narrowly defined are not sufficient. Without a new expanded sense of ethical responsibility that extends to the whole human family, the greater community of life, and future generations, a clear sense of direction and the motivation, aspiration, and political will needed will be lacking. For over three decades, United Nations (UN) Summits at Stockholm (1972), Rio (1992), and Johannesburg (2002) have recognized the challenge and set promising agendas for action, but governments have mostly failed to vigorously pursue implementation. In the words of the Earth Charter, the achievement of sustainability requires "a change of mind and heart" (The Way Forward, paragraph two).

More specifically, the Earth Charter focuses attention on the need for global ethics. It is concerned with the identification and promotion of ethical values that are widely shared in all nations, cultures, and religions—what some philosophers call universal values. Global ethics are of critical importance in the Great Transition because we live in an increasingly interdependent, fragile, and complex world. The mounting scientific evidence that Earth's climate is warming and that the primary cause is the human generation of greenhouse gas emissions provides one dramatic example of humanity's growing interdependence. In this matter, each and every nation is being affected by the accumulated impact of the behavior of all others.

In the twenty-first century, global interdependence means that no community or nation can manage its problems by itself. Partnership and collaboration are essential, and the dramatic innovations in communications technologies and the sharing of knowledge are making all sorts of new national, regional and global networks and partnerships possible. However, effective cooperation in an interdependent world requires common goals and shared values. This is especially true when communities endeavor to address problems like poverty, inequity, economic instability, global warming, the loss of biodiversity, the depletion of resources, nuclear proliferation, and terrorism. The Earth Charter Preamble, therefore, states that "we urgently need a shared vision of basic values to provide an ethical foundation for the emerging world community" (paragraph 6). The Earth Charter principles, which are the product of a decade-long, cross-cultural dialogue, endeavor to address this need.

One of the major achievements of the twentieth century has been a wide-ranging, international dialogue that has led to articulation of an expanding vision of shared values. This vision is found in the Charter of the United Nations, the Universal Declaration of Human Rights, the World Charter for Nature, and in many other covenants, treaties, and declarations issued by UN Summits and intergovernmental partnerships. In addition, the emerging global civil society has issued over two hundred people's treaties and declarations in the last three decades. In developing its vision of "interdependent principles for a sustainable way of life," the Earth Charter builds on and extends the ethical vision in these UN and civil society documents.

One especially important contribution of the Earth Charter to the shaping of the new global ethics is the document's recognition of the interdependence of all its principles and presentation of a holistic and integrated ethical outlook. More concretely, the Earth Charter appreciates the interrelation of humanity's environmental, economic, political, social, and spiritual challenges, and, therefore, its ethical principles include, for example, respect for nature, environmental conservation, poverty eradication, human rights, gender equality, economic justice, democracy, and a culture of tolerance, nonviolence, and peace. Attempts to deal with problems in isolation will, at best, have only limited success. An inclusive, well-coordinated, long-term strategy is part of the meaning of living and acting sustainably.

Taken together the sixteen main principles and sixty-one supporting principles of the Earth Charter provide a vision in rough outline of the ideal of a sustainable world community. These principles provide an ethical compass for charting the way forward. The Earth Charter can also serve as an educational tool for clarifying the meaning of sustainable development as a general concept. Narrowly defined, sustainable development means ensuring ecological sustainability, but, beginning with the Brundtland Commission, there has been a deepening international realization that given the interrelation of humanity's goals, the more inclusive conceptualization found in the Earth Charter is appropriate. When discussing the concept of sustainable development, however, it is important to keep in mind that implementation at the local level of the general principles set forth in the Earth Charter will take many different forms. As "The Way Forward" states: "Our cultural diversity is a precious heritage and different cultures will find their own distinctive ways to realize the vision" (paragraph two). In addition, when the Earth Charter Commission approved the final version of the document, there was recognition that the global dialogue on shared values would, and should, continue.

The Earth Charter is made up largely of general ethical guidelines and broad strategic goals supported by a world view that includes a sense of belonging to the larger evolving universe and "reverence for the mystery of being, gratitude for the gift of life, and humility regarding the human place in nature."[2] Concerned to keep the document fairly brief, the Earth Charter Commission made a decision not to include discussion of mechanisms and instruments for implementing the principles. "The Way Forward" does, however, make these observations about what implementation will require:

> Life often involves tensions between important values. This can mean difficult choices. However, we must find ways to harmonize diversity with unity, the exercise of freedom with the common good, short-term objectives with long-term goals. Every individual, family, organization, and community has a vital role to play. The arts, sciences, religions, educational institutions, media, businesses, nongovernmental organizations, and governments are all called to offer creative leadership. The partnership of government, civil society, and business is essential for effective governance. (paragraph three)

In addition, a specific reference is made to the important role of the UN and the need for a new international covenant that synthesizes and consolidates international law in the fields of environmental conservation and sustainable development:

> In order to build a sustainable global community, the nations of the world must renew their commitment to the United Nations, fulfill their obligations under existing international agreements, and support the implementation of Earth Charter principles with an international

legally binding instrument on environment and development. (paragraph four)

Since the Earth Charter was drafted, it has become increasingly clear that if the UN is to be an effective instrument of international cooperation and global governance in the twenty-first century, it must undergo major reforms. The Secretary General and a number of member nations have made constructive proposals, and the future of the UN hinges on the willingness of the international community to implement a reform agenda. Just as the soft law principles in the Universal Declaration of Human Rights have been translated into several legally binding human rights covenants, so there has been hope that the Earth Charter principles would, in time, find expression in "an international legally binding instrument on environment and development" (The Way Forward, paragraph four). The elements of such a treaty have already been assembled by the IUCN Commission on Environmental Law in its Draft International Covenant on Environment and Development, which was first presented at the UN in 1995 and which has since been updated and revised. This Draft Covenant provides a solid basis for intergovernmental negotiation, but, to date, the international community has not been prepared to take the next step in advancing international law in the field of environment and development.

What progress is being made in deepening and expanding the ethical vision that guides the international community? What role has the Earth Charter played in this matter? Shortly after the launch of the Earth Charter at the Peace Palace in The Hague in June 2000, the Millennium NGO Forum, which included over one thousand non government organizations (NGOs), endorsed the Earth Charter and recommended that the UN Millennium Summit recognize and support the document. While this did not happen, the UN Millennium Declaration did reaffirm, for the first time in two decades, the principle of "respect for nature" as among the "fundamental values essential to international relations." It also identifies as fundamental shared values, freedom, equality, solidarity, tolerance, and shared responsibility and calls for "a new ethic" of conservation and environmental stewardship. In addition, the document sets forth the Millennium Development Goals (MDGs), which are entirely consistent with the Earth Charter, and established some targets and timetables that involve important steps toward the implementation of a number of Earth Charter principles. For example, the MDGs include commitment to reduce by half the number of people living in absolute poverty by 2015, to eliminate gender disparity in primary and secondary education, and to integrate the principles of sustainable development into nation state policies.

Further progress was made at the World Summit on Sustainable Development (WSSD) held in Johannesburg in 2002. Even though many NGO groups endorsed the Earth Charter during the Summit and South Africa, the host nation, led an effort to recognize the Earth Charter in the Johannesburg Declaration,

this was not to be largely due to the opposition of the United States. However, the Johannesburg Declaration does use language almost identical to that found in the Earth Charter Preamble to affirm in broad outline the Charter's vision of "global interdependence and universal responsibility":

> From this continent, the cradle of humanity, we declare, through the Plan of Implementation of the World Summit on Sustainable Development and the present Declaration, our responsibility to one another, to the greater community of life and to our children. (Paragraph 6; emphasis added)

This statement is the first time that an international law document has made an explicit reference to the community of life. Furthermore, the Johannesburg Declaration deepens the meaning of respect for nature by affirming that people are responsible to, as well as for, the protection of the greater community of life. From the perspective of the Earth Charter, there is implicit in this formulation recognition that people are members of Earth's community of life and, as with communities in general, all the members of the community of life – non-human species as well as people – are worthy of moral consideration. In other words, non-human species as members of the greater community of life have intrinsic value as well as instrumental value.[3] It is also noteworthy that the ethic of care central to the Earth Charter finds expression in the Johannesburg Declaration's reference to a "caring global society." The WSSD Plan of Implementation in its Introduction states that "we acknowledge the importance of ethics for sustainable development" (I.5).

In 2003, the UNESCO General Conference of Member States adopted a resolution introduced by Jordan that recognizes the Earth Charter as an ethical framework for sustainable development and as a valuable teaching tool. A year later the World Conservation Union (IUCN), which includes seventy-seven state governments and over 800 NGOs among its members who are from 140 countries, adopted a similar resolution at its World Conservation Congress in Bangkok. Over two thousand NGOs, including many religious groups, have also endorsed the Earth Charter. Coupled with the wide use of the Earth Charter as a teaching tool in schools and universities, all of these developments mark a significant, even if very gradual, shift in humanity's ethical awareness.

Is there actual progress being made in moving toward the goal of sustainable development? Is there evidence that a heightened sense of social and ecological responsibility is leading civil society, business, and government to undertake efforts that involve implementation of Earth Charter principles? It is very easy to become discouraged and pessimistic about the human future when one reads the steady stream of grim reports on global warming, the destruction of forests, biodiversity loss, shortages of water, poverty, HIV/AIDS, rising military expenditures, nuclear proliferation, and terrorism. However, in 2002, two environmental leaders, David Suzuki and Holly Dressel, published a book entitled *Good News for a Change: How Everyday People are Helping the Planet.*[4] In fact, there is much good news that suggests attitudes are changing and an increasing number of individuals, corporations, religious organizations, and governments are finding ways to reverse dangerous trends and to implement Agenda 21 and the ideals and goals of the Earth Charter. The remainder of this essay considers some examples.

The dramatic growth in population during the twentieth century is one factor contributing to the depletion of resources and the degradation of ecosystems. The world population has more than doubled over the past five decades, reaching 6.3 billion in 2004. The UN Population Division estimates that the world's population will continue to grow in the twenty-first century increasing by forty percent before stabilizing and that this growth will occur largely in the world's fifty poorest countries. This will put added stress on ecological and social systems. The good news is that the annual rate of population growth has declined over the past three decades from 2.1% to 1.14% in 2004. Median fertility is projected to decline from 2.6 children per woman to just over two children by 2050. Demographers, therefore, predict that in 2050, human numbers will peak at around 9.1 billion rather than 10 or 11 billion as estimated earlier.[5] They may then begin to decline. It is largely the decisions and actions of women in countries like Brazil and India that account for the unanticipated decline in birth rates, and there is wide international agreement that the key to sustainable population growth in the developing world is gender equality and the empowerment of women through access to health care, education, and economic opportunity.[6] These values and goals have been incorporated to a large extent in the Millennium Development Goals.

The 2002 World Summit on Sustainable Development identified poverty eradication as a cornerstone of a sustainable future. Over a billion people live in absolute or extreme poverty, struggling to exist on a dollar a day or less. In 2005, Jeffrey Sachs, an economist who is the director of the Earth Institute at Columbia University and special adviser to the United Nations Secretary-General on the Millennium Development Goals, published an important book with the optimistic title: *The End of Poverty: Economic Possibilities for our Time*. Noting that the world community has made a commitment to halving absolute poverty by 2015, Sachs argues that "Our generation can choose to end that extreme poverty by the year 2025." *The End of Poverty* systematically explains what must be done to overcome the basic causes of poverty and how this can be achieved at affordable costs. Sachs calls for a global poverty eradication coalition that would organize the scientific research required and generate the necessary financial assistance and with these resources help poor countries create the basic infrastructure (roads, power, and ports), health care, and education systems needed so that they can take advantage of the world's markets as engines of development.[7]

Some critics argue that Sachs is an overly optimistic liberal with too great a faith in reason, science, and the malleability of societies and with too little appreciation of the obstacles presented by traditional culture, corrupt governments, undemocratic institutions, and armed conflict.[8] It is certainly important to keep these concerns in mind when designing strategies to assist developing nations. However, the Millennium Development Goals and studies such as *The End of Poverty* present a challenge that an increasing number of international leaders are taking seriously. One indication is a recent decision by the Group of Eight (G8), the world's wealthiest nations, to cancel $40 billion of debt owed to international agencies by the eighteen poorest countries, reducing their annual debt burden by $1.5 billion.[9]

Democracy and sustainable development are interdependent, and democracy is now the dominant form of government in the world and is widely viewed by people in all regions as a universal value and the only legitimate form of government.[10] Historians view democracy as having spread during the modern period in three waves. The "third wave" involved a global democratic revolution that began in Portugal in 1974 and then swept through Latin America and into Asia and Africa and, with the fall of the Berlin Wall, into central and Eastern Europe.[11] By 2003, 117 or sixty percent of the world's countries were democracies.[12] One great advantage of democratic forms of government is that criticism is built into the system and people are able to hold their leaders accountable for how they respond to environmental and social problems. The democratic trend in modern history is a cause for hope.[13]

In addition to population numbers, the major factor determining a society's ecological footprint is the technology it uses in energy production, agriculture, manufacturing, transportation, and the operation of households. A sustainability revolution requires a technology revolution that 1) greatly increases the efficiency with which energy and material resources are used with the goal of doing more with less, 2) generates a shift from the use of fossil fuels to renewable energy sources, and 3) facilitates the prevention of pollution and elimination of all waste except what can be assimilated by ecological systems.[14] The technological revolution is gaining momentum and the world community has the scientific and technological expertise to achieve the innovations and advances that are needed. In order to expand and quicken the pace of the sustainability revolution in technology, there will have to be larger budgets for research and development, increased consumer demand, and stronger markets for green products. A special effort must be made to transfer green technology to the developing nations as their economies mature and modernize.

A sustainability revolution also requires new systems of global governance that better manage the process of globalization, promoting the eradication of poverty, environmental protection, human rights, a more equitable process of economic development, and world peace.[15] The market by itself does not protect the environment or ensure social and economic justice. This problem is magnified when governments subsidize unsustainable activities, which they often do, and when the prices of goods and services do not reflect the full environmental and social costs, which is generally the case. Full-cost pricing should be high on the agenda of those working for a sustainable economic system.[16]

On the one hand, the achievement of good global governance requires well-constructed systems of international law, responsible national governments, democratically managed and accountable transnational institutions (such as the UN, World Bank, World Trade Organization, and International Monetary Fund) and effective methods of enforcement. On the other hand, global governance in our complex world is also increasingly a responsibility shared by civil society and corporations acting both independently and in collaboration with governments. This dimension of global governance involves decentralized, voluntary, and creative initiatives on the part of citizens' campaigns, consumer advocacy groups, and human rights and environmental NGOs, as well as businesses.[17]

Prime examples of the sustainability revolution in technology and positive developments in global governance are the innovations and collaborations taking place in the field of energy production and consumption, especially as it relates to the problem of climate change. Many experts view global warming as the most serious environmental problem facing the world. Scientists report that global warming is melting mountain glaciers and the ice sheets at Earth's poles and weather-related disasters are on the rise, and they warn that climate change may lead to a rise in sea levels that threatens coastal ecosystems and communities, a disruption of ocean currents such as the Gulf Stream, a further increase in catastrophic weather events, and the spread of disease.[18] Considerations of this nature have led many business leaders to conclude that global warming is the major environmental threat to a healthy economy. In a "Special Report" on global warming *Business Week*, a USA publication, stated in 2004: "Consensus is growing among scientists, governments and business that they must act fast to combat climate change. This has already sparked efforts to limit CO2 emissions. Many companies are now preparing for a carbon-constrained world."[19] The formation of The Climate Group illustrates the point. The Climate Group is an international coalition with a secretariat in the United Kingdom. Its members are representatives of corporations, cities, states, and national governments committed to collaborating on reducing greenhouse gas (GHG) emissions and sharing best practices. These members have joined in a commitment to develop new clean technologies, maximize energy efficiency, increase the use of renewable energy sources, build markets for green power, and promote best practices.[20]

In the last decade, the primary obstacle to corporate and government action on GHG emissions and other environmental problems has been the assumption that implementing sustainability measures will be too costly and will slow or halt economic growth. The experience of The Climate Group is providing significant evidence that this assumption is false and that major advances in energy efficiency and innovations in the use of renewable energy sources leading to substantial GHG emissions reductions are being made in ways that are cost-effective and often highly profitable. For example, a recent study of The Climate Group found that:

> BP reports a savings of $650 million from emissions reductions efforts. IBM reports a saving of $791 million. DuPont claims $2 billion in efficiencies. Alcoa is looking at saving $100 million by 2006. STMicroelectronics expects $900 million in savings by 2010. Germany reports its efforts will lead to the creation of 450,000 jobs, many of them within the renewable energy sector...."[21]

Reinforcing these trends, 150 national governments have ratified the Kyoto Protocol which entered into force in 2005. As a result of these and many other initiatives, the Worldwatch Institute reports that "total use of solar and wind energy is expanding at a thirty percent annual rate" and that wind energy is now cheaper than natural gas and "closing in on coal."[22] The industrialized world may be approaching the tipping point with regard to a willingness to take action in response to global warming and the need for more sustainable energy policies and practices.

Many of these developments reflect the growing power and influence of global civil society which is exercised in and through consumer campaigns, shareholder initiatives, political movements, and Global Public Policy Networks (GPPN) all involving the work of thousands of NGOs.[23] The role of NGOs is well-illustrated by the new ways in which social and environmental standards are being set for corporate behavior and compliance is verified. There was a time when corporations wrote their own codes of conduct and performance audits were generally an internal affair. In the twenty-first century, standards are being set in open negotiations between industry representatives and all the relevant stakeholders, including NGO experts associated with initiatives such as CERES, the Global Reporting Initiative (GRI), the GHG Protocol, the Forest Stewardship Council, and the Equator Principles. Verification of compliance is conducted by outside organizations that require full disclosure. In addition, NGOs have learned how to skillfully use market campaigns to put pressure on corporations to comply with performance and reporting standards. From the perspective of the Earth Charter, which is itself a global, civil society endeavor to promote ethical principles that are in turn translated into binding government and business standards, all of these developments contribute to the implementation of the Charter's principles and are part of the way forward.

The critical role of the emerging global civil society in building just, democratic, participatory, and sustainable societies underscores the great importance of education for sustainable development in schools, colleges, and universities and in non-formal programs that encourage life long learning.[24] The UN Decade of Education for Sustainable Development (DESD), which the UN General Assembly has charged UNESCO with organizing, focuses much needed international attention on this urgent task. As UNESCO recognizes in its International Implementation Scheme for the Decade, the Earth Charter can serve as a valuable teaching tool in ESD programs.

As this essay suggests, it is possible to identify the beginnings of the Great Transition, but there are no grounds for complacency. Some would argue that what has been accomplished to date is too little too late. It is certainly true that fully achieving sustainable patterns of development remains a distant and very challenging goal. There is an urgent need to strengthen and accelerate the positive trends, and civil society can make the difference. Citizens, NGOs, and religious organizations must keep the pressure on government and business. However, there are many examples of a new sense of social and ecological responsibility taking hold in the corridors of economic and political power supported by the realization that sustainable development is sound economic practice, especially if one takes a long-term view. The Earth Charter can continue to serve as an ethical guide, teaching tool, and source of inspiration—a vision of what the human family can choose to be and to create. If the dangers and risks today are great, so are the opportunities. In the closing words of the Earth Charter: "Let ours be a time remembered for the awakening of a new reverence for life, the firm resolve to achieve sustainability, the quickening of the struggle for justice and peace, and the joyful celebration of life." ●

**Notes**

1   Raskin. P. et. al. (2000). *Great Transition: The Promise and Lure of the Times Ahead*. Boston: Stockholm Environment Institute.
2   See Earth Charter Preamble.
3   See Earth Charter Principles 1 and 15.
4   (2002). Douglas and MacIntyre Publishing Group: Vancouver, Toronto, and New York: Greystone Books.
5   United Nations Department of Economic and Social Affairs, Population Division. (2005). *World Population Prospects: The 2004 Revision – Highlights*. New York: United Nations. Document ESA/P/WP.193 24 February 2005. See also Worldwatch Institute, *Vital Signs 2005: The Trends that are Shaping our Future*. New York: W.W. Norton, 64-65.
6   See Earth Charter Principles 7 and 11.
7   Sachs. J.D.(2005). *The End of Poverty: Economic Possibilities for our Time*. New York: Penguin, 1-4, 364-68.
8   Brooks, D. Liberals, Conservatives, and Aid. (2005, June 26). *New York Times*. , sec. 4.
9   Colwell, A. Finance Chiefs Cancel Debt of 18 Nations. (2005, June 12). New York Times, Final edition. sec. 1.
10   Sen, A. (1999). *Development is Freedom*. New York: Anchor Books, Random House, xi-xii, 146-88. Sen, A. (1999, July). "Democracy is a Universal Value, Journal of Democracy 10:3(July 1999):3-16. Diamond, L. (Winter/Spring 2005). "The State of Democratization at the Beginning of the 21st Century. *The Whitehead Journal of Diplomacy and International Relations* 6:13-18. Gershman, C. (Winter/Spring 2005). "Democracy as

Policy Goal and Universal Value," *The Whitehead Journal of Diplomacy and International Relations* 6:119-37. Gershman provides a very useful summary of the eight ways that democracy benefits people in developing countries and contributes to sustainability.
11   Huntington, S.P. (1991). *The Third Wave: Democratization in the Late Twentieth Century*. Norman: University of Oklahoma Press, 3-30.
12   Diamond, 13.
13   See Earth Charter Principle 13.
14   See Earth Charter Principles 6 and 7 and Speth, J. G. (2005). *Red Sky at Morning: America and the Crisis of the Global Environment*. New Haven: Yale University Press, 157-61.
15   See Earth Charter Principles 5, 7, 10, 12, 13, and 16.
16   Speth, 161-66.
17   Speth, 172-90, 222-27, and Afterword. The World Business Council on Sustainable Development has labeled the spontaneous innovations of corporations and NGOs JAZZ, and Speth provides a very good description of the nature and extent of green JAZZ. See also *Vital Signs 2005*, 106-07.
18   The Arctic Climate Impact Assessment (ACIA) (2004). *Impacts of a Warming Arctic* (Cambridge: Cambridge University Press and *The Millennium Ecosystem Assessment: Synthesis Report*. (2005). Washington, DC: World Resources Institute, as well as the reports of the Intergovernmental Panel on Climate Change. For a more complete discussion of scientific research on global warming and what can be done to address the problem, see Speth, Afterword. See also *Vital Signs 2005*, 40-41, 50-51, and 88-89.
19   *Business Week* (2004, August, 16):60.
20   Northrop, M. (2004). "Leading by Example: Profitable Corporate Strategies and Successful Public Policies for Reducing Greenhouse Gas Emissions," *Widener Law Journal*, 14:1:57.
21   Northrop, M. "Leading by Example," 55.
22   *Vital Signs 2005*, 14, 34-37.
23   Speth, 222-27. Speth provides an overview of the activities of dozens of leading environmental NGOs that are contributing to global governance.
24   See Earth Charter Principle 14.

Klaus Bosselmann and Prue Taylor, New Zealand. A thematic essay on the significance of the Earth Charter for global law

# The Significance of the Earth Charter in International Law

**Klaus Bosselmann** is the founding director of the New Zealand Centre for Environmental Law at the University of Auckland. Before coming to New Zealand in 1989, he was a judge and law professor in Berlin. In 1980, he co-founded the Greens ('Die Grünen') in Germany and, in 1990, the Greens in New Zealand. He has been a delegate at the two World Summits on Sustainable Development in Rio (1992) and Johannesburg (2002) and was involved in negotiating the first Earth Charter at the 1992 Rio Global Forum. He later served as a legal adviser to the Earth Charter Drafting Committee. He is Chair of Earth Charter Aotearoa New Zealand and a member of the IUCN Environmental Law Commission Ethics Specialist Group.

**Prue Taylor** is a Senior Lecturer at the Department of Planning, University of Auckland, New Zealand. She teaches environmental and planning law to undergraduate and graduate students. Her specialist interests are environmental ethics, international environmental law, biotechnology, climate change, and environmental governance structures. She was part of in the first drafting sessions for the Earth Charter that took place at the Global Forum in Rio de Janerio in 1992. She became involved again in 1998 as part of the team of legal experts advising on the Charter. Dr. Taylor has worked actively in support of the Charter as a member of the IUCN Ethics Specialist Working Group. She has published a number of articles exploring the Charter in a legal context, and uses the Charter regularly in her teaching of university students.

From the perspective of international law, the Earth Charter is a new and fascinating instrument (Bosselmann, 2004, 69; Taylor, 1999, 193). This is partly due to its origins. The world-wide dialogue of thousands of civil society groups and individuals, over a period of several years, is impressive in itself. Unlike Agenda 21, the state-negotiated soft law document of the 1992 Rio Earth Summit, the Earth Charter represents a much broader consensus. It is probably the first time that global civil society has produced a document with such a wide consensus on global principles. Concepts like ecological integrity, precautionary principle, democratic decision-making, human rights, and non-violence are well-established in international law, yet not always so clearly defined as they are in the Earth Charter. More importantly, the interaction between all these concepts has not been spelled out in any other single document, not even in Agenda 21.

The reputation and credibility of the Earth Charter rest largely on its transnational, cross-cultural, inter-denominational approach. In what most perceive as a crisis of global governance, this approach is highly significant. While the Earth Charter does not represent global civil society in its entirety including, for example, corporate interests, it does represent a very significant sector of it. States will not, for example, be able to overlook its leading role in the light of their endorsement of Type 2 partnerships for sustainable development in Agenda 21 and the 2002 Johannesburg Plan of Implementation. States will certainly need partnerships with civil society if they want to gain control over anarchistic global corporate power.

Meanwhile, the Earth Charter continues to foster its moral-political leadership within global civil society. The promotion of its principles in more than fifty national Earth Charter campaigns, and the ever-increasing number of endorsing institutions, are evidence of its success and strengths.

In terms of international law principles, the Earth Charter represents *prima facie* a draft legal document. It enjoys considerable recognition and discussion among legal educators and scholars (Kiss and Shelton, 2000, 70; Taylor, 1999; Taylor, 1998, 326). While the legal status of a number of the Earth Charter's principles is disputed, most of them are frequently referred to in treaties, conventions, and other binding documents. Key concepts such as the precautionary principle or sustainable development are not (yet) recognized as custom or general principles of international law. However, they have become an integral part of international law (Birnie and Boyle, 2002, 84, 115; Kiss and Shelton, 2000, 248, 264).

In recent times, "soft law" has become an important "new" source of international law (Kiss and Shelton, 2000, 46). In contrast to "hard law" (treaties, custom, general principles), "soft law" is not legally binding. It cannot be ratified and does not have direct legal effect. However, the political strength of Agenda 21, another soft law document, has emerged as a powerful document in international environmental law. Since 1992, Agenda 21 has been recognized and implemented by wide sectors of civil society all around the world. Local governments, small and mid-sized businesses, educational institutions, and professional organizations have enacted statutes or guidelines for sustainable development, citing Agenda 21 as their main source. This new kind of "bottom-up ratification" has put enormous political pressure on governments to implement some form of governance for sustainable development. Among all the treaties and international documents promoting sustainable development, none has had as much impact on practice as the soft law Agenda 21. The Earth Charter can benefit from this precedent. Although not yet recognized as a soft law document, it has all the ingredients to become one.

Earth Charter Commissioners and the International Secretariat laboured for a year to gain the Charter recognition at the World Summit on Sustainable Development (WSSD), held in Johannesburg in 2002. In his address to the opening session of the Summit, President Mbeki of South Africa cited the Earth Charter as a significant expression of "human solidarity" and as part of "the solid base from which the Johannesburg World Summit must proceed." In the closing days of the Summit, the first draft of the Johannesburg Declaration on Sustainable Development included recognition of "the relevance of the challenges posed in the Earth Charter" (paragraph 13).

On the last day of the Summit, in closed-door negotiations, the reference to the Earth Charter was deleted from the Political Declaration (Rockefeller, 2002, 2). However, the final version of the Political Declaration included, in paragraph 6, wording almost identical to the concluding words of the first paragraph of the Earth Charter Preamble, which states that "it is imperative that we, the peoples of Earth, declare our responsibility to one another, to the greater community of life, and to future generations." Furthermore, Article 6 of the WSSD Plan of Implementation contains indirect reference to the Earth Charter: "We acknowledge the importance of ethics for sustainable development, and therefore we emphasize the need to consider ethics in the implementation of Agenda 21."

The WSSD documents reflect growing international support for sustainability ethics, as expressed in the Earth Charter. Since Johannesburg, international recognition has progressed. In October 2003, the 32nd General Conference of the United Nations Educational Scientific and Cultural Organization (UNESCO) adopted a resolution recognizing the Earth Charter "as an important ethical framework for sustainable development." In November 2004, the International Union for the Conservation of Nature and Natural Resources (IUCN) World Conservation Congress in Bangkok, approved a resolution recognizing the Earth Charter "as an ethical guide for IUCN policy" and encouraging its Member states "to determine the role the Earth Charter can play as a policy guide within their own spheres of responsibility."

A decisive step toward soft law recognition would be a resolution of recognition by the United Nations General Assembly. But, even without such recognition, there can be little doubt about the Earth Charter's potential. A number of pathways could lead to the Earth Charter being acknowledged as a legally binding international instrument.

One of these pathways is the continued promotion of the Earth Charter within countries and among international organizations. The target here is to increase endorsements (in their various forms) up to a point were the Earth Charter reaches a certain omnipresence. This process could lead to its gradual transformation from soft law into a hard law instrument, in much the same way as nascent principles of law gradually gain recognition and status as binding "customary" international law.

Another path would be its conversion into a United Nations Draft Earth Charter, either together with the IUCN Draft Covenant on Environment and Development, or as a stand-alone document, eventually opening it up for negotiation among states. A further path could be to focus on the Earth Charter's content and seek dialogues with governments on desirable principles and their implementation in law and policy. Here the Charter could have a "blueprint" function not dissimilar to Agenda 21.

However, the most promising path of all is to insist on the Earth Charter's validity as a novel instrument of global law. Never before have so many people, in so many different countries, representing so many cultures and religions, reached a consensus on a central theme of humanity. To some extent, the Earth Charter can be celebrated as global civil society's first and foremost founding document. Such an achievement, both in terms of quantity and quality, puts the world's states on the back foot. States, having failed for so long to fulfil their promise of sustainable development, are rapidly losing their political and intellectual leadership.

Since the Westphalian Age (1648), we have seen inter-national law, i.e. law between nation states – but not transnational law or global law. Transnational or global legal thinking is not new: civil society promoted universal human rights in the French and American revolutions, for example. It found its international legal recognition in the Universal Declaration of Human Rights in 1948. States have reluctantly, and not without setbacks, accepted the idea of human rights as pre-state, universal entitlements. Equally, the UN Charter 1945 is a document of transnationalism, at least in its underlying principle of collective responsibility for peace and security. The fact that states have, by and large, struggled to foster human rights, peace, and security does not discredit global agreements such as the Universal Declaration or the UN Charter. To the contrary, the failure of states stresses the need for such instruments.

The Earth Charter qualifies as a founding document for global law, as no other international document has described the failure of states and peoples so clearly and forcefully. It is the failure to accept a three-fold imperative: "…that we, the peoples of the Earth, declare our responsibility to one another, to the greater community of life, and to future generations" (Preamble, Earth Charter).

In law, such imperatives and responsibilities are usually captured by notions of distributional justice. But what concept of justice is intended when we think of responsibilities to one another, to the greater community of life, and to future generations?

The Brundtland Report (WCSD, 1987) derived two forms of justice from the idea of sustainable development, i.e. intragenerational justice (between people living today) and intergenerational justice (between people living today and in the future). Responsibility to the greater community of life is not reflected in this idea – an omission common among state-negotiated documents on sustainable development (e.g. 1992 Rio Declaration, 2002 Johannesburg Declaration).

By contrast, care and respect for the community of life are central to the Earth Charter. They are central simply because, in an evolutionary process, human life cannot be separated from other forms of life. From the perspective of ecological integrity and sustainability, care for one another and for future generations is useless if we ignore the community of life that we are part of. If this is a moral imperative, it should also be a legal imperative.

Thus, lawyers debate whether the nonhuman world can be part of the *justitia communis* or must stay excluded from the *justitia communis*? The former approach reflects a new concept, the latter follows the traditional, anthropocentric concept of justice.

John Rawls, who shaped contemporary theories of justice more than anyone, has been very clear: "(the) status of the natural world and our proper relation to it is not a constitutional essential or a basic question of justice" (Rawls, 1993, 246). Rawls acknowledges "duties" to the nonhuman world, but he describes them as mere "duties of compassion and humanity" rather than duties of justice. To him, any "considered beliefs" to morally include the nonhuman world "are outside the scope of the theory of justice." (Rawls, 1999, 448). Efforts to reconcile Rawls' political liberalism with ecological justice (Wissenburg, 1998; Barry, 2001; Bell, 2002) underestimate the persistence of paradigms. How could Rawls, or any legal theorist, trade their

anthropocentric liberalism for non-anthropocentric ecologism? The Earth Charter challenges the anthropocentric idea of justice. As humans have put the Earth's ecological integrity at risk, no level of social organization – economics, politics, law – can be exempt from the moral imperative of care and respect for the community of life. The test lies in the current state of affairs. If the Earth Charter is right, then we are in desperate need of a new framework of thinking. Justice needs to include the community of life (Bosselmann, 1999; 2005). Perceived in this way, people of all cultures and nations may be able to give the dream of global law some solid foundation. ●

### References

Barry, J. (2001). Greening liberal democracy: Practice, theory and economy. In J. Barry & M. Wissenburg (Eds.). *Sustaining liberal democracy: Ecological challenges and opportunities*. Palgrave: Publisher?

Bell, D. (2002). How can political liberals be environmentalists? *Political studies, 50/4*, 703.

Birnie, P. & Boyle, A. (2002). *International law and the environment* (2nd ed.). New York: Oxford University Press.

Bosselmann, K. (forthcoming 2005). Ecological justice and law. In B. Richardson & S. Wood (Eds.). *Environmental law for sustainability: A critical reader*. Oxford: Hart Publishing.

Bosselmann, K. (2004). In search of global law: The significance of the Earth Charter, (8) *Worldviews: Environment, culture, religion 1*, 62.

Bosselmann, K. (2002). "Rio +10: Any closer to sustainable development?" *New Zealand Journal of Environmental Law 6*, 297.

Bosselmann, K. (1999). Justice and the environment: Building blocks for a theory on ecological justice. In K. Bosselmann & B. Richardson (Eds.). *Environmental justice and market mechanisms*. London: Kluwer Law International.

Kiss, A. & Shelton, D. (2000). *International environmental law* (2nd ed.) Ardsley, New York: Transnational Publ.

Rawls, J. (1999). *A theory of justice* (revised ed.). New York: Oxford University Press.

Rawls, J. (1993). *Political liberalism*. New York: Oxford University Press.

Rockfeller, S. (2002). *The Earth Charter and Johannesburg*. Unpublished communication.

Taylor, P. (1999). The Earth Charter. In *New Zealand Journal of Environmental Law 3*, 193.

Taylor, P. (1998). *An ecological approach to international law*. London: Routledge.

WCSD, World Commission on Environment and Environment and Development. (Ed.). (1987). *Our common future*. Oxford: Oxford University Press.

Wissenburg, M. (1998). *Green liberalism: The free and green society*. London: UCL Press.

# Building Support for the Earth Charter Movement

**Joan Anderson** is originally from Scotland. She has worked since 1997 in the public information office of Soka Gakkai International (SGI), based in Tokyo, Japan. Her career to date has combined work as an editor, writer, and information specialist with experience in development. She first encountered the Earth Charter preparing a supplement on it for the *SGI Quarterly* magazine, and then in January 2000, she spent several weeks traveling around Asia to promote the Earth Charter in Singapore, Malaysia, Hong Kong, The Philippines, Korea, and Japan. This total immersion made her a convert and since then she has often joined international meetings on the Earth Charter and Education for Sustainable Development as a representative of SGI.

Being part of the Earth Charter movement gives those of us in faith-based organizations that are working for social change an important sense of belonging to a wider community of concerns and values. It is a bridge and it builds bridges. It enables us to find and explore our common ground.

In order to examine the question of how to build support for the Earth Charter, I will draw on my experience of doing this within the Soka Gakkai International (SGI) network. SGI is an international lay Buddhist association with the broad aim of spreading peace, culture, and education based on the philosophy and ideals of Nichiren Buddhism. There are currently around twelve million members of SGI around the world, with the largest concentration still in Japan, where the organization began as an educational reform group with Buddhist underpinnings in 1930. The SGI Charter, adopted in 1994, articulates many of the same concerns as the Earth Charter, stating:

> We recognize that at no other time in history has humankind experienced such an intense juxtaposition of war and peace, discrimination and equality, poverty and abundance…that humanity's egoism and intemperance have engendered global problems, including degradation

of the natural environment and widening economic chasms…. (Preamble, paragraph two).

Since 1997, when the SGI-affiliated Boston Research Center for the 21st Century began consultations on the Benchmark Draft of the Earth Charter, and the president of SGI, Daisaku Ikeda, first stressed the importance of the Earth Charter in his annual peace proposals, individual SGI members in many countries have been inspired by the vision articulated in the Charter. There are now two main e-networks linking these individuals. One links around seventy SGI members in thirty countries, and the other brings together key Earth Charter people within SGI-USA. Many of the latter group have been actively involved with helping to organize the local Earth Charter Community Summits which take place annually in October in a range of locations throughout the USA, and internationally, to inform, educate, and engage ordinary people, including youth, with the Earth Charter through music, the arts, and dialogue.

Two core principles of Buddhism generally make it easy for SGI members to relate to the Charter – the injunction to respect Earth and life in all its diversity and the recognition of the interdependency and interconnectedness of all life. The call for action as responsible global citizens also resonates with our members as it is in line with our belief that even a single individual's actions do make a difference.

In some cases almost the entire SGI organization in a particular country has become engaged, as in Canada and Taiwan; but, in most cases, it is at the individual and local level that the Charter has affected people most deeply. One SGI member who created a bilingual school in Beijing made the Earth Charter the ethical foundation for the school. Another is creating an Earth Charter-based learning center for sustainable development in rural France and another has worked within SGI-Italy to develop innovative youth forums and talk shows where young people meet in small groups and use the Charter as a tool for reflection on their real-life concerns.

This widely-scattered response is partly indicative of the autonomous nature of respective SGI organizations around the world. But maybe there are other reasons why the Earth Charter has not yet been taken up by very many SGI organizations as a major theme. As one SGI member who has been using the Charter in her work as an educator said, "There is no simple way to describe it and that is a problem." Another commented, "It's rare that I begin a conversation about planetary ethics and values without a listener's eyes glazing over at some early point in the exchange." And people's initial impressions – that the Charter is just about environmental protection – may also often not be accurate.

After all, the concept of sustainability is barely understood and not skillfully articulated by many, including those who promote it. This is one reason why the Earth Charter resources produced by SGI, such as the "A Quiet Revolution" film and the "Seeds of Change: The Earth Charter and Human Potential" exhibition are aimed at communicating with a wide non-specialist audience and connecting with viewers as individual human beings.

There seems to be a particular kind of person who is typically captivated by the Charter – someone who is concerned about many social issues and aware of the linkages among them, who immediately responds to its holistic vision. It could be said that we are merely "preaching to the choir;" however, based on our experience, the more people are exposed to the principles of the Earth Charter, the more empowered they become.

There are other challenges in the process of spreading the word about the Earth Charter. There may be the suspicion that it was created by one particular group with a particular agenda. It is ideal for Earth Charter events and programs to be jointly conceived and organized by more than one organization and, particularly in the case of religious groups, through interfaith activities.

During the process of learning about the Charter, I would identify several stages. First, comes knowledge and awareness but with no sense of involvement or ownership. Then, either through discussion or a more right-brain activity, such as viewing a cultural performance or artwork inspired by the Charter, there is a moment of conversion where the person concerned begins to feel passionate about its vision and that she or he has the right to be an active proponent of it and its values.

Small dialogue groups or one-to-one discussions are frequently mentioned as the key, as is speaking of the Earth Charter in terms of how it has impacted one's own life. One SGI Earth Charter enthusiast complains, "Westerners take a very theoretical approach to the Charter, as something to get others to do. It is difficult for them to apply the principles to themselves or others personally." She has held "Earth Charter Dinner Dialogues" and says, "I notice that the dialogues develop and grow into other things. So starting very simply, but regularly, is the key."

As SGI President Ikeda said in his message for the Hague launch of the Charter in 2000:

The process by which the Earth Charter has been developed is one of dialogue. Truths arrived at through discussion and dialogue are warm, living truths. Nothing sparks a more profound and lasting transformation in the human heart than such interactions....

My own experience has included heartwarming conversations with youth in Singapore, for whom the Earth Charter caused reflection on their materialistic outlooks. Another experience was listening to emotionally moving stories at a conference in Australia in which individuals shared their personal histories of encountering the Charter and how it had rekindled their hope.

I have found it useful to consider a fifty-year time span over which awareness and practical implementation of the Charter will grow, mainly driven by creative, spontaneous, bottom-up initiatives, which can be amplified by skillful use of the media. Hopefully these will increasingly be matched by recognition and endorsement by professional associations, cities, and even governments. As another SGI member comments, "Bringing the Earth Charter to fruition is like running a marathon instead of a 100-meter dash."

We might ask how important it is that people actually know about the Earth Charter when they may be already living and acting in a way that puts its principles into action. I would argue that it does have an important function as a catalyst in giving people who share common concerns a loose sense of unity. But in today's pluralistic world, it will never be the one vision of a sustainable world, and Earth Charter advocates need to also consider how to join forces with other broad value-based movements.

There is a need to amplify and communicate more widely the message of the Earth Charter and its success stories – something which the "Seeds of Change" exhibition attempts to do. Faith-based groups such as SGI have strong grassroots networks and a wide reach into local communities which offers great future opportunity. Further, with a particular focus on youth and use of the Earth Charter in education during the UN Decade of Education for Sustainable Development, the potential is vast. Let us continue to scatter the seeds of Earth Charter awareness widely, making sure that they land in places where inspired individuals can continue the human connection that enables its values to thrive in people's daily lives. ●

# The Way Forward for Coalitions of Workers and Businesses for Sustainability

**Herman H.F. Wijffels** is Chairman of the Netherlands Social and Economic Council. In 1981, he joined the Executive Board of the Rabobank Group, a financial institution headquartered in the Netherlands and active internationally in financing agri-business. In 1986 he was appointed as its Chairman. From 1968 until 1977, he was a civil servant at the European Commission and in the Dutch administration. From 1977 until 1981, he was Secretary General of the Dutch Federation of Industries. Wijffels is also Chairman of the Society for Preservation of Nature in the Netherlands. He is Chairman of the Supervisory Boards of the Rijksmuseum, Tilburg University, and the University Medical Centre Utrecht. Wijffels serves on a number of corporate boards and as a director of several charities.

A growing number of companies have come to realise that they cannot afford to neglect their wide circles of stakeholders. In our information society, news spreads fast, reputations turn out to be fragile. In a globalising world in which modern information and communication technologies play a central role, critical consumers and interest groups demand not only decent and responsible behaviour from businesses and their CEO's, but also transparency about their mission and the way it is implemented in daily practice. In this climate, the concept of Corporate Social Responsibility (CSR) has become the catch-all term. The key message of this concept is reflected in Principle 7 of the Earth Charter: "Adopt patterns of production, consumption, and reproduction that safeguard Earth's regenerative capacities, human rights, and community well-being."

What is the business of business? For Milton Friedman, the recipient of the 1976 Nobel Prize for economics, it was simple. In a market economy, the enterprise has one – and only one – social responsibility: "to use its resources and engage in activities designed to increase its profits so long as it stays within the rules of the game, which is to say, engages in open and free competition, without deception or fraud. Similarly, the 'social responsibility' of labour leaders is to serve the interests of the members of their unions".[1]

Society nowadays expects more from both business and trade unions in terms of corporate citizenship. Citizens and interest groups increasingly hold companies directly accountable for their social responsibilities. Public acceptance and a good reputation are important conditions for the continuation of many companies. The need for public acceptance is expressed in terms of a "license to operate," which must be earned and renewed from time to time.

In my view, a modern company is a co-operation of a number of different stakeholders.[2] One of the conditions for the proper functioning of such a partnership model is the ability to maintain a certain balance in the degree of control and influence exercised by the various stakeholders in the company. An imbalance in these relations can lead to poorer performance and, in the longer term, damage the credibility and reputation of the company. Employees and shareholders together represent the primary stakeholders in the company. It is crucial to the company's operations that it is able to create an effective bond with these stakeholders as well as with customers, suppliers, creditors, and others, including government bodies, non-governmental organisations (NGOs), and local residents. It is in the company's interest to invest in good relations with these stakeholders. It comes down to the conviction that, in the long run, optimising stakeholder value will best serve the interests of shareholders.

Corporate social responsibility encompasses the core business. This means that concern for the social effects of the company's actions is part of that core business. For the purpose of sustainable development, this entails consciously directing business activities towards creating value in three dimensions in the longer term, the Triple P bottom line: Profit, People, Planet: Profit refers to the creation of value through the production of goods and services and through the creation of employment and sources of income. The financial returns reflect the appreciation of consumers for the company's products and the efficiency with which factors of production are used. For investors, it is the criterion against which the company's performance is measured through shareholder value. People include not only the company's own staff, but also the outside community. Concern for this dimension starts with good labour relations and a stimulating social policy. And it certainly relates to respect for human rights and fundamental labour standards in other countries and the promotion of good labour relations in developing countries. Planet means that care for the natural environment – for the integrity of Earth's ecological systems, as the Earth Charter puts it – is fully integrated into day-to-day business operations as well as the company's strategic decision-making process.

In so far as the international capital market, under Anglo-Saxon influence, only looks at shareholder value, there is a tension with a balanced and coherent implementation of the three dimensions of corporate social responsibility. There are also counter forces: in the US, of all places, there has been a sharp rise in investment funds which concentrate specifically on ethical investing. In the Netherlands, the growth of specific "green" investment products has been greatly stimulated by a special tax scheme.

In addition, the financial services sector is showing growing concern for insufficient sustainability – because of the associated risks. Taking the performance of companies in the social and environmental areas into account when compiling an investment portfolio is not necessarily at the expense of investment performance. Research has shown that so long as the selection is sufficiently diversified, an investor can secure roughly the same results as with similar conventional stocks. It is encouraging to note the increasing popularity of the Dow Jones Sustainability Indexes (DJSI)[3] – the world's first global sustainability indexes launched in 1999. The growing amount of assets that investors are putting behind the DJSI, as well as the public recognition of these benchmarks, indicate that more and more companies perceive the indexes as an incentive for continuous sustainability improvements.

In the public arena, the individual enterprise is subject to a number of forces: what it must do because of legislation and regulation and public expectations, what it should do from personal conviction, and what it finds profitable to do. It is up to the individual company to decide exactly how it wants to position itself with respect to these forces.

The number of companies that voluntarily draw up a corporate code setting out their basic responsibilities towards their environment, and the core values, standards, or rules they observe, has rapidly increased. Corporate codes provide a strong institutional foundation for values to which the company attaches importance and for the standards which provide guidelines for the actions of management and employees and help in finding solutions to dilemmas or conflicts. Corporate codes commit managers and staff to making certain efforts. It is important that a corporate code is not imposed from the top down by the company's management. The more the employees are involved in drafting the code, the better for its acceptance and implementation.

Corporate codes can build on various systems of standards in which the international community has enshrined public expectations and values. Besides the Universal Declaration of Human Rights (1948) and the international treaties concerning civil and political rights and concerning economic, social and cultural rights (both 1966), these include the International Labour Organisation (ILO) Conventions and the Organisation for Economic Co-operation and Development (OECD) Guidelines for Multinational Enterprises.

In 2000, the Secretary General of the United Nations, Kofi Annan, initiated a Global Compact for the New Century.[4] The aim of this compact, which sets out nine principles, is to involve companies, trade unions, and non governmental organisations (NGOs) in the promotion of human rights, fundamental labour standards, and ecological sustainability. Although governments are primarily responsible for guaranteeing and protecting human rights and fundamental freedoms, enterprises can nevertheless also be expected to do everything in their power to promote compliance with these principles. Enterprises, trade union organisations, and NGOs have adopted the Global Compact.

What the Earth Charter adds to this variety of international standards and initiatives is, first and foremost, a comprehensive set of common principles and shared values that fully reflect our global interdependency. I strongly feel that the principles of the Earth Charter provide us – workers, business people, consumers, citizens – with a reliable compass to help us find the way forward towards sustainable development on this one world of ours. The need for such a compass is evident in an era of swift and profound changes in the world economy, increasing ecological pressures, continuous underdevelopment in big parts of the world, and a growing fear of international terrorism.

In our world-in-transition, traditional institutes are outdated and inadequate. The Earth Charter provides the ethical terms of reference for realising the ambitions of the twenty-first century such as the Millennium Development Goals, as an important step towards global sustainability. Transnational companies and the international division of labour are prime carriers of the globalisation of production and consumption. Safeguarding Earth's regenerative capacities, human rights, and community well-being demands the conscious and active commitment of workers and businesses, as well as consumers. Captains of industry and trade unions can take an important step forward by paying tribute to the principles of the Earth Charter. May I invite you to endorse the Charter and act accordingly? ●

**Notes**

1    Friedman, M. (1962). *Capitalism and freedom*. Chicago: University of Chicago Press. p. 133.
2    SER (Social and Economic Council), *Corporate social responsibility - A Dutch approach*, Assen 2001.
3    See: www. sustainability-indexes.com
4    See: www.unglobalcompact.org

Nigel Dower, Scotland. A thematic essay on global interdependence and universal responsibility

# The Earth Charter and Global Citizenship: A Way Forward

**Nigel Dower** is Honorary Senior Lecturer in Philosophy and Academic Consultant, University of Aberdeen. His main academic interests in the last twenty years have been in exploring ethics in a globalised world. He brings a cosmopolitan perspective to issues like development, environment, international relations, global governance, war and peace, and human rights. Dr. Dower has given lectures on the Earth Charter and its relationship to global ethics, development, and environment, in the UK, USA, Honduras, Italy, and South Africa. His publications include *World Ethics – the New Agenda* (Edinburgh University Press 1998), and *Introduction to Global Citizenship* (Edinburgh University Press 2003) in which he featured the Earth Charter. He is currently President of the International Development Ethics Association and Fellow of the Royal Society of Arts.

In this chapter, I make the case for seeing the Earth Charter and global citizenship as complementary to each other. I shall argue that, at one level, one provides the content – the Earth Charter as a global ethic – and the other, the form – the motivating sense of being a citizen of a global community. At the same time, the juxtaposition of the two rather different ideas – both in general thinking and in education – provides the context of critical debate, discussion, and dialogue about both, and thus generally strengthens commitment to each. This, at least, has been my experience as a teacher in trying to teach students at college level to think constructively about global ethics issues, and as someone who has been interested in the Earth Charter and in global citizenship for some time – engaging with others in discussions about global issues. The former has been mainly based on part of what I taught as my contribution to two courses I co-ordinated from 2000 to 2004 in the University of Aberdeen on "Challenge of the Environment" and "Global Citizenship." The latter has emerged from lectures and talks I have given which either include or focus on the Earth Charter. The main thrust of this chapter in practical terms is in giving examples of types of issues in which the relationship between the Earth Charter and global citizenship can be focused on mutual benefit.

For the purposes of this discussion, the claim that we are global citizens is a claim: first, that there are certain universal values which are either accepted across the world, or should be so accepted; second, that we all belong in some sense to a global community understood in a variety of ways – moral, political, legal, social, etc. The global ethic generally put forward by global citizens in the modern world is one which has two further features: first, the ethic stresses the idea of transnational obligations or responsibilities; for instance; we have significant obligations of assistance across national borders towards any human being who needs help; second, the global ethic endorsed is one that is accessible to people from many different backgrounds of faith, culture, or philosophy – that is, the ethic is not tied for instance to the theological premises of a particular religion.

The Earth Charter is, in essentials, for the purposes of this discussion, a global ethic in the following three respects: first, it is a set of universal principles which are comprehensive in the sense of covering all the major areas of values applicable to human existence, but not comprehensive in the sense that they are tied to any one comprehensive world view, such as Buddhism and secular anthropocentrism; second, it is global in that it is actually accepted by large number of people from all over the globe; third, it is global also in that it was formed as a result of a wide process of global consultation. Furthermore, the Earth Charter is a public document available for endorsement by individuals who do so in the knowledge that they endorse something endorsed by hundreds of thousands of others. The values of the Earth Charter are not merely shared in the sense that they are the same for different people; they are shared in the stronger sense of people belonging to a community of shared values.

Apart from the fact that the Earth Charter explicitly invites us to think of ourselves inter alia as citizens of the world (Preamble, paragraph five), it is clear from the above characteristics of the two ideas that they go closely together. A global citizen who is in search of reasonable global ethic can find it in the Earth Charter, since the latter is wide-ranging but accessible to many viewpoints; she can find in it further reason to endorse it, apart from its inherent reasonableness, the fact that it arises from worldwide consultation and is, in fact, endorsed by many; and she can find through the Earth Charter a genuine and real community of like-minded people across the world united in its inspirational power. Conversely, someone who is an advocate of the Earth Charter can see that the Earth Charter is at heart a global ethic – though this exact language is not used in it. As such, it is something a global citizen would endorse. She can see, too, that more specifically the Earth Charter, in advocating global responsibility (Preamble, paragraph two and Subprinciple 2.b), stresses one of the key elements that a global citizen is keen to stress – obligations across borders. She can recognise, too, that what global citizenship adds to global ethics, as such, is that we are or should become citizens of the world and in so doing stresses both the inner motivational resources of individuals and the external social structures and institutions which make a global ethic such as the Earth Charter more likely to be realised in practice.

The complementary relationship between the two cannot be assumed though. It is perfectly possible that someone who is an advocate of the Earth Charter rejects the discourse of global citizenship – perhaps questioning its "political" connotations on the grounds that the Earth Charter is about transformation of ordinary lives, not about forms of governance. Or, he may question the "anthropocentric" character of citizenship which may be seen to be restricted to humans, whereas we really belong to an "ethical community" or "commonwealth of life;" or he may even question the whole idea of a "global ethic," and so not regard the Earth Charter as a global ethic, perhaps because it simply is not – or is not yet – globally accepted. Conversely, someone committed to global citizenship or a global ethic may not be particularly keen to associate this with the Earth Charter if, for instance, he thought the Earth Charter principles were wrong in significant respects; too pluralistic, allowing too much diversity; too idealistic or bland so that in either case it is not relevant to making decisions; or, too detailed to be the right candidate for a global ethic. Responses like these have certainly arisen in discussions I have had in university discussion groups.

Given that for various reasons there could be a perception that they do not go together, one needs to say two things in response. First, whilst such antagonisms are possible and have certainly surfaced in my teaching from some students, it is probable that the outcome of bringing the two together is that they are mutually reinforcing – each providing what may be missing, or at least a weaker element in the other. For most people then, if they start with the one and get to think about the other, the result will be acceptance of the other and through that acceptance the strengthening of both, partly because one has access to a wider range of conceptual tools and ideas for articulating either. A full picture of the form and content of a global ethic is provided. At least from my experience of trying to teach around these ideas, positive responses are more common than negative ones – but this, if generalised, is an act of faith since I have not done or seen sociological confirmation of it!

Second, putting the two together brings out the issues and potential sources of opposition to either and thus creates the context of a more vigorous and constructively critical discussion of the issues. Certainly, an attitude towards the Earth Charter of critical loyalty and of constructive criticism is important to the Earth Charter in maintaining it as a living ethic and not some kind of holy writ about which there cannot be critical debate and interpretation. Likewise global ethics and the advocacy of global citizenship benefit from contestation.

It is also an act of faith, to some extent, to suppose that where there is open debate, the outcome will generally be in the direction of what one believes to be right! But, my general experience of teaching in this area is that although there will always be individual students who reject global citizenship and/or reject the Earth Charter, on the whole most warm to the ideas in the light of critical discussion, and that bringing the two ideas together helps to create a rounded framework for discussion, precisely because each complements the other, as indicated earlier.

One way of putting this point is to note that global citizenship discourse rather more explicitly takes on board the facts of globalisation than does the Earth Charter, which can seem rather detached from the realities of global, socio-political processes. Those interested in global citizenship recognise the processes of globalisation which have given global citizenship many different avenues for expression and embodiment, in non government organisations, and global civil society, and thus helps to embed the Earth Charter in the emerging global community of which it is part.

Conversely, the global citizen can find in the Earth Charter a concrete expression of a global ethic which otherwise might seem too abstract and undefined. Furthermore, insofar as she feels her global ethic should actually be shared by agents from all over the world, and not just be an idea in the mind of the global citizen herself, then the Earth Charter fits the bill perfectly since it is, if nothing else, a global ethic which is actually shared, and perceived to be shared, by people throughout the world. ●

# The Spiritual Way, the Gandhian Way

 **Kamla Chowdhry** was a Professor at the Indian Institute of Management, Ahmedabad and a visiting Professor at the Harvard Business School, USA. She also worked in the Ford Foundation in India as Programme Advisor for Public Planning and Management. She has published several papers relating to forestry, environment, sustainable development, and ethics and development. Dr. Chowdhry is a founding trustee of the National Foundation for India and was involved in setting up the Institute of Rural Management. She is also a trustee of the Vikram Sarbhai Foundation and Chairperson of the Society for Promotion of Wasteland Development.

Earth's pain is becoming humanity's pain. We have consistently ignored the dark side of development and we continue to do so. Earth, which is our home, and home to all living creatures, has been used ruthlessly and mercilessly and unsustainably. The very existence of life on Earth is at stake. We must reverse this trend if life on Earth as we have known it for millennia is to continue.

There is also emerging a growing yearning for the individual's and Earth's healing. The Earth Charter is a response to this widespread yearning for the spiritual healing of humans as well as Earth God's creation and Mother Earth, as others call it. At the heart of the Earth Charter is the need to consider and strengthen the inner spirit of humans, to make moral and ethical choices, to move towards a technology with a human face, and towards a non-violent economics that would cooperate with Earth and with nature rather than exploit it.

The Earth Charter, we hope, will be a turning point in our history. We live in a world which has obsessive preoccupation with growth and unlimited confidence in new technologies. Modern technology has been responsible for our disappearing forests, disappearing rivers and wetlands, disappearing biodiversity, disappearing fossil and mineral wealth, and increase in deserts, arid lands, and wastelands. We have pursued the philosophy of the cancer cell which grows and expands on its host, eventually killing it. We are behaving like the cancer cell, killing Earth with our expanded economic growth.

The Earth Charter has become necessary if we are to survive. It recognizes the crisis is not only in our economic growth and in our consumerism, but also recognizes the crisis in our social, moral, and spiritual life. The confidence that scientific and technological methodologies are the only valid approaches to truth and knowledge is changing. In the last two to three hundred years, science and technology in the West have been extensively used by man for his greed, and for acquiring power. In the process, he has deeply damaged and poisoned the Earth and also deeply damaged and spiritually contaminated himself as well. The Earth Charter provides the vision, the spiritual and the ethical basis, the direction and limits of the scientific and technological change. It helps in having an holistic, an ecological, and an ethical view of knowledge a view which in many ways is similar to those of mystics and of spiritual religious people.

The Earth Charter holds Earth as sacred, as did the belief systems of indigenous people, and of Hindus, Jains, and Buddhists. They treated Earth as sacred and did not exploit nature without concern for its well-being, for its sustainability.

As Gandhi said, "Earth has enough for our needs, but not enough for our greed." If we are concerned about sustainable development, about poverty and equality, about violence and crime and wars, we must turn to Mahatma Gandhi, a man of deep spiritual, moral, and ethical values, as well as a man of action who could transform millions and lead a non-violent revolution. If we are to save Earth and move towards a sustainable future we have a great deal to learn from the Mahatma.

Gandhi's method was "satyagraha" – the literal meaning being "holding on to truth." Essentially satyagraha is a moral principle, converted into a method to fight for social and political justice.

In everything Gandhi did, he introduced the spirit of religion in his politics. When he was asked whether he was a saint or a politician he replied, "I could not be leading a religious life unless I identified with the whole of mankind, and that I could not do unless I took part in politics."

If the general principles of the Earth Charter are to be achieved and transferred into action, the action must be religious, spiritual, and political as Gandhi's was. We will have to apply Gandhi's principles of truth and non-violence if the Earth Charter is to be won for humanity.

In the Earth Charter, we propose a new paradigm for development, a people-led development, a development which is pro-poor, pro-nature, and pro-woman. Like Gandhi, we must practice what we preach. If Gandhi was concerned about the poorest of the poor, he adopted a life style reflecting his constituency. "If I come in my loin cloth," he said, "it is because I represent the half-starved, half-naked dumb millions of India."

And we know from Gandhi, if the voice of the Earth Charter is to become a living reality, then the starting point of change is with oneself. If we cannot change ourselves, we cannot change the world. We need the inner strength to be able to say to ourselves and to the world, "My life is my message." If we cannot do this, the Earth Charter will fail.

Ultimately, Earth's sustainability is based on deep spiritual and religious experience. Earth is sacred and spiritual and needs to be treated as such. In India, we have Vedic hymns dedicated to Earth, which have been recited and sung over the centuries, for at least three thousand years or more. The Earth Charter also needs our dedication and our commitment as the Vedic hymns do, and I promise it will change the world. We must treat the Earth as sacred, with respect and compassion, and use it only as sustainability allows us.

Like the Gita, the Bible, the Quran, or whatever holy book you may follow, the Earth Charter, too, requires serious consideration, re-reading, re-interpreting, and mediation. It will help us to reconnect with what our cultures consider sacred and spiritual. We need to weave the Earth Charter around our own living traditions, our values, and our concepts of sacredness and spirituality. ●

# The Only Way Forward

Her Royal Highness **Princess Basma bint Talal** has worked extensively to promote a wide range of global issues related to sustainable human development. Princess Basma founded and heads the Jordanian Hashemite Fund for Human Development, a non-governmental organization that promotes sustainable development interventions within local communities. On the international level, Princess Basma is Honorary Human Development Ambassador for the United Nations Development Programme, Goodwill Ambassador for the United Nations Development Fund for Women, Global Goodwill Ambassador for the United Nations Population Fund, and Member of the Jury for the Equator Initiative. Princess Basma holds a doctorate in development studies from Oxford University and is the author of *Re-thinking an NGO: Development, Donors and Civil Society in Jordan*, an analysis of the impact of changing paradigms of development. As a member of the Earth Charter Commission, Princess Basma has generated commitment and endorsement for the Earth Charter in Jordan and the region. In 2002, Jordan's ninety-nine municipalities endorsed a declaration to support the Earth Charter. In 2003, the Jordanian Ministry of Education successfully presented the Earth Charter Resolution for adoption by the UNESCO General Conference.

I consider myself to be extraordinarily privileged to be invited to contribute this Afterword to *The Earth Charter in Action: Toward a Sustainable World*. It is always inspiring to read the work of others, and to gain an insight into different ways of seeing and understanding the world around us. I hope that I will be able to do justice to the rich diversity of views presented in this unique volume.

The book demonstrates that, in the few years since the idea of an Earth Charter was first put forward, much has been achieved. The Earth Charter has stimulated intellectuals to rethink fundamental concepts and theories; it has led politicians to revise their own policies; it has led economists to review the very assumptions on which they base their prescriptions for develop-

ment; and it has inspired grassroots activists to challenge the "wisdom" of experts. We are witnessing the realisation that a paradigm shift in the way we theorise development is the only way forward.

We are often reminded that we live in a globalised world. But, economic growth is often dependent on the culture of consumerism and built-in obsolescence. It is hardly surprising, then, that so many of the authors acknowledge that the political, economic, business, and social systems that globalisation seeks to replicate are, in essence, obsolete. In the words of Albert Einstein, often cited in this volume, "You cannot solve problems with the way of thinking that led to their creation."

In finding new solutions to the urgent challenge of global survival, one size does not fit all. It is essential that we recognise the specificity of local contexts and respect local solutions. In the fight against disease, we now know that local knowledge is often far more effective than western science. Such insight leads us to discover remedies in the flora and fauna of the Amazonian rainforests, the arid deserts, and the frozen wastes. The people of these regions also have insights into social and economic organisation that will help us achieve the necessary paradigm shifts in global systems. If we are to understand their local views and learn from them, it is necessary that their voices be heard, and that we listen to them. We must celebrate biodiversity of thought. As many contributors noted, in the words of the Earth Charter, "This requires a change of mind and heart" (The Way Forward, paragraph two).

Our contexts are diverse, but our vision and values are shared. My own cultural heritage lies in the Arab Bedu tribes of the desert, yet I found a resonance with the essay concerning the challenges facing the Inuit communities of Greenland. The article reminded us that "We have to deal with our situation bottom-up, asking ourselves, 'What part do I play here, however small and insignificant. What can I do to push things in the right direction, however humbly?'"

This directs the reader to the title: *The Earth Charter in Action*. We are urged to translate lofty statements into local concrete actions. This will not be difficult. Across the world, there are grassroots organisations that help poor and marginalised people secure a more sustainable livelihood. Their "people-centred" work provides a solid foundation from which to broaden efforts and become "Earth-centred." The two issues are intertwined, for poor and marginalised people have most to gain from the sustainable use of finite resources.

Women, for example, play a central role in ensuring the survival of the human race. For generations, women have been at the forefront in campaigns to protect the world's resources. One advantage of the technological revolution is that the actions of such women are now broadcast and validated world-wide. Finally, their extraordinary role is being recognised through global awards, such as the Nobel Peace Prize.

The Charter also provides a unifying focal point around which young people can express their commitment to protect Earth. Never has this been more essential – more than fifty percent of the global population is under the age of twenty-five. The network of the Earth Charter Youth Initiative is designed to serve as a platform where young people celebrate diversity of religion, class, and ethnicity as a positive value, rather than a potential fault line. The more young people work together, the more the ripples of change are created around the world. Our three billion young people should be treated, not as the potential consumers of global products, but as the providers of global solutions. They will have to lead the way to change the priorities that promote material wealth over personal well-being and justice. They will be the active global citizens who use creativity as a tool for action.

This volume illustrates the ways that this youthful creativity can be harnessed. The Ark of Hope, for example, where young people are encouraged to deposit messages and materials that symbolise their vision for the future is an idea that can be adapted easily to different cultural and religious contexts. The Brink Expedition Team raises awareness of the threats presented by global warming, but they do so in the spirit of their beliefs – by travelling without using fossil fuels. Theirs is an adventure which inspires young people to express, in positive, life-enhancing terms, their alternative visions for a better way of organising the world.

In all these endeavours, the role of education is central. Across the world, the movement to promote a more holistic approach to learning is taking hold. The necessary new knowledge, skills, and behaviours cannot be achieved through formal education alone, but must be instilled through access to life-long reflection and learning. This requires that we constantly open our minds to new ideas, that we challenge existing paradigms, and that we engage in genuine dialogue that embraces the diversity of world views. Such interactions bring about more profound and lasting transformation in the human heart and mind. The future is not pre-ordained but is determined by human choices and

actions. We can, to some degree, choose our future – and this book provides insights into the choices that we should make.

This may be the Afterword, but it is certainly not the last word. This is a debate that will continue and will be reflected in action. I look forward to reading a future volume where we celebrate our achievements and, hopefully, a United Nations declaration recognising the Rights of Earth. ●

# Acknowledgements

From the Editorial Team

In our task to create this book, we were honored to work as a team and to connect with the many inspirational individuals involved in the Earth Charter Initiative from all over the world. We especially acknowledge the valuable guidance we received from the members of the Editorial Advisory Group: Joan Anderson, Rick Clugston, Ruud Lubbers, Mohit Mukherjee, Steven C. Rockefeller, and Michael Slaby. We are also grateful to Betty McDermott and Marina Bakhova, our colleagues at the Earth Charter International Secretariat in Costa Rica. We gratefully acknowledge Henny Helmich, Director of NCDO and Ron Smit, Co-director of KIT Publishers, for their extraordinary support and commitment to make this book possible. In addition, we give thanks to Frank Langedijk and Frans Bieckmann for helping with the book design and certain chapters, respectively.

We would like to express our gratitude to the authors of each chapter in this book. Their valuable insights have greatly enriched this project.

We would like to acknowledge the role of the Center for Environmental and Sustainability Education of the Florida Gulf Coast University for its institutional support. The Center works toward a sustainable world through scholarship, education, and action. We would like to thank all those assisting and contributing to the making of the book, in particular: Richard Tchen, Diane Wakeman, and Brandon Hollingshead.

*Peter Blaze Corcoran, Alide Roerink and Mirian Vilela*

From the Editor-in-Chief

"Dank u wel" to my Dutch colleagues and friends who have made me feel so at home in Wageningen and so welcome to collaborate on publishing in The Netherlands. I am particularly grateful to Arjen Wals, to Alide Roerink, and to Ron Smit for the opportunities they have shared with me. I am honored to have seen work on behalf of the Earth Charter by so many around the world. I especially acknowledge the daily work of Betty McDermott, Mohit Mukherjee, and Mirian Vilela in leading the Earth Charter Initiative. I am uplifted by the commitment of the Earth Charter Youth Initiative. I especially acknowledge the assistance and friendship of Michael Slaby of Germany and Lucky Moyo of South Africa. Thanks to my colleagues and students at Florida Gulf Coast University for their forebearance in giving me the opportunity to do the work of the Earth Charter. I thank my faithful student assistants at the Center for Environmental and Sustainability Education. In particular, I am deeply indebted to the members of the in-house editorial team at the Center: Richard Tchen, Diane Wakeman, and, especially Brandon Hollingshead–their work has made this book possible. The inspiration for everything I do is drawn from my mother in Maine and from my family in the Fijian Islands. Their love is my daily sustenance. Finally, I wish to acknowledge and thank an unsung hero of the Earth Charter movement–Rick Clugston. He also introduced me to the Earth Charter and my gratitude abounds.

*Peter Blaze Corcoran*

The Center for Environmental and Sustainability Education at Florida Gulf Coast University works toward realizing the dream of a sustainable and peaceful future for Earth through scholarship, education, and action. It advances understanding and achievement of the goals of environmental and sustainability education through innovative educational research methods, emergent eco-pedagogies, and educational philosophy and practice based on an ethics of care and sustainability.